RESEARCH FOR WRITERS

Advanced English Composition

Second Edition

Margo L. Martin
Charles D. Smires

FLORIDA STATE COLLEGE
at Jacksonville

KENDALL/HUNT PUBLISHING COMPANY
4050 Westmark Drive   Dubuque, Iowa 52002

CONTENTS

PREFACE

To the Student

As a college student, you will have many opportunities to write academic essays as you continue to take courses. In fact, you may already have taken classes that required you to research and then write about discipline-related topics. No matter what area of study you are researching—literature, the humanities, the social sciences, the behavioral sciences—you will probably be expected not only to write about your research findings, but also to document them appropriately.

The purpose of this book is to provide you with a broad-based text that will guide you through the research-writing process and documentation formats used in a variety of disciplines beyond the freshman English composition class. In addition, you will be introduced to writing for the workplace. No matter what your chosen profession will be, written communication will be a key component of your career. This book will present some of the formats and characteristics of several common business documents. In accomplishing its goals, this text has several features that will help you write.

First, the book reviews essay-writing basics, including essay structure and the modes of writing. Then, the text thoroughly explains the research process step by step. You will first learn strategies for writing paraphrases, summaries, and quotations. Next, you will learn about conducting research, selecting and narrowing a topic for your paper, and taking notes. The book then takes you through the process of writing the paper itself, from the thesis statement and outline to the final draft.

Additionally, the text discusses the following different types of research essays: an argumentative research paper, a literary analysis essay, a critique and review, and the technical report. Also included in this text are strategies for writing business correspondence.

In-class essay writing is a different type of academic writing that you will encounter in many courses that you take. The final chapter of the book provides strategies for writing such timed essays under pressure.

Another strength of the text is that each chapter provides a variety of model essays written by both students and professionals. Be sure to look for them. These sample papers will give you some ideas regarding ways to proceed with your own writing assignments.

A final feature of this book is that it serves as a companion to the *Research for Writers* telecourse lessons. If you are enrolled in such a course, you will find that each chapter provides a more in-depth explanation of the concepts covered in each telelesson. Keep in mind that every instructor teaches a little differently than all other instructors, and your instructor may choose to assign chapters differently than we have chosen to arrange them. Your instructor will decide the best way to pair the chapters of this textbook with the telelessons.

Happy writing!
Margo and Charles

To the Teacher

Research for Writers is designed to guide students in all major aspects of research and writing required in college coursework. The chapters are arranged to follow a logical sequence of instruction but are self-contained to allow the instructor to select appropriate chapters to fit a particular instructional design. We realize that there are numerous textbooks available that target specific areas of writing, so we have chosen instead to provide a textbook that offers a broader range of basic research and writing concepts. Contemporary students no longer have opportunities to take unlimited coursework; thus, we recognize the need to provide instructional tools that are broader in scope and design.

One of the major strengths of this textbook is its attention to writing about literature, the humanities, business, and the social and behavioral sciences. The text offers specific directions for the kinds of writing students will encounter in each of these disciplines. The fourteen chapters are written for the standard 45-50 contact-hour term.

First, the book reviews essay-writing basics, including essay structure and the modes of writing. Then, the text thoroughly explains the research process step by step. Students will initially learn strategies for writing paraphrases, summaries, and quotations. Next, they will learn about conducting research, selecting and narrowing a topic for their papers, and taking notes. The book then takes students through the process of writing the paper itself, from the thesis statement and outline to the final draft.

Additionally, the text discusses the following different types of research essays: an argumentative research paper; a literary analysis essay; a critique and review, and the technical report. Also in this text are strategies for writing business correspondence.

As you know, in-class essay writing is a different type of academic writing that students will encounter in many courses that they take. The final chapter of the book provides strategies for writing such timed essays under pressure.

Another strength of this book is that, wherever possible, we have chosen to provide models for the various forms of writing discussed. Many of these examples are taken from students' writing samples, though some are borrowed from professional writers. While the student models may contain some flaws, they do exemplify the preferred written response to typical college assignments.

This new edition of *Research for Writers* maintains all of these strengths of the previous edition with several additional benefits. Most of the student and professional examples and model papers have been updated and in some cases, expanded. The conducting research section has been broadened to include a more thorough discussion of online research and the associated conventions that accompany such research. Finally, the documentation sections of the text have been updated to reflect the current practices of the most recent MLA and APA style guides.

Finally if you are using this text to support and supplement the telecourse series *Research for Writers*, each chapter provides a more in-depth explanation of the concepts covered in each telelesson.

The textbook chapters correspond with the telelessons as follows:

ACKNOWLEDGMENTS

We would like to thank the following people for their help in writing this textbook

Kathleen Clower

Joe A. Davis

Rawlslyn Francis

Suzanne Hess

Barbara Markham

Victoria McGlone

Sally Nielsen

Wendy Perniciaro

Stephanie H. Powers

Barbara Salvage

Susan Slavicz

In particular, we would like to thank the students who were willing to share their writings

Gerald Pine

Bowen Barrs

Luther Buie

Stephanie Hughes

Romana Lopes

Casey McKinney

Cherie Brunelle Risley

Celena Soto

Rebekah Trotter

Barry Underwood

Darcy Webb

Chris Weed

ABOUT THE AUTHORS

Margo L. Martin, Ed.D., Dean of Arts and Sciences at Florida State College at Jacksonville, South Campus, has twenty-eight years of college-level teaching and administrative experience.

Charles Smires, retired Dean of Liberal Arts at Florida State College at Jacksonville, South Campus, has thirty-six years of community college teaching and administrative experience.

Both authors have taught various courses in English composition, literature, humanities, and technical report writing. Additionally, the authors have taught via different course delivery methods, including telecourses, online and blended instruction, and interactive television as well as the traditional classroom setting.

Chapter 1

Reviewing the Essay

When you are assigned an essay to write, you may ask yourself, "What exactly is the task at hand?" The first step is understanding what makes an essay an essay. Simply stated, an essay is a group of three or more related paragraphs that are connected by a single unifying idea. This chapter will guide you in writing a well-developed essay by reviewing the elements of the essay.

Objectives

- delineate the parts of an essay;

- discuss the connections and transitions needed to establish coherence within an essay;

- explain each of the multiple strategies available for the development of your ideas in essay form.

▼ PARTS OF AN ESSAY

Like many students, you may find having to write an essay to be a somewhat intimidating task. You may see an enormous challenge ahead of you. Writing an essay is by no means a simple, one-step process, but it is certainly a manageable one. One way to help alleviate essay-writing anxiety is to understand, one by one, each of the essay's three distinct parts: introduction, body, and conclusion.

THE INTRODUCTION

The introduction serves several purposes. In the opening section of your paper, you will capture your reader's interest, clearly lay out your paper's topic and organization, and guide your reader to the body of the essay. An essay's introduction is not limited to one paragraph. Certain essays may require two or more introductory paragraphs to provide sufficient background information before reaching the main point of the essay. However, you may find that keeping your introductory material within one paragraph will help you to stay focused.

Purpose

One of your first goals should be to define clearly for both yourself and the reader why you are writing. The challenge here is managing to move past the fact that you are writing an essay for an English class or for some other academic purpose. One way to do so is to select a topic that truly interests you and possibly one about which you already know something. You will find that the task of writing an essay is not quite so grueling or stressful if you explore a topic that intrigues you. Furthermore, your audience will sense your interest in the topic through the tone and unity of your final product. In turn, your readers will enjoy reading what you've written!

Audience

In addition to establishing your purpose for writing, you must clearly identify your audience—the person or people for whom you are writing. Identifying your expected readers will help you to determine the tone and vocabulary that are appropriate for developing your essay. Your audience's interests, values, and education should all be considered. These factors affect the tone that you should use in writing your paper. If your readers aren't interested, or if they feel that you are being condescending, insulting, or threatening toward them, then it doesn't matter how wonderful your paper is—no one will willingly read it once you have alienated your audience. Think of your paper having to reach three potential types of readers: those who don't know, those who aren't certain they want to know, and those who are adamant about not knowing.

Think about the chain of events that occurred during your first two weeks of this school term. Surely, your experiences went beyond the academic. Now consider having to write a letter to three different individuals regarding your reaction to these first two weeks: one will go to your grandmother, who helps to fund your education and who worries excessively about your well being; one will go to the president of the college that you are attending; and one will go to your best friend. How will the letters differ from one another? Could you get away with writing just one letter? Probably not. Chances are that the vocabulary, tone, and content you select for each letter will be specifically geared to each specific audience. Your grandmother will want to know if you are eating properly and if your teachers are capable, not whether your first party of the semester was a success.

In most academic writing situations, considering your classmates as well as your instructor as your audience is quite appropriate. You should write honestly and as interestingly as you are able.

<table>
<tr><td rowspan="4">**Phrases to Avoid**</td><td>• I think</td></tr>
<tr><td>• I believe</td></tr>
<tr><td>• I feel</td></tr>
<tr><td>• in my opinion.</td></tr>
</table>

Unless you have quoted someone else, the reader will believe the ideas in your paper to be yours, so such phrases are unnecessary.

Attention Grabber

Getting your reader's attention is probably the most important task of all. If you fail to intrigue the reader enough to read your paper, then the skill with which you develop the remainder of the paper does not matter! There are several lead-in strategies that you can try. Begin with background information such as the history behind your topic or a timeline of events that have led up to the period you plan to discuss in detail. Start with an anecdote, dramatic statement, or appropriate quotation. Asking rhetorical questions and presenting startling statistics can also pique the curiosity of your reader and can be effective ways of snaring your reader's attention.

Thesis Statement and Essay Blueprint

The thesis statement is the one sentence in the introduction that lets your reader know the controlling or main idea of the entire essay. The thesis statement is often followed or preceded by a sentence that serves as an "essay blueprint." The thesis presents the point of your paper as well as the topic of the paper—it's the "why" as well as the "what." Consider the following sentence:

Organic food has become increasingly popular among consumers in the last several years.

Such a sentence answers "what" the paper is about, but so what? What is the point? "Why" might a reader want to know about organic food? Try this sentence instead:

Organic food is a healthy food choice for consumers.

This sentence offers a reason for reading about organic food. Now let's give the thesis statement some direction by adding an essay blueprint sentence:

> Organic food is a healthy food choice for consumers. It provides more nutrients, reduces pesticide exposure, and curtails antibiotic intake.

By adding an "essay blueprint" to the thesis statement, the reader now knows how the paper will be organized topically. The thesis statement and essay blueprint together serve as a contract between the writer and the audience—all of the main points of the paper as indicated in the thesis/blueprint must be included within the paper as a whole, and nothing extra should be added as an afterthought. If you find it necessary to add to or subtract from the paper's primary points after establishing the thesis statement and essay blueprint, simply expand or contract the thesis statement and essay blueprint as appropriate. Consider the primary thrust of your paper to be a working thesis statement until the paper is finished. As with the introduction, it's difficult to be definitive about the thesis statement until after the paper has been written and, time permitting, revised. Other considerations when writing a thesis statement are to avoid posing a question rather than making a statement; avoid stating the obvious; and avoid statements such as "In this paper, I will address..." or "This essay will be about...."

Once you have written a tentative thesis statement, you must decide where it should be located within the introduction. There is no one correct place for it. The thesis statement can appear at the beginning, middle, or end of the introduction. Even so, it is often easier to introduce the paper deductively by starting with general ideas and funneling more specifically to the primary focus of the essay. (Though it usually appears early in an essay, a thesis statement can sometimes be placed effectively in the essay's conclusion.)

While it's okay to begin with the introduction when writing, oftentimes it's easier to write a more effective introduction after you have written most or all of the body paragraphs of the paper. Think of beginning your paper the same way you might present a guest speaker to a group. If the speaker is someone whom you've only just met, your introduction of him or her will more than likely be brief and perhaps only loosely connected to the speech he or she plans to give to the group. However, if the speaker is someone whom you have known for a while or whose background you have at least researched, your introduction of that individual will have more depth and relevance to his or her topic.

THE BODY

The second, or middle, part of the essay is the body of the paper. The body of an essay can be comprised of one or many individual paragraphs. Many instructors expect their students to write a minimum of three paragraphs to flesh out the body of an essay. Let's focus on the contents of an effective paragraph: the topic sentence and supporting details.

Topic Sentence

Each body paragraph should include a topic sentence, which is a general statement that has two purposes: to reveal the controlling or main idea of the entire paragraph and to link the paragraph with the thesis statement and essay blueprint provided in the introduction. A topic sentence indicates to the reader the main idea that will be discussed in that particular paragraph—it should be general enough to capture all of the elements within the paragraph, but not so broad that it reaches beyond the content of the paragraph. The topic sentence can appear at the beginning, middle, or end of the paragraph. While not every paragraph that you will read in professional writing will provide you with a clearly stated topic sentence, including a topic sentence in each of your own paragraphs will help to guide your reader through each of your main points and will also help you as a writer to stay focused as you develop each point.

Supporting Details

Along with a topic sentence, each body paragraph should include supporting details. Such details should include a variety of clear and convincing concrete examples to support all general points made within the paragraph. Such evidence as statistics and testimonials can be effective means of support for general statements. As you begin to develop the body of your essay, you may ask yourself, "Just how many supporting details are enough?" Truly, "enough" depends on your audience, your purpose for writing, and the form in which you will present your essay. As a general rule of thumb, academic papers should include well-developed body paragraphs that begin with topic sentences, include several supporting details augmented with concrete examples, and end with concluding sentences that lead into following paragraphs.

THE CONCLUSION

The conclusion of the essay is just that: the end of the paper. The reader should not have to wonder if he or she is about to finish reading your paper. Several approaches can result in an effective conclusion. For a particularly lengthy essay, you may want to summarize the paper's main points in a fresh way. Beware of simply restating the thesis, however. In a shorter paper, where restating the paper's main points might be redundant, you may wish to draw conclusions or identify implications. The conclusion is also a good place to include personal observations and evaluations. Criticisms often fit well here. Other options include ending with a quotation, specific example, or forceful statement. Ultimately, you want the conclusion to be brief, and you want to avoid merely repeating the introduction. Also, you do not want to bring up any new points that are not mentioned in your essay blueprint.

▼ COHERENCE

You should not construct an essay like a house of cards. In a house of cards, one card precariously rests against or atop another. The slightest disturbance causes the "house" to collapse. You should build your essay more like a log cabin with the notches in the logs interconnecting. For an essay, the interconnecting "notches" are the coherence devices you use to hold your essay together.

To cohere means to stick together. If your essay is to "stick together" and convey its message, your reader must understand the flow of ideas and the interrelatedness of the concepts. Comprehension for your reader is achieved when you show the logical relationships between sentences and paragraphs in your essay. Without the coherence devices, your essay will fall apart for your reader like the analogous house of cards.

You can achieve coherence in your essay through the use of various devices and techniques: organization, repetition, restatement, parallel structure, transition words and phrases, tagging, internal previews, and internal summaries.

ORGANIZATION

The primary way to build a sturdy foundation for your essay is to use a clear organizational pattern. Essays can be arranged in either deductive or inductive order. Deductive essays (going from the general to the specific) have their thesis statements located in the introduction. Inductive essays (going from the specific to the general) ha ve their thesis statements located in the conclusion.

In addition to the overall organizational pattern for your essay, your body paragraphs need to follow a logical pattern. The logical sequence of ideas will help your reader see the connection between your paragraphs and their relationship to your thesis statement.

Organizational Patterns for Body Paragraphs	• **Chronological**—arranging paragraphs according to how the events/ideas occur in time sequence • **Spatial**—arranging paragraphs according to how the details occur with regards to location (left to right, front to back, top to bottom) • **Emphatic**—arranging paragraphs according to how the ideas are presented in order of importance (least to most important, most important to least) • **Causal**—arranging paragraphs according to how the events/ideas relate in a cause/effect chain (from effect to cause or cause to effect) • **Problem/Solution**—arranging paragraphs in an argument essay according to the issue and its solution(s) (also can be problem-cause-solution format) • **Topical**—arranging paragraphs according to topics discussed (used when one of the other patterns is not appropriate, i.e. discussing the four types of dangerous drivers on the road when they are all equally dangerous)

REPETITION

An easy way to obtain coherence in your essay is to repeat key words and terms. This device can be used to provide flow within a paragraph as well as to provide flow between paragraphs.

For example, examine this concluding paragraph from an education paper about teaching comprehension skills to reading students:

> The reader who has not developed successful metacognitive *strategies* should be taught a variety of *strategies* to improve his or her comprehension process. The teacher should not overwhelm the student with too many *strategies* but should introduce the approaches one by one. The teacher should model the process until the student is able to model it properly. Continued practice in the use of a *strategy* should be provided by the teacher, and the teacher should encourage the student to use the *strategy* independently. The teacher should make occasional checks to verify the student is, in fact, using the new *strategy*. Once this stage is reached, additional *strategies* can be taught to the student.

As you can see, the repetition of the concepts of "*strategies*" and "*strategy*" provides the linkage between the sentences and ideas in this paragraph.

Repetition can also be used to provide coherence between paragraphs. By repeating the key terms from the thesis statement in your essay in the topic sentences of your body paragraphs, you can help to link your whole essay together.

For example, look at the thesis and topic sentences from a student essay, analyzing the effects of his ignoring his diabetes.

Thesis: Severe muscle cramps, disorientation, and loss of vision are definitely *signs* that I have failed to take my sugar levels seriously.

Topic Sentences: The first *sign* of my uncontrolled diabetes is severe leg cramps.

As a result of my continued stubbornness to acknowledge my condition, I have discovered another alarming *sign* of uncontrolled diabetes – disorientation.

The most eye opening *sign* of my high glucose level has been the loss of my vision.

RESTATEMENT

Another coherence technique that is very similar to repetition is restatement. Instead of repeating the same word or term, you repeat the same concept, but you restate it in different words or terms, as is the case in this commentary written by Leon Botstein for *Time*.

> The new changes to the SAT are harmless. But these modest *reforms* will do little to stem the rising tide against such testing.

PARALLEL STRUCTURE

In mathematics, you learn that parallel lines are two or more lines that are an equal distance apart at all points along the lines and thus never intersect. This idea of equality holds true for parallel structure in writing. Parallelism in writing refers to the concept that two or more ideas are expressed according to the same grammatical pattern or structure. This similarity or equality in pattern aids coherence because it enhances the flow of ideas for your reader and emphasizes the equal importance of the ideas being expressed.

Notice the use of parallel structure in this following paragraph taken from a health article written by Laura McMullen for *U.S. News and World Report*.

> Alcohol is a drug with two stories. *There's one story of feeling relaxed* after a glass of wine and *another of being unconscious* after a bottle. *There's one story of feeling social* after a margarita and *another of feeling reckless* after tequila shots. *There's one story of feeling alive* and in the moment at sunset and *another of feeling nothing* at all by sunrise.

TRANSITION WORDS AND PHRASES

A common technique for achieving coherence in an essay is the use of transition words and phrases. Transition means "change," so transitional words and phrases are used to indicate to your reader that a change in ideas is about to occur. Your choice of transition words gives your reader the logical connection between the sentences to help him or her understand the relationship between the ideas.

Some of the most common transition words and phrases are listed below according to their meaning or the relationship they show between ideas.

Adding Ideas

These transition words are used when you want to add an idea or concept to your previous one.

also   furthermore   moreover   in addition   additionally

Giving Examples

When you want to give an example to illustrate an idea, you can use these transition words and phrases to introduce your example.

to illustrate   for example   for instance

Showing Contrast

Many times you want to present an idea or concept that is opposite of the one you just presented. These transition words and phrases indicate for your reader that you are showing this contrast.

however   nevertheless   in contrast to   though   on the other hand

Showing Comparison

Other times you want to show that an idea or concept is similar to the one you just presented. The following transition words and phrases provide the bridge to the new idea.

likewise   similarly

Providing a Summary

This group of transition words and phrases indicates for your reader that you are about to sum up what you previously stated or are about to conclude your point.

in summary   in conclusion   in brief   to sum up

Emphasizing a Point

Some transition words can be used to emphasize a point or to call attention to a clarification of an idea.

in fact   indeed   to be sure   certainly   in other words

Signaling an Effect

When you are discussing how one event led to another, you can use the following transition words to show how your second event is the result of the first one.

therefore   consequently   as a result   thus   so

The following transition words indicate that the second event is the cause of or the reason for the first.

because   since   for

Indicating a Sequence

These transition words are helpful when your ideas follow a particular order.

<table>
<tr>
<td rowspan="3">

Primary Sequences

</td>
<td>

1. Time

    first, second, etc.   now   next   then   later   finally
meanwhile

2. Location

    to the right   to the left   above   below   next to   opposite to

3. Value

    most importantly   the most important   the least important
foremost

</td>
</tr>
</table>

Identify the types of transition devices used in the following paragraph, and see if you can explain the meaning of each as it relates to the connection between ideas. The transition words and phrases have been italicized.

> I have been taking niacin for several years as a way to lower my "bad" or LDL cholesterol and to raise my "good" or HDL cholesterol. *Recently, however,* I have been experiencing two side effects from this vitamin. The *first* effect is flushing. *Although* not dangerous to my health, the flushing is uncomfortable. *In addition* to causing reddening of my skin, I experience a burning and itching sensation. *Another* effect has been an increase in my glucose levels. This *more serious* effect could lead to the onset of diabetes. *Despite* its positive impact on cholesterol levels, current research shows that niacin does not reduce the risk of heart attacks. *In fact,* it may cause more harm. *As a result* of these side effects and current research, I am no longer going to be taking niacin as a supplement.

TAGGING

A technique that can be used to provide transition from one paragraph to the next can be called "tagging." Just as in the game of tag, in which one person touches someone else to pass on who is "it," you can transition from one paragraph to the next, by passing on the point from one paragraph to the next. With this technique, you achieve coherence by referring to the idea in the previous paragraph in a dependent clause or phrase and announcing the idea of the new paragraph in an independent clause.

In a student essay on how to surf entitled "Surfing 101," the student writer has just discussed the need to learn the language of surfing and is getting ready to describe how to catch a wave. Her transition into her next point and paragraph is as follows:

> *Once a would-be surfer understands some basic terms,* one is ready to go on to the next step, which is paddle, paddle, paddle.

INTERNAL PREVIEWS AND SUMMARIES

In essays of longer lengths, two coherence devices that can aid your reader in following the flow of your ideas are internal previews and internal summaries. Just as the "essay blueprint" lets your reader know what the major points or divisions of your essay will be, an internal preview lets your reader know what major points will be covered in one of your body paragraphs. For example, in an essay on energy drinks, the writer wants to discuss the most common side effects of such drinks. She begins her body paragraph with the following sentences:

> Several serious side effects are very common from the use of energy drinks. *These side effects are irritability, anxiety, and insomnia.*

An internal summary is very similar to an internal preview. However, just as the term indicates, you provide your reader with a summary of your major point(s) at the end of a body paragraph before going on to a new point and the next paragraph.

For example, in the essay on energy drinks, after writing about the ingredients in energy drinks, the writer concludes her paragraph with the following sentence:

> This combination of caffeine, sugar, and herbal stimulants produces the detrimental health effects that make energy drinks such as risk for adolescents and adults.

▼ DEVELOPMENT WITH MULTIPLE STRATEGIES

Imagine that you are a server at one of your local restaurants. In discussing your experience at the restaurant with your family and friends, they have probably asked you a variety of questions about your job. What is the atmosphere of the restaurant like? What was the funniest or most embarrassing incident you have encountered since you have been working as a server? How did you go about getting a job at the restaurant? What types of customers do you encounter? How does this job compare to a server's job at another restaurant? How has this job impacted your schooling and your other activities? Why did you choose to work at this restaurant? What do you consider a good tipper to be? In responding to these questions, you are asked to view your experience on this job in a particular way, deliberately selecting the relevant information and organizing it so it will address the appropriate question. Although you may not consciously realize it, your response has followed an organized pattern. When writing an essay, once you have decided on your topic, your purpose, and your audience, you will now consciously consider what will be the best development strategy to focus your topic and to clarify your ideas. There are a variety of patterns or *strategies* that allow you to discuss your experiences in a number of different ways and to give other people the opportunity to view those experiences from different perspectives. The major strategies employed in writing are *description, narration, examples, process analysis, comparison and contrast, classification, causation,* and *definition*. In writing your essays, you will more than likely use multiple strategies to develop your ideas. Following is a brief explanation of each of these strategies.

DESCRIPTION

Description provides the sensory details of a person, object, or place so the described person, object, or place becomes real for your reader. You want your reader to visualize and experience what you did. Although a description tends to be primarily visual, the other senses of smell, sound, taste, and touch enhance the reality of your description for your reader. Good description, though, not only describes the sensory details, but also establishes a *dominant impression,* so that the reader understands why this description is important. Look at this student's description of her parents' garage and notice how all of the details contribute to impression of total disarray:

My parents' two-car garage is an unbearable vision of chaos and clutter, An innumerable number of brown, tattered boxes overflowing with holiday decorations and garb are stacked aimlessly throughout the area. Second-hand dining room chairs, damaged light fixtures, and two broken vacuums occupy one side of the room; the other side is consumed by a bulky, rusted lawn mower, bundles of intertwined electrical cords, and piles of musty old clothing, dirty sheets and soiled towels. At the back of the garage, two dingy brown racing bikes and one tandem bicycle are propped against my dad's old work bench, which is now home to various hammers, wrenches and screwdrivers, cleaning products, and half-opened, sticky paint cans. Rickety, mildew-ridden cabinets, once strong and sturdy containing all of the aforementioned items, dangle precariously over the bench. To top it all off, my mom's canine obedience class instructional materials, multiple dry-erase easels, foul-smelling dog treats, and giant tubs of plush, squeaking toys are situated right in the middle of the garage, making navigation virtually impossible. Although my parents may still refer to this edifice as their garage, I call it a labyrinth of disaster.

Description, like anything you write, should be relevant.

NARRATION

A narrative is a story. It has a *plot* (the sequence of events in the story) and a *theme* (the main idea). A narrative also has characters, a setting, and a conflict. A good narrative leads the reader to the story's *climax* and then resolves the original conflict in a *resolution*. A narrative outline has the following parts and can be visualized as a leaning pyramid:

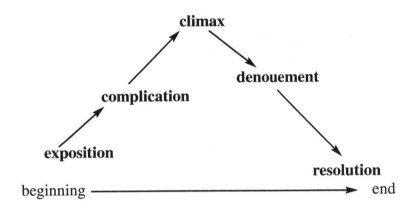

The *exposition* of the narrative should describe the major characters and the setting, and the conflict should emerge either stated directly or implied in some way. All of these elements then interact as the *complication* develops the narrative towards the *climax*, or turning point. After the climax, the narrative quickly wraps up the loose ends in the *denouement* and finally resolves the original conflict. A good narrative is quite effective in supporting a major point you are trying to make in an essay. Readers often relate much better to a well-told narrative than to a long list of statistics. Look at this short narrative in which the writer relates the humorous side of a potentially serious accident in the home.

Just my luck! If someone had been present with a camera, I would be now viral on *YouTube*! I was watching *Jeopardy* while walking on the treadmill when I got to the end of my ten minutes. I reached out to the minus button to slow down, but hit the plus by mistake. That started me off running and reaching wildly for the minus again, but hitting the darn plus once again! Well, that took my feet out from under me, and I went down on my knees and hands and off the end of the belt onto the floor. Fortunately, the only damage was a skun elbow (as in skin, skan, skun), although the next day my whole body felt like I had been run over by that proverbial Mack truck. Maybe I should get one of those I've-fallen-and-I-can't -get-up buttons for these "special" occasions.

Examples

A frequently used strategy for developing your essay is the use of *examples*. Examples come from personal experience or from research, but their use is critical in establishing the importance or relevance of the point you are trying to make. Examples allow the reader to connect an abstract point in an argument with something that is real in his or her experience; without such a connection, the point may be lost to the reader or lack enough significance to make it useless.

Reminders about Using Examples

- Be sure the examples you use in your essay are relevant to the reader. An example may work for you, but it may be beyond the experience of your reader.

- Be sure the example supports the point you are trying to make. If it doesn't connect the reader to the point of discussion, it adds nothing to your essay or to the value of your argument.

- Be sure the example is concrete and makes only one point. If the reader has to figure out what part of the example is important, he or she may decide to ignore it.

- Be sure to give enough examples to make your point, but avoid "overkill." Too many examples may tire your reader and cause him or her to lose interest.

Notice in the excerpt below how examples are used to show how expensive television viewing can be:

Watching television today has become a very costly endeavor. It is not just the advertised channel packages you need to consider, but also the "hidden" costs associated with cable or satellite television. For instance, some channels you might like to have are not part of the channel packages but have separate fees. These include premium channels such as HBO, Showtime, and Cinemax and certain sport channels such as the Tennis Channel, the Major League Baseball Network, or the National Football League Network. Another example of "hidden" fees is the equipment charges. For high density (HD) quality television and the ability to record shows, you will need to lease an HD DVR. If you have more than one television, you will pay additional charges for adapter/receivers for each of your televisions. Then, of course, you will want to get some type of service protection in case of equipment or wiring failure, adding another fee to your total bill. The final "hidden" cost is the taxes, surcharges, and regulatory fees associated with your cable/satellite service. Although you will probably have anticipated this added "hidden" cost, you will be surprised at how much money these three items can run. Although that advertised cable or satellite television special deal sounded attractive, once you get your monthly bill, you will soon realize that television viewing has become an expensive luxury thanks to all of the "hidden" costs.

PROCESS ANALYSIS

Another strategy you might use in developing your essay is *process analysis*. You may find the need to explain how something occurs—how a jury reaches a decision or how a car thief methodically breaks into and steals a locked car. Process analysis requires the writer to identify the major steps of an operation and to discuss them in a logical order. Giving someone directions to get from point A to point B may seem an obvious exercise in process analysis, but instructions differ in that they require the reader to *act;* process requires only that the reader *understand* the operation. You might, for example, give instructions to someone about how to write a check, but what happens to that check after it is written is the substance of good process. *Reader's Digest* wrote a series of articles explaining how different parts of the body work under the titles "Joe's Kidney" or "Joe's Brain." In these articles, the various physical and chemical process of the body are defined and explained, often using metaphor and analogy so that the lay reader can gain the greatest appreciation of the terribly complex bodily functions. Technical writers are faced with this dilemma, and they must constantly find ways to explain new technologies to a not-so-technical audience. The background of the audience is an important factor in how the process is explained. Listen to how your advanced physics professor explains a process to you; then, imagine how you would explain that same process to your six-year-old brother or sister. As an example of this strategy, read this brief excerpt below from the "Surfing 101" essay previously mentioned in which the student writer discusses one of the steps in learning how to surf:

> Next, you will need to "pop up" onto your board. It may be helpful to practice "popping up" in the privacy of your own home. To do this step, you will need to straighten out your arms while lifting your torso up and then "pop" your legs up and under your body until your feet are planted securely on the board. You have only a second or two to execute this step, so don't try to get up on your knees first. You will surely "eat it" if you do, meaning you will swallow a lot of water because you didn't have enough time to stand up and went crashing into the wave.

COMPARISON AND CONTRAST

To clarify a particular point, you will often find the need to compare or contrast something with something else. By showing similarities or differences, you help your reader to see relationships they may not have noticed or to see distinctions that will aid their understanding. In the excerpt below, the student writer uses contrast to help his reader understand the traits of an anti-hero:

> Although aspirin and Tylenol are commonly used as pain relievers, there are several differences between the two drugs that one should consider when using them. Aspirin, an acetylsalicylic acid, is absorbed in the bloodstream, and through a chemical reaction, attacks the causes of the pain. Besides lowering fevers and relieving aches and pains, aspirin reduces inflammation, such as with arthritis. Aspirin has the ability to thin the blood and, thus, has been used effectively as a treatment for heart attacks and strokes. The negative aspect of aspirin is that it does have side effects. Aspirin can cause nausea, dizziness, indigestion and heart burn. Aspirin is usually not recommended for use with children and should not be used by patients with bleeding disorders. In contrast, Tylenol, known as acetaminophen, reduces pain and fever, but does not attack the underlying cause of such symptoms. In addition, Tylenol does not treat arthritic inflammation. Tylenol cannot be used for the treatment of heart attacks or strokes because of its lack of anti-clotting ability. Unlike aspirin, though, Tylenol generally does not irritate the stomach or cause other gastric side effects. Also, Tylenol is safer for use with children and patients with bleeding disorders. When deciding on which pain reliever to use, one should remember these differences.

How would you describe the taste of a boiled river eel or shark fin soup? More than likely, and perhaps out of exasperation, you will finally say it tastes like chicken. A comparison brings the unfamiliar into the range of experiences the reader can relate to. You might need to explain an experience by comparing it to something you know the reader has experienced or with which the reader is familiar.

Note the comparison below in this excerpt from the book *An Astronaut's Guide to Life on Earth* in which Astronaut Chris Hadfield describes his initial reaction to having returned from space:

> "It's like being a newborn, this sudden sensory overload of noise, color, smells and gravity after months of quietly floating, encased in relative calm and isolation. No wonder babies cry in protest when they are born."

In your essays, you will probably use comparison frequently as a strategy to re-enforce your major points.

CLASSIFICATION

Another strategy you will find effective is *classification*. Classification is the dividing of the whole into parts or categories. If you are asked to talk about a large group or something with many parts or aspects, you may wish to identify the sub-groups within the whole. For example, in biology, you learned about the classification of plants and animals. Books are classified for arrangement in your library. Classification also allows you to create your own sub-groups. Think about how you might group the people in the class you're in right now based on how they are dressed or how they participate in class. If you are a fan of reality shows on television, how would you classify/group this large variety of shows into meaningful categories so a non-viewer of such shows could understand what they are like? In another form of classification, *division*, the writer simply divides the whole into its pre-existing parts. You might analyze a football team's prowess by grading each of the positions, from center to quarterback. Classifying and dividing can be very helpful in trying to discuss groups or concepts that are too large to be handled effectively by themselves; sometimes you can see the forest when you look at the trees! Here is an excerpt from an essay in which the writer is discussing one of the categories of reality television programming.

> The most popular category of reality television shows is the competitive show. In this category of reality television, contestants compete at some task, either individually or as team. At some select interval, contestants are eliminated one person or team at a time until the last person/team left is declared the winner of a grand prize, usually a large sum of money. Contestants are usually eliminated through voting either by a panel of judges, by audience viewers, or by contestants themselves. Often, contestants of a competitive show must live together in a confined environment. Some examples of reality competition shows are *Big Brother, Survivor, Project Runway, The Amazing Race, Top Chef,* and *The Voice.*

CAUSE AND EFFECT

With causal analysis, you help your reader understand the impact of an event, experience, or decision; or you explain to your reader why this event, experience, or decision occurred. In the first situation, you are discussing effect and in the second, you are discussing cause. In analyzing impact, you need to decide what were the primary effects that resulted and what were the secondary ones. Analyzing causes can often be complex because you need to distinguish between what actually contributed to a situation as opposed to what indirectly caused it or just happened to occur prior to the situation but didn't lead to it. Thus you must be careful to give concrete explanations in presenting causes in your essays to show the connection to your topic. For example, in the excerpt below the writer explains one of his reasons or causes for wanting to attend college:

> *Most of all, I want to fulfill my own dream – to be an English teacher. As far back as I have memories I have loved the study of English, especially literature. During English classes in high school and even in junior high school, I would listen intently to every word my teachers uttered, trying to grasp as much knowledge as I could, whether they were explaining the intricacies of the English language or the symbolic meaning of poetic verse. I remembered dreaming of standing in front of a classroom, exploring with students the tragedy of* Romeo and Juliet, *the suspense and horror of Edgar Allen Poe, and the romantic vision of Lord Byron. To realize my dream, I knew I would have to attend college, so here I am today listening to my professor expounding on the simplistic, but powerful writing style of Ernest Hemingway, looking forward to the day when I will be known as Dr. Franklin, Professor of English.*

Now let's take a look at impacts. Below is another excerpt from an article in *Sports Illustrated* by Grant Wahl. In this excerpt, the writers points out the effects on Qatar if it were to lose its hosting of the 2022 FIFA World Cup.

> *What would happen if Qatar lost the World Cup? The country would save upward of $30 billion of stadiums and infrastructures, for starters. But that would pale in comparison to the loss of prestige, says James M. Dorsey, author of the respected blog The Turbulent World of Middle East Soccer. After spending years and billions of dollars building influence in the region – not least through Al Jazeera television, which is funded by the Qatari royal family – Qatar's status in the Middle East took a hit when the government backed the failed Muslim Brotherhood government in Egypt. Losing the World Cup would hurt Qatar's standing even further.*

Definition

One of the most important strategies you might employ in your essays is definition. Many times, people are unable to resolve their differences because they can't agree on the terms of their argument. Other times, people may reach a common definition, but interpret it differently. Abstract concepts such as humility, integrity, courage, pride, or justice are particularly prone to different interpretations. Think about this: How do you define the term "team player"? How would your boss define it? How would your colleague at work define it? How would your son, a member of a little league baseball team, define it? How would his coach define it? You cannot assume that everyone defines the world the same way you do, so paying attention to definitions in any discussion increases the likelihood of reaching some degree of consensus.

The most common form of definition is the *formal definition*. The formal definition has three parts: the *item* or term to be defined, the *class* or group that item falls within, and the *differentiation* by which the item can be separated from other items in the same group. For example, you might define a linguistic *character* (the item) as a written symbol (the class) that has both a sound and a physical association (the differentia). The formal definition of an aircraft carrier might look like this: "an aircraft carrier is a large military ship that launches and retrieves fixed-winged and other aircraft from its surface deck." Notice that a formal definition is always written as a complete sentence, beginning with the item. There may be several differentia. Take this definition from a student essay on the meaning of beauty: *Beauty is the quality that gratifies and appeals to both the mind and senses of an individual. It's important that the focus is on the word "individual."*

Below are two brief excerpts showing two different approaches to definition. The first is an excerpt from a humorous student essay on the definition of "wazoo." Note that one way to define is to tell what it is not. The second excerpt is from the satiric essay "Why I Want a Wife" by Judy Brady. In this essay, she details all of the qualities of the "ideal" wife.

> I dismissed the silly meanings that people had conjured up. The wazoo is not the Washington Zoo, a battle cry for amazons, the goop that snails leave behind, or the great leader of the Wa people. I want a wife who cooks the meals, a wife who is a good cook. I want a wife who will plan the menus, do the necessary grocery shopping, prepare the meals, serve them pleasantly, and then do the cleaning up while I do my studying.

Another way something may be defined is by *metaphor*. Look at J.B. Priestley's definition of the Internet:

> You can't escape the metaphor: the Internet as the Interstate. In one way, the I-way metaphor is right: being on-line is like driving. You can read the manual, but you have to try it to really learn.

Or, look at how Michael Callen defined AIDS:

> ...as the moment-to-moment management of uncertainty. It's like standing in the middle of the New York Stock Exchange at midday,

buzzers and lights flashing, everyone yelling, a million opinions. AIDS is about loss of control—of one's bowels, one's bladder, one's life.

Comparing an unfamiliar item or concept to one that is familiar helps the reader to understand the topic; the danger, of course, is that in doing so, the reader creates a false comparison and misleads the reader. If the writer is careful, though, definition can go a long way in clarifying major points in your essay, both for the reader and the writer.

In writing essays, you will find all these strategies helpful in making your points understood. Most essays employ a combination of these strategies, using each to make a particular point or support a larger discussion. Using multiple strategies gives your essay a variety of perspectives and makes it easier for the reader to understand what you are trying to say. Being aware of these strategies makes your writing tasks much easier and, more importantly, you can be confident your essay conveys the meaning and purpose you intend.

▼ A Sample Essay Using Multiple Strategies

Consider the following essay, "Texting Your Feelings, Symbol by Symbol" by Nick Bilton. In this reaction essay, the writer uses multiple strategies to communicate his thoughts on the use of textual symbols to convey feelings. Look carefully to see if you can spot the author's inclusion of specific examples, comparison and contrast, definition, and narration within the essay.

Texting Your Feelings, Symbol by Symbol
Nick Bilton

I recently had to sit my friend down for a modern-day digital intervention. It wasn't that he was using his phone at dinner, or that he was hitting "reply all" on e-mail threads, or leaving unnecessary voice mail messages. No, this was much worse.

A few weeks ago my friend, Michael Galpert, who is 30 yearold [sic] and is founder of SuperCalendar, a personal assistant Web site, lives in New York City and was visiting the West Coast for work. I set him up on a date with a friend who lives in Los Angeles. The first date went well and the two decided to see each other again.

When Michael returned to New York, he and his new romantic interest started text messaging, and, as you often do if you are of a certain tech-savvy set, were communicating via emoji. As my colleague Jenna Wortham explained this year, emoji are the cartoonlike and more elaborate cousins of emoticons—those combinations of colons, parentheses and other punctuation that can convey expressions like a smile or a wink. ;-)

The woman Michael was courting would type sweet nothings to him using emoji icons— a lady dancing, high heels or a martini with an olive—and this is where things went awry.

Michael would respond with the "thumbs up" emoji, a hand that looks as if it belongs to an inflated cartoon character. When she would text "I'm excited to see you," followed by a pink heart, Michael would respond with a thumbs up.

The woman confided to me and a friend that she believed that based on his use of emoji, Michael was clearly not interested in her and just wanted to be friends. ""It's like he's saying 'Hey, dude' or 'Sure, bro' when he sends me that emoji," she told me. "It's not cute."

That's when I had to intervene.

Sure, it might sound a bit odd that a new, long-distance relationship could fizzle because a tiny icon was misused, yet these types of messaging miscommunications happen often (though perhaps not quite as comically). The emoji icons can be baffling to the American adults who, whether they realize it or not, are taking their social cues from Japanese teenagers.

But American adults are not the first grown-ups with a tin ear for emoji.

"In Japan, there was a similar, interesting moment when you started to see older folks and men start using these kind [sic]of cute aspects—these emoji—that originally came from middle-school girl, mobile-phone culture," said Mimi Ito, a cultural anthropologist at the University of California, Irvine, who studies how young people use digital media in Asia and the United States. "Now, as emoji are seeing more adoption in the U.S., you're seeing a form of communication being used that was clearly developed and marketed to a different demographic."

Emoji date back to 1995, when people used pagers instead of smartphones and NTT DoCoMo, Japan's biggest cellular phone operator, added a small heart icon to its pagers. The heart spread rapidly among Japanese teenagers because it allowed them to express an emotion that was almost impossible to portray in small snippets of text.

While emoji made their way to America a few years later, not many people used them until 2011, when Apple included the symbols in iOS 5, the company's mobile operating system. But Apple was not trying to woo American customers when it introduced the colorful pictorial icons. It was going after Japanese teenagers, said Fred Benenson, a data engineer at Kickstarter and the author of "Emoji Dick," a recreation of Herman Melville's classic novel, "Moby Dick," told entirely in emoji.

Mr. Benenson said that once Apple added emoji to iOS—they required a separate downloadable app but are now available in a manually activated keyboard—it was apparent that they could be used to tell a much longer story. But, he warned, sometimes emoji can be lost in translation.

"There are these blind spots with emoji, as a lot of choices for the icons bias towards Japanese culture," he said.

There are plenty of emoji for Japanese food like sushi, ramen noodles, and mochi balls on a skewer. There are also lots of animals, including a dog, cat, mouse, bunny, frog, and two camels. Unfortunately, emoji for slices of Americana like tacos and hot dogs are hard to find.

American companies like Facebook have recently taken to emoji. But Facebook has been learning that the billion-plus people who communicate across its social network not only speak many different languages but also use emoji differently. Greg Marra, a Facebook product manager, recently traveled to India and Japan to better understand the differences.

"We discovered that in the Asian culture, the expression on an emoji face isn't necessarily what conveys emotion. It's the context of where that face is located," Mr. Marra said.

In Asian cultures, an emoji face in dark clouds would show that someone is sad and having a bad day. A face on a beach with the sun glaring means they are happy. In the United States, the emotion on the face tells the story, not the surroundings. Also, "stars for eyes could mean something completely different in Asia than using dots for eyes," he said.

Eventually, though, Americans will catch on.

"Usually we see about a 10-year lag from when a new communication is adopted and when it becomes a norm," Ms. Ito said. "We're somewhere in the middle of that curve right now as an American-specific emoji culture forms in the U.S."

As for Michael, things didn't work out with the woman he was inadvertently insulting. But he said he learned a lesson along the way. "I'm no longer using the thumbs-up emoji," he said recently. "I've switched it out for the star emoji."

Chapter 2

Summarizing, Paraphrasing and Quoting

In this text, you are learning how to use researched material to explain a point or support a contention. You will present your researched information in your paper in one of three formats: as a summary, as a paraphrase, or as a quotation. Sometimes when you try to include outside sources in an essay, the paper sounds as though it was copied directly from an encyclopedia or from a choppy series of sources. This problem can be avoided if you understand how to put researched information in your own words and how to select specific details to quote directly. Chapter 2 will help you master the skills of summarizing, paraphrasing, and quoting.

Objectives

- define the concepts of summarizing, paraphrasing, and quoting;

- explain the use of all three formats in a research paper;

- identify the common mistakes to avoid.

▼ Summarizing

In a research paper, you are using information from other sources to support or add credence to your points or assertions. Most of the time you will present that information in the form of a summary. When you summarize a passage, you are stating the main ideas of that passage and eliminating most of the detail. Whether you summarize a sentence, a paragraph, several paragraphs, a page, or several pages, you are always following the same process: you are condensing or shortening the material to its key points.

Before you begin to write a summary, you first need to read the entire passage carefully. After getting an understanding of the whole passage, you should reread the passage, looking for all the key points. If the passage is an essay or several paragraphs, you are looking for the thesis or main idea and the sentences that support it. If the passage is a single paragraph, you are looking for the topic sentence and the sub-topic ideas. Remember you are not concentrating on the specific details in a summary. You may want to highlight the key ideas in the passage you are reading if you can. If not, then write down these key ideas on a sheet of paper. Once you have determined the key points of the passage, you are ready to write your summary. Referring to the ideas you highlighted or wrote on the sheet of paper, express these ideas in your own words. Do not use the exact wording from the original passage in your summary.

Mistakes to Avoid When Writing a Summary

- Adding too much detail that distracts from the key points you are trying to make.

- Using the exact words from the original passage and not quoting them.

Let's say for a history class you are writing a research paper on the establishment of a Jewish homeland after World War Two. For your paper, you might want to summarize the following paragraphs from the *Eleanor: The Years Alone* by Joseph Lash.

In Palestine, the British rejection of the joint commission's recommendations turned the desperate Jewish settlers toward acts of terrorism against the British forces and illegal immigration organized by the Jewish defense force, the Haganah. Bridges were blown up and British officers kidnapped. There were pitched battles between British and Jewish troops. The British, with 50,000 troops in Palestine, decided on some drastic action. The Zionist leaders were jailed. That strengthened the influences of the terrorists. The King David Hotel, headquarters of the mandatory and the British Army, was blown up with forty-three killed and forty-three injured.

Your summary of this paragraph might read as follows:

> After the British repudiated the commission's proposals, terrorist acts by Jewish occupants and armed conflict between British and Jewish forces occurred in Palestine. In retaliation for the imprisoning of Zionist leaders by the British, Jewish extremists bombed the British Army headquarters, the King David Hotel, killing and injuring many.

The type of summary we have been discussing up to this point is the type you use as a part of a larger work. The summary is used to support other information. There are times, though, when you may be required to write a stand-alone summary. Two types of summaries that fall into this category are the abstract or *précis* and the annotated bibliography.

An abstract, also called a précis, is a summary of an entire text, whether it is an article or a book. Because you are summarizing an entire text in this instance, the length of an abstract is longer than the type of summary we previously discussed. You are highlighting for your reader the main premise of the text and the key topics covered in that text. You are letting your reader know the major points being made. As mentioned previously, make sure you express all the points in your own words. Keep the major points in the same order as they appear in the original work. Also, keep your ideas in the same proportions as the original. For example, if there are three main points in the article you are summarizing and the author devotes approximately one-third of his article to each, you should devote approximately one-third of your summary to each point. Begin an abstract by identifying the source, giving the author, title, and publication date of the work. Also, mention the type of source it is, such as a book, article, movie, or play. For example, the beginning of an abstract might read: "John Horgan in his March 2013 *National Geographic* article "The drones come home" discusses...." After reading your abstract, the reader should have a good understanding of what is being discussed in the text by the author and what the author's main contentions are without having to read the original text.

A bibliography is a listing of references. An annotated bibliography is a listing of references that includes a brief summary of the text listed. The annotated bibliography gives your reader an overview of the main premise of the text and the key topics. It generally does not go into as much detail as the abstract or précis. Chapter 7 discusses the development and use of a bibliography in greater detail.

Many times a professor will ask you to compile an annotated bibliography on a topic. This assignment provides you and your reader with a handy resource. You will remember, and your reader will know, if a particular source would be a valuable resource to consult when writing a paper on that topic. For example, here is an abstract of the John Horgan article from the *National Geographic* of March 2013 as it is presented in the *Academic Search Complete* database:

> The article looks at potential non-military applications for unmanned aerial vehicles (UAVs), also known as *drones*, following the approval of their use in domestic airspace by the U.S. Federal Aviation Administration (FAA) by September 30, 2015. Possible UAV uses include police surveillance, crop monitoring, and traffic control. Other topics include research into *drone* navigation systems, miniature UAVs which mimic birds or insects, and terrorism, safety, and privacy concerns.

▼ Paraphrasing

When you paraphrase, you take someone else's ideas and put them into your own words. Unlike a summary, a paraphrase conveys all the ideas of the original passage. You may change the order of the ideas from the original, but you do not omit any of the points or details. Consequently, your paraphrase of a passage will be approximately the same length as the original.

Before you begin to write a paraphrase, first make sure you understand the meaning of the original passage. Read the original passage carefully and thoroughly. If there are any words you do not understand, make sure you look up the words in a dictionary. If you are having trouble interpreting the original passage, ask your instructor, a family member, or a friend to help you clarify your understanding. You will not be able to write a clear and accurate paraphrase if there is any part of the original passage you do not understand.

After you are sure you understand the original passage, you are ready to write your paraphrase. To make sure you do not mimic the wording of the original passage too closely, put the passage aside that you are paraphrasing and do not look at it as you write. After you have put together your first draft, then refer to the original passage to see if there are any points or details that you have omitted. If you cannot think of a synonymous word for a word in the original passage, you may want to refer to a thesaurus. However, be very careful when using a thesaurus so that you do not select a word that changes the original connotation of the passage.

As you are writing your passage, make sure you use your own writing style. Use the sentence patterns that you traditionally use when you write. Don't change your style to match the style of the original passage. Too often trying to imitate the style of the original author results in a stilted and awkward paraphrase that is not clear to the reader. Choose words that are comfortable for your vocabulary.

Remember you can change the order of the ideas from the original passage. You may combine points or separate points from how they appear in the original. Re-ordering ideas will change the writing style of the original author's to your own. Just do not leave out any of the points or details from the original passage in your paraphrase.

Mistakes to Avoid When Writing a Paraphrase	• Misinterpreting the original passage • Keeping the wording of the paraphrase too much like the original • Keeping the writing style of the paraphrase too much like the original • Writing an unclear or awkward paraphrase • Using similar words in your paraphrase to the wording in the original passage that do not have the correct connotation of the original • Omitting ideas or details from the original passage • Inadequately documenting the paraphrase

For an art paper on Dadaism, you might want to paraphrase to the following two sentences from the *History of Art*:

> It is hardly surprising that the mechanized mass killing of the First World War should have driven Duchamp to despair. Together with a number of others who shared his attitude, he launched in protest a movement called Dada (or Dadaism).

Your paraphrase of these sentences might read this way:

> Duchamp was predictably despondent over the "mechanized" atrocities of World War I. Consequently in reaction to these horrors, he, with several like-minded colleagues, began the art movement known as Dada, also named Dadaism.

Please note that the word *mechanized* is in quotation marks to indicate that it was used in the original passage. Because of the importance of the word in association with World War I and the growth of Dadaism, it is used as is in the paraphrased version.

▼ Quoting

You will find that there are times you will want to use researched material in its original wording. You do not want to condense the information, nor do you want to present it in your own words. In these cases, you will quote directly from the original passage. There are three primary reasons for presenting researched information as a direct quotation:

1. You want the direct words of an authority to support your contention to add credibility to your position.

2. The impact of the original passage will be diminished if you use your own words.

3. You really cannot think of another way to reword the passage.

When quoting, you will want to be familiar with three different punctuation marks that will simplify and add clarity to your direct quotations.

ELLIPSIS MARKS

The ellipsis marks are three dots that work together as a unit to indicate that you have omitted words from the original passage when you quoted. The three dots represent the location of the omitted words. Words are omitted in a case of parenthetical ideas or unnecessary detail to the main idea you want to quote. When the omitted material comes at the end of a quoted statement, use four dots, with the fourth one serving as the period at the end of the sentence.

For example, take this sentence from an article from the *AARP Bulletin* of April 2014 dealing with tax delinquency and senior citizens:

> Although most foreclosures are triggered by homeowners falling behind on their mortgage payments, the number of foreclosures tied to delinquent tax payments is rising, according to the National Consumer Law Center, a nonprofit advocacy group.

Depending on how you used this sentence as a direct quotation in your paper, it could look as follows:

> "...the number of foreclosures tied to delinquent tax payments is rising, according to the National Consumer Law Center, a nonprofit advocacy group."

or

> "Although most foreclosures are triggered by homeowners falling behind on their mortgage payments, the number of foreclosures tied to delinquent tax payments is rising...."

BRACKETS

Brackets are used when you want to add your own words to a quotation to help with clarification or to make a comment.

Generally you use brackets to explain the reference of a pronoun found in the quoted material or to clarify an idea being discussed that might have been lost because of omitted words.

For example, instead of writing a summary of the passage taken from *Eleanor: The Years Alone,* you wanted to take the first line as a quotation. It would look like this:

> "In Palestine, the British rejection of the joint commission's [the Anglo-American Committee of Inquiry] recommendations turned

the desperate Jewish settlers toward acts of terrorism against the British forces and illegal immigration organized by the Jewish defense force, the Haganah."

The brackets are used to identify the joint commission that is referenced.

SINGLE QUOTATION MARKS

Single quotation marks are used when quoted material already appears in the passage you want to quote. In this situation, you convert the quotation marks in the original passage to single quotation marks. For example, you want to use the following sentence from the *History of Art* as a quotation in your paper:

> Picasso's *Three Musicians* shows this "cut-paper style" so consistently that we cannot tell from the reproduction whether it is painted or pasted.

As presented in your paper, the quotation would appear as follows:

> "Picasso's *Three Musicians* shows this 'cut-paper style' so consistently that we cannot tell from the reproduction whether it is painted or pasted."

Mistakes to Avoid When Quoting	<ul><li>Quoting a passage incorrectly</li><li>Changing any of the original wording in a passage, including spelling and grammar errors</li><li>Leaving out words, causing the meaning of the original passage to change</li><li>Taking the quotation out of context and thus changing the meaning</li><li>Inserting your own words in a quotation without using brackets</li><li>Not using single quotation marks around quoted material in the original passage</li></ul>

▼ Using Summary, Paraphrase, and Quotation in a Paper

When you write a research paper, you use summaries, paraphrases, and quotations to help clarify a point, support an assertion, and verify a contention. For your research paper to be effective, you want the researched information to blend in smoothly with your own ideas. To achieve this coherence, first present the point you are trying to make and any explanation needed. Then, include your researched information as support, no matter what format or what combination of formats you use. After including your researched material, comment on that information to explain how it substantiates your point.

When you include the researched information in your paper, make sure you adequately document this information. You do not want your reader to think that the information is from your own knowledge or experience if you are getting it from another source. You need to tell your reader who originally wrote or said the information, who this person is, and where you found the information. Such documentation will prevent you from committing *plagiarism*, the stealing of someone else's ideas. Chapter 6 will explain how to present documented information in your essay.

Chapter 3

Researching a Topic

You are a basketball fan and want to know how your favorite professional team is doing. You are getting ready to travel to Iceland this summer and want to know what the average temperature is there in July. You need a new truck and want to know which model provides the best gas mileage. To find the answers to these questions, you might check your local newspaper, do a Google search, or read about the most recent data in *Consumer Reports*, respectively. In each scenario, you are performing research, conducting an investigation to gather information.

Throughout your academic and professional career, you will be asked to write about topics that require you to explain, describe, or argue a particular point of view. In personal essay writing, you support your point of view with information gathered from your own experience. With research writing, though, you are dealing with topics that you do not know have the sufficient background or knowledge to discuss, so you must rely on outside sources to provide you with that information. The major difference between the type of research described in the opening scenarios and the type of research performed for academic writing is academic research requires a formal, organized plan. Chapter 3 introduces you to the initial steps in the research writing process.

Objectives

- ◆ discuss the importance of audience;

- ◆ suggest ways to select and narrow your topic effectively;

- ◆ describe the two types of research sources;

- ◆ explain the current approaches to accessing information.

▼ CONSIDER YOUR AUDIENCE

At this point in your life, you probably have noticed that, despite the spiritual admonishments to do so, you can't treat everyone with whom you come into contact the same. Early on, you probably noticed that the way you talk to your best friend may not be the same way you talk to your mother. The words you use when you hit your hand with a hammer while repairing your roof are probably different from the words you use when you hit a slice on the golf course while playing golf with the local rabbi. Indeed, most successful people are very adept at knowing the appropriate action and words to use in any particular situation. Sizing up your audience, knowing what they expect to hear, and knowing the appropriate tone and delivery that will be most effective for that audience will enhance your ability to make your point of view understood and appreciated.

Questions to Ask Before Deciding on Topic/Strategy	1. What are the demographic variables (age, sex, race, religion, and so forth) of my audience? 2. What are my audience's interests? 3. What are my audience's beliefs, attitudes, and values? 4. What does my audience already know? 5. What does my audience need to know?

The answers to all of these questions will help you decide on a topic and the appropriate strategy and tone as you plan your essay. Remember that, while the facts seemingly may support your point of view, the audience's *perception* of those facts may be more important in determining the success of your essay. The audience for whom you are writing should always be an important consideration as you plan and develop your research paper.

Let's say that you have been given the assignment to research the day you were born. If you were writing to a general audience with varied backgrounds, you would concentrate on the major national events reported that day, for they would have the most impact on people in general. If you were writing for your economics professor and classmates, you would explore the business stories in the newspaper or on the Internet to find out what were the important economic stories on that day. If this assignment were for your humanities class, you would research websites and databases that focus on the arts, looking for the highlights in theater, art, and music. As this example shows, knowing your audience is key to selecting your topic, the first step in the research writing process.

▼ Selecting and Narrowing Your Topic

When it comes to selecting a topic for a research paper, you face two situations: one in which your professor assigns you the topic and one in which you get to write on any topic you choose. In this second situation, follow a few guidelines in your topic selection. First, select a topic about which you care deeply. You will be doing much reading about your topic, so it definitely should be one you find very interesting. Second, choose a topic about which you have some knowledge. With such a background, you will have a better understanding of the abundance of material you will be reading. There is certainly nothing wrong, though, with researching a topic that interests you but about which you have no knowledge; however, even in this case, you should be certain you will understand the issues, concepts, and terminology you will encounter in your research.

Once you have selected your topic, you will soon find that your work with that topic is still not done. Let's say your humanities professor asks you to write a research paper, and based on your interest, you select the Romantic Period. Your first response is to head for the library or a popular Internet search engine such as Google and immediately start a search on the Romantic Period. What you quickly find is that there are *thousands* of published items listed under the broad heading of Romantic Period, and you are left floundering, unsure of what exactly to examine. Encountering an overwhelming number of sources is a very common dilemma, but one you can quickly remedy by a simple process of narrowing your topic.

One way to approach the narrowing process is by looking at a general discussion of the broad topic. An encyclopedia or a history book that offers a historical survey might provide a good start. As you read, note some recurring topics. Perhaps you notice that the French Revolution is regularly mentioned and that several literary names—Wordsworth, Coleridge, and Keats are prominently discussed. Perhaps you also read that nature and the concept of the "noble savage" are also mentioned as Romantic themes. With these various concepts in mind, you can now begin the process of discovering any relationships that might exist between them. You wonder, "What exactly is a 'noble savage' and what is the connection with Coleridge?"

A second approach to narrowing your topic is to do an Internet search. Going to one of the search engines, such as Google, you type in Romantic Period. You then get several categories from which to choose, such as literature, periods and styles, music, and art. You decide to click on music. Your search brings up a site on Romantic music, and upon reading, you see such names as Wagner, Chopin, Liszt and such concepts as nationalism, expressionism, and chromaticism. With these various concepts in mind, you again begin the process of discovering any relationships that might exist between them. This time you ask, "What is the connection between nationalism and Wagner's operas?"

The process of discovery and association will help you narrow your topic to a more specific focus, such as Coleridge and the "noble savage" or Wagner and nationalism. However, you have a long way to go before you actually determine what your final topic and point of view will be. You first must thoroughly investigate your narrowed topic. To conduct this investigation, you need to know where and how to locate your information.

▼ CONDUCTING YOUR RESEARCH

Once you have narrowed your topic and have identified the major concepts you need to research, you must now consider the kind of research sources you need. Researchers identify two kinds of sources available: *primary sources* and *secondary sources*. Primary sources are actual records and materials that relate to your topic. For example, an original poem written by Coleridge, a collection of Coleridge's letters, and drawings of "noble savages" by Romantic artists are all primary sources. Secondary sources are not original works, but are accounts and explanations of people and events, usually written some time after the people lived or the events happened. A history book is a secondary source, but quotations of eyewitnesses to an event or quotations of famous people within those history books are primary sources. Most visual documents such as photographs, films, and historical drawings are also primary sources. It is important to remember, though, that being a primary source does not necessarily make it truthful or accurate. Any person, including photographers, can distort truth with bias and omission. A photographer who publishes a photo of looters in a natural disaster chooses *not* to show pictures of the countless acts of heroism and courage that are just as much a part of the event. This limited scope is a common criticism of news reporting—that its focus is only on the negative events of our daily existence and not on the many good things that are happening, too. The point is that whatever kind of sources you choose to use, the reliability of the sources and the value of their contribution to your research is not necessarily determined by whether they are primary or secondary; you will have to use other criteria to determine their reliability.

▼ ACCESSING INFORMATION: THE LIBRARY

Perhaps in no other area of your educational program has change been more apparent than in the contemporary library and the way you access information. In this age of information explosion, we are constantly experiencing the modern affliction of information "overload." The fact is, we are facing a major challenge of handling the tremendous onslaught of textual information—how we find it, how we classify and organize it, how we store it, and how we access and use it are all the dilemmas of the modern researcher. While the task can seem challenging, let's look at some of the tools available to you as you try to find the information you need to complete your class writing assignments or research projects or just to learn more about things that are of personal interest to you.

First, remember the library is still the best place to begin your search for information. Unless you are a professional information specialist yourself, simply going to your personal computer and typing in a topic will usually only provide you with thousands of "hits" on the topic you are researching. How will you know which ones are useful? How will you separate the scholarly text from the rantings and ravings of a radical blogger? How can you focus and narrow your search in order to maximize your time and get the most relevant documents? Again, unless you are a specialist, you probably won't be able to do many of these tasks and will waste valuable hours weeding through the thousands of documents confronting you.

Libraries offer you the services and the experts to find quickly the answers you need for your research. Whether you access your documents electronically through websites and databases or through magazines or books, the library is best equipped and staffed to help you find the material you require. Don't overestimate your own research abilities; when you have access to public services that are free, you are wise to take full advantage of them and use the time you save for that "life after research."

So, what will you find when you get to the library? First, remember the library has its own way of classifying information so you can readily locate what you need. Most academic libraries use the Library of Congress (LOC) system (public libraries use the Dewey Decimal System) to arrange information. The LOC arranges materials by subject and assigns a letter to designate the particular area. For example, the letter N deals with arts, and any number beginning with N deals with art. A second letter will further narrow the broad arts category. NA deals with architecture while NB deals with sculpture. Further numbers and letters, called "call numbers," narrow the topic even further until a specific book is identified. A book titled *Modern American Sculpture* has an LOC call number of NB212.A8. Once you write down the call number, the library stacks and bookcases are usually clearly marked to allow you quick access to the particular book you seek. If you can't find it, the librarian can help you or tell you whether the material has been checked out.

Most modern libraries provide an online catalog of all call numbers so that you can access the material you need through a keyboard search. You can perform these searches by author, subject, keyword, or title. If you have trouble finding your book, article, or documentary, the librarian can show you ways to focus your search or help you locate an alternative source. Increasingly many libraries carry electronic books or ebooks. If you have a member of that library or have access to its holdings, you will be able to download an ebook on your computer for your use. (Similarly, many audio-visual resources are now in electronic form for download.)

In many instances, the online catalog allows you to access the library's holdings from your home or workplace. Even at home, though, you can still get help from the librarian by chatting online or calling the reference desk if you have any questions or problems with your research. Many libraries now offer reference service via live online chat and e-mail. You can send the librarian a question, and a response is usually guaranteed within a certain time period. Remember, you don't have to be a computer genius to navigate the library catalog; the time you save in getting the document can be spent analyzing its contents.

While books provide you with a great deal of information, periodicals (magazines, journals, and newspapers) are rich sources of more up-to-date research. Magazines and journals are published at frequent intervals and are excellent documents in which to locate opinions and data about recent events and the latest research. Certainly, newspapers print information about events within hours of their occurrence. To locate articles in periodicals, you should consult online periodical subscription databases. General interest magazine databases available are *Reader's Guide* and *Info Trac*. Some helpful newspaper databases are *NewsBank, New York Times*, and *Wall Street Journal*. The first database will help you locate your topic in articles in newspapers across the United States and the other two in articles in those specific newspapers. Another valuable source of information is scholarly journals. Scholarly journals are usually sponsored by professional organizations in various academic disciplines and the articles included have undergone peer-review. Some examples of general academic databases are *Academic OneFile, Academic Search Complete*, and *JSTOR*. There are also other databases for specialized academic disciplines or areas. For instance, **ERIC** is the leading index for educational articles, **MedLine** covers medical literature, and **Business Source Complete** covers business materials. While research libraries carry a wide selection of newspapers and periodicals from all over the world, your local library may carry only the most popular periodicals and newspapers. Even if you live in a small town with a small library, you may still be able to get the article you need. Many on-line indexes offer not only the periodical's citation but also the full text of the article as well. Since access to these indexes and full-text articles may be restricted by licenses, you may need to have the appropriate identification and password to gain access, so check with your school or public librarian about how you can obtain entry. Another service your library may offer to access articles and materials not locally available is that of interlibrary loans. Though this process may take some time, critical sources you need for your research are often only available through this service, and the wait to get your materials sent to you is well worth the effort to access the materials.

Some libraries may also provide a repository of government publications that may prove helpful to your research. Again, your reference librarian can help you research government publications, and if the library doesn't carry the documents, the librarian can certainly direct you to their source or provide them to you via interlibrary loan. Government documents can also be located in the Government Reporter section of your library's SIRS KnowledgeSource database. Most government documents are now appearing, though, on Internet sites and are freely accessible to anyone. **FedWorld (www.fedworld.gov)** is an Internet site that will allow you access to numerous government web locations, and **Thomas (Thomas.loc.gov)** is the web page for the United States Congress.

Finally, you can access government documents on the appropriate government agency website, whether local, state, or federal.

▼ USING ELECTRONIC SEARCHES

When using online databases, you should first consult the database's "help" or "about" section that explains how to search. Often, your search will provide you with other subject headings, but finding the right key words or appropriate subject headings can be a problem. Your librarian can help you focus your search if you can't locate the information you seek.

If your topic is too general and your selection of possible materials too large, you might want to use a Boolean search, named after George Boole, who developed the major concepts of symbolic logic. A **Boolean search** simply combines your key words using the words *AND, NOT,* or *OR* (the so-called "Boolean operators"). For example, if you are looking for "service dogs," that word alone might give you too many articles to explore. If you are really interested only in the use of service dogs with veterans suffering from post-traumatic stress, you could try combining "service dogs" and "PTSD." The search will then give you only those articles that deal with these concepts.

If you want to examine the use of service dogs with veterans with post-traumatic and with children with autism, you might try "service dogs AND (PTSD OR autism)." Notice that OR is usually used in parentheses like a math equation. Finally, you can exclude information in order to narrow your search by using NOT: "service dogs NOT blindness" finds articles dealing the use of service dogs for use with a range of disabilities, except blindness. A Boolean search will help you quickly narrow a broad topic and will provide you with a smaller list of articles for you to browse.

With so much of today's research being done on the Internet, you need to understand some of the systems you will be using and some of the terms and procedures you might encounter. The Internet itself is a configuration of networks of computers from every country in the world. From your terminal, you can access and communicate with other computers in the configuration. To contact a Website, you must have an address, called its "URL" (Uniform Resource Locator), which has three parts. The first is the prefix, which is usually "www." Next is the name of the owner – a person's name, a company, a school, or an organization. Finally, the last part of the URL is the type of site. If it is a company, it is "**.com**." An educational site would be "**.edu**" while an organization is "**.org**." Dots separate each of these three parts. Two major concerns with the Internet are that it is so large, with millions of addresses, and that it is dynamic, adding new addresses continuously. As a result, you may have difficulty finding the particular addresses you need for your research. While much of the Internet is free, a number of commercial sites require a subscription for access.

If you are a frequent visitor to the Internet, you already are familiar with **search engines**, which give access to information on the Web. Search engines allow you to search multiple sites at once and will give you the top results of your subject. Generally, these results are listed in order of popularity of the sites or with paid advertising sites appearing first. The two most popular search engines are Google and Yahoo.

Because of the wealth of information on the Internet, you will need a search strategy to make the finding of research on your selected topic manageable. For example, if you were writing a research paper on service dogs and type those words in the Google search engine, you will come up with 417,000,000 results. However, if you include those same words with quotation marks around them, only those articles with that exact phrasing will appear. In this case, "service dogs" results in 539,000 listings. If you narrow the focus of service dogs to their use with individuals suffering with post-traumatic stress disorder, you could type in "service dogs" and "PTSD" resulting in 151,000 entries. As you can see, as you refine the search, the number of hits decreases.

▼ PROBLEMS ON THE INTERNET

Besides the huge volume of information available to you on the Web, you need to be aware of other concerns about using the Web. Remember that the Internet will probably not allow you to do an in-depth study unless you are willing to pay for the resources or you have access to copyrighted materials through your library or organization. If you are serious about the quality and accuracy of your research, the Internet cannot yet replace the library for finding reliable information. For materials you do find on the Web, you must also be aware that there is very little censorship or quality control for materials that are published on-line. Almost anyone can put an opinion on the Web, regardless of its accuracy or bias. Whatever you find on the Web, you must assess its credibility. First, double-check any statistics you glean from the Web against known and reliable sources. Don't assume the data has already been verified! Second, try to assess the credibility of the author. Can you verify whether he or she is an expert in the field? Has he or she published other works? What do other professionals say about this person? Remember, people can claim many things about themselves in order to assert an opinion; be aware that people often are more concerned with expressing their personal opinions and biases than with presenting carefully researched data. The more objective you judge the author to be, the more likely the research has value to your study. Always look at the URL to help you decide the degree of objectivity. URLs ending in *.edu* or *.gov* are usually good indicators they are reliable sources of objective research and data. Sites ending in *.org* will give you information that particular organization wants you to have. Sites with *.com* will give you positive information about the products they are marketing; it is not likely you will see that company providing studies that are negative toward their products except by court order (as was the case with tobacco companies who, as part of court settlements, were required to publish sensitive research reports that showed negligence or false information in the industry's studies of smoking and cancer). Finally, watch for blogs and other personal web pages. With these types of sites, you are generally looking at someone's personal opinion and not a legitimate piece of research. Make sure you carefully investigate the credentials of the blogger or the person whose website you have found before you would even begin to consider including information from such sites in your paper.

Another problem when using the Web is plagiarizing. Correct citation format is explained in Chapter 6, but be sure you understand that just because you find information on the Web, you are not exempt from citing your source. As with all research, the validity of your information is based, in part, on the ability of the reader to locate your information. If you don't cite the source, the reader cannot consider the information in his assessment of your work and your research will be weakened or rendered invalid as a result.

The twenty-first century researcher has many new ways to access the information that has become the fuel and force driving the Information Age. Libraries have re-defined themselves in order to provide you with the tools you need to access and utilize the flood of information available. The computer, which is largely responsible for the new age, has also provided us the means to harness and control this information. In many ways, research is much easier today than it was in the past, but it does require more deliberate thought and process in order to find the information required. If, indeed, knowledge is power, every world citizen has been empowered with the ability to use information that was previously only the domain of the elite. With the tools you have available to you, you can research and find almost any topic known, and the library is the gateway to that knowledge.

Gathering Your Information

Once you have selected a topic, you are ready to begin gathering the information for your research paper. As you learned in Chapter 3, you will be researching both primary and secondary sources. You learned how to use the library and Internet to find these sources on your topic. Chapter 4 will discuss the process for gathering your information and for recording it for possible use in your paper. By having a well-established plan for obtaining the information, you will simplify the writing process.

Objectives

- explain guiding questions;

- provide guidelines for developing the working bibliography;

- delineate steps for taking notes;

- establish criteria for evaluating sources.

▼ CONSTRUCTING GUIDING QUESTIONS

Even though you have narrowed your topic selection, you need direction in determining what information you should be looking for with regard to your topic and what information you should record. You do not have the time to read and record all the information you find on your topic. To help you focus your research, begin the gathering process by creating some guiding questions. These are possible questions to which you would like to find the answers in your research. Although only one question will eventually be the focus of your paper, you should begin with several because you are not yet sure how much information you can find on a particular question. Also, as you research, you might find that what initially interested you may shift to another aspect of the topic.

As you construct guiding questions, remember to create questions that will allow you to develop a thesis, in other words questions that require you to take a position on your topic or draw some conclusion. In writing your questions, avoid questions that are too narrow or too broad. Develop guiding questions whose answers provide enough support to meet the assigned length of your paper. If a question is too narrow, you will be able to answer it in a word, a sentence, or brief paragraph. The question does not lead to sufficient development of ideas. If the question is too broad, you will not be effectively guided in your research. Your question will be so vague or open-ended that too much material will be needed to answer, thus not helping you to focus your topic.

Also, avoid guiding questions that are biased. Such questions, by their wording, already imply the position you will take on your topic. Controlling questions should be objective. You should not have a particular viewpoint in mind before you begin to write. If you already know what your position is on a topic, then you will be biased in your reading and may overlook important material that disproves or does not substantiate your viewpoint.

Finally, avoid guiding questions that are not researchable. Be careful that you do not create a question whose focus is so local or regional that you will find limited research on that topic.

▼ PREPARING A WORKING BIBLIOGRAPHY

If you have a minor repair project around the house that you are going to take care of yourself, you make a written or mental list of those items you wish to purchase. Let's say that you are going to install a new faucet in your kitchen sink. Since this may be the first time you ever attempted such a project, you might decide to purchase a book on home repairs. You, of course, will need to purchase a new faucet and the other necessary parts to install it. Finally, you might not have the proper tools, so you will need to buy a wrench and a screwdriver. However, before purchasing these items, you actually compile another written or mental list, a list of stores at which you are going to make the purchases. You might decide to purchase the book at a bookstore, the faucet and supplies at a plumbing supply house, and the tools at a hardware store, or you might decide to purchase all your needed items at one of the mega-hardware stores. In any case, you are not exactly sure what you are going to find at these stores, but you, at least, know where you are going to look. By preparing this list of places, you have a plan to follow, so you are not driving all around town, wasting time and money, determining where you will find the items to complete your project.

When you are preparing to write a research paper, a working bibliography is similar to this list of stores for your home-repair project. A bibliography is a just a list of resources on a particular subject. A *working* bibliography means it is a starting point for finding the information on the subject about which are you writing. You have not actually found any of the sources yet or read any of the information; you just have given yourself a working plan as to where to find the material. Such a bibliography prevents you from walking aimlessly around the library, looking for books or magazines on your topic or endlessly surfing the Internet, trying to locate information.

When you have finished writing the final draft of your research paper, you will end with a *Works Cited* or *References* page that lists all the resources used in your paper. Chapter 7 discusses such bibliography lists in greater detail. For the working bibliography, you can create a file of index cards to help guide your research or you can maintain the bibliographic information on your computer allowing it to sort and alphabetize your possible sources for later transfer to your final draft. When using cards, you will use one index card for each possible source for your paper. (You should use 4″ x 6″ sized index cards for your working bibliography.) Remember that the key word is "possible." Your working bibliography just gives you possible sources for your paper; after you find the source, you may decide that the information is not relevant to your topic and not use that source at all for your paper.

As you locate various sources through the research methods described in the previous chapter, you will complete one index card or one entry on your computer for each source. You should complete such a card/entry at the time you discover a possible source, whether in your library's computer database or through a search engine over the Internet. Each index card/entry should include the author, title and publishing information for that source as well as the cataloguing reference number, if the source is a book located in a library. You should follow correct bibliographic format. You will use either the Modern Language Association (MLA) format or the American Psychological Association (APA) format, depending on the discipline for which you are writing. You want to make sure that you include all information specified by the appropriate format and follow the punctuation guidelines. By using the correct format on each bibliography card/entry, you will simplify the process when it comes to preparing your final *Works Cited or References* page.

Following are three different examples of working bibliography cards using the MLA format on the topic of antibiotic-resistant bacteria:

For *a book*, your entry should include the name of the author(s), the title of the book, and the publishing information. Consider the following example:

> Salyers, Abigail A., and Dixie D. Whitt. *Revenge of the*
>
> *Microbes: How Bacterial Resistance is Undermining*
>
> *the Antibiotic Miracle.* Washington, D.C.: ASM Press, 2005.
>
> QR177
> .S26
> FSCJ Library

For *an article from a periodical (weekly or monthly) in an online database,* list the name of the author (if one is identified), the title of the article, the name of the magazine, the date of the magazine, the page number(s) of the article, the title of the database, the medium of publication, and the access date.

> McKnight, Whitney. "Antibiotic-Related Illness in U.S Tops 2
>
> Million Annually." *Internal Medicine News* 1 Oct. 2013: 14.
>
> *Academic One File.* Web. 6 Nov. 2013.

For *an article from an online website,* give the author's name (if given), the title of the article, the name of the website, the publisher or sponsor of the site, the date of publication, the medium, and the date of access.

> Laskaway, Tom. "Finally, a Smoking Gun Connecting Livestock
>
> Antibiotics and Superbugs." *Grist.Org.* Grist Magazine,
>
> 24 Feb. 2012. Web. 13 Nov. 2013.

▼ EVALUATING YOUR SOURCES

After creating your working bibliography, you will need to determine which sources you will be using for your research paper. An important factor in that determination is the credibility of that source. Your readers may not accept your position and support if they feel your sources are not reliable or objective.

In analyzing the credibility of your sources, consider several factors. First, determine the qualifications of the author. You can find such information many times in bibliographical sketches included with the source, or you can research the person in a biographical reference work, such as *Who's Who in America*. In reviewing credentials, determine this person's educational preparation and work experience. Your goal is to verify that this person is truly an expert in the field about which he or she is writing. A good indication to determine if an author is a recognized expert is if you read references about this person in a variety of sources.

Besides verifying the credibility of the author, also remember to verify the credibility of any person referenced in the text whom you would like to quote or paraphrase for your paper. Before using this person to support a point, determine this person's credentials as you did for the author.

Similarly, when you use a journal, magazine, or newspaper, be aware of the credentials of that publication. Determine if that publication is considered a reputable and reliable source. For example there is a big credibility gap between *The New York Times* and a supermarket tabloid. Also, when it comes to scholarly journals, you should check with practitioners in a particular field to see which journals are considered to be the most respected and accepted for research in that discipline.

Another factor to consider in evaluating the credibility of the author is to see if there is any bias involved with the author's work. Does the author have a financial interest in the results of the study he conducted? Was the author paid to conduct the research by a particular company, clouding the objectivity of the work? Does the author have a particular political or religious bias, or has the author encountered some personal situation that might affect his or her objectivity when it comes to certain ideas?

A final factor to think about in determining the credibility of a source is the date of the publication. In most cases, you may consider that the more recent the publication, the more credible the source. With the speed with which information is obtained in today's technological and electronic age, information quickly becomes outdated. When dealing with online sources, be aware of several dates: the date the site was created, the date it was last updated, and the date you accessed it. The key date for the purposes of credibility (and documentation) is the date the site was last updated. Again, consider that the more recent the update, the more reliable the information should be.

▼ TAKING NOTES

After you have created your working bibliography, located your sources, and begun your reading, you are ready to begin the note-taking stage in the research writing process. This stage is the most important part of this process. It is the accuracy and thoroughness of your notes that will lead to your convincing your reader to accept the position you established in your thesis. Just as important, though, before you begin to write your paper, your notes will help you to refine your thesis and to construct an outline and, as you write your paper, will help to simplify the writing process.

The most effective way to take notes is to use note cards. Note cards will allow you to organize your paper more efficiently as well as to add and delete ideas more easily. You should use 4″ x 6″ index cards for your notes. If you prefer, you can type your notes electronically on your computer or laptop. However, you want to follow the same principles for taking notes on cards. Through copying and pasting, you can organize your notes into folders as discussed below.

No matter what approach you use for your notes to be effective, you need to remember two key points before beginning your note-taking. First, make sure you understand what you are reading. Before taking notes on a passage, you must understand the ideas being expressed. If there are any words you do not know in the passage, look up their definitions before trying to take notes. The only way for your notes to be accurate and eventually to be comprehensible in your paper is for you to have complete comprehension of the original passage. Second, write only one idea on a card. One idea does not necessarily mean one sentence. One idea could be one sentence, but it could also be one paragraph or a series of paragraphs. The important point is that when you read the information on one of your note cards, it expresses only one main idea. By having only one idea on a card, you will be able to shuffle your cards, moving information around easily when it comes to outlining your paper and writing your rough draft.

When you take notes, use one of three formats for your information: direct quotation, paraphrase, or summary. Chapter 2 discusses the conventions for handling these three formats for researched information. Which format you use depends on the original material and how detailed that material needs to be for your paper. If you need a specific piece of information to support your contention and you want someone's exact words to provide that support, then transfer the information onto your note card as a direct quotation. Of course, you will place quotation marks around that piece of information to remind you that it is a direct quotation. If you want the detail from the original source as support but you can simplify the wording, then paraphrase that information. Finally, if detail is not important, but the basic concept expressed in your source is, then summarize the information on your note card.

To be able to document the researched material included on your card correctly in your paper, label each card with certain information. In the left-hand corner of the card, if you know the author of your source, write the last name of that author. If the source has two or three authors, then list the last names of each author. If you have used more than one source written by the same author, include not only the last name but also one or two key words from the title of the source so that you will know which source by that author you used. If the author of the source is not identified, then in the left-hand corner, write one or two key words from the beginning of the title. In addition to the author or title information, also include the page number or numbers from that source where you found the material you have written on your card. Note that if you are using an online source, you will not have a page reference. The reason for needing only abbreviated information on your note cards regarding your sources is that you have already created bibliography cards/entries that list the complete source information.

You may run across the situation that the author of your source has quoted another person, and you want to use that other person's quotation in your paper. To remind yourself of this situation, when you transfer this quotation to your note card, include at the top of the card the name of the person quoted. Identify this information with the use of brackets. So in the top left-hand corner, write the last name of the author of the source you used plus the page number of the quotation. Then, in brackets beneath this author information, write the name of the person whose quotation you have taken down on your note card.

In addition to providing source information on the top of your note cards, include one other important item: in the right hand corner, write the topic of the card. Write one word or brief phrase that reminds you of the key idea found on that card. Any card that deals with that particular topic or idea should have the same label. These topic labels will be key in your organizing your notes and outlining your paper before you begin to write your rough draft.

When typing your notes on a computer, use a similar approach for the labeling of your notes. Make sure you have the appropriate source information on the top of each page. Also, for each note taken, assign the relevant topic label. These topic labels can then be used to create different folders for your notes. You can then cut and paste your notes from various sources into the relevant folder. Just remember when you transfer a note into a folder, that you copy the source information with that note.

Below are two examples of note cards on the topic of antibiotic-resistant bacteria, the first showing a direct quotation and the second a paraphrase:

McKnight	rate of infection
"Each year in the United States, more than 2 million people contract drug-resistant infections and 23,000 die."	

Salyers and Whitt 2	definition of antibiotics
Antibiotics are medicines made from natural substances such as mold or bacteria that inhibit or attack and kill the growth of other bacteria.	

(Note: Because the first note is from an online source, there is no page reference.)

▼ Note about Topic Labels

Reread your note cards daily to make sure you have labeled each card correctly. If you feel a better topic label would be more descriptive, re-label each card that has that topic with the new label.

Not only are the topic labels on your note cards important for helping you organize your paper, but also they will be helpful in guiding your research. As you review daily your note cards and the topic labels, you will see which topics have limited research gathered up to that point. If a particular topic is crucial to the support of your thesis, you will need to devote more attention to finding information on that topic.

▼ Writing a Tentative Thesis Statement

After you feel you have gathered enough research to begin to answer your guiding question, you are ready to craft a tentative thesis statement. It is called "tentative" because your thesis will become more defined as you outline your paper, continue to research your topic, and write your rough draft. The tentative thesis gives you a starting point for organizing your research and for drawing a conclusion based on that research.

Think about this....

Let's say that you have chosen your city's *Beachside neighborhood* as your topic after reading in your local newspaper that this neighborhood was built next to a landfill and residents are now experiencing health issues. Before researching this topic, you create such guiding questions as, *What are the health issues being faced by the Beachside residents?, What factors have contributed to these medical effects?,* and *What has been the city's response to this situation?* After conducting your research, you decide to answer the first question as the basis of your paper. Based on your initial research, you construct the following tentative thesis:

> Beachside residents are suffering serious medical problems caused by toxic pollution from their local landfill.

As you proceed with the next steps in the research-paper-writing process as described in the following chapter, this tentative thesis will serve to give you a helpful direction. However, as, or after, you write your first draft, you might find yourself needing to change that direction or at least to make it more specific.

With the construction of your tentative thesis, you are ready to move on to the writing stage. If you have found various reliable sources on your topic and taken thorough notes to answer your guiding question, you will find the actual writing of your paper to be a relatively simple task. However, keep in mind that just because you are ready to write does not mean the information-gathering stage is completely over. As you proceed with your writing, you will probably find that there are still gaps in your research. When you do, simply continue to gather information as described in this chapter.

Writing a Research Paper
Part I—Developing a Thesis Statement and Outline

At this point in the research writing process, you've probably spent a great deal of time reading about your topic in a variety of sources, and you've most likely generated quite a few notes. By now, you also should have a fairly clear idea of the direction your paper is headed and the points you will need to discuss in the paper. Chapter 5 will help you get started in writing your research paper.

Objectives

- provide strategies for writing an effective thesis statement and essay blueprint;

- explain the construction of a balanced outline.

▼ REFINING THE THESIS STATEMENT AND ESSAY BLUEPRINT

Before you begin writing, you need to spend a little time refining your thesis statement and essay blueprint. As Chapter 1 explained, the thesis statement is the one sentence in the introduction that lets your reader know the controlling or main idea of the entire essay. The thesis statement is often followed or preceded by an "essay blueprint," a sentence that helps the reader to see the paper's organizational plan. Also, the thesis should not be written as a question, nor should it begin with phrases such as, "In this paper, I will address…" or, "This essay will be about…."

At this point, you want to be certain that your thesis expresses a clear idea, perhaps even a course of action to be taken. Thesis statements can be written on three levels of action, depending on the reaction you are seeking from your reader: stimulation, motivation, and activation. If you simply want to stimulate your audience to think about an idea or an issue as a means of creating an awareness, you might write a thesis statement like the following:

> Beachside residents are suffering serious medical effects caused by toxic pollution from their local landfill.

A sentence such as this one might be followed by an essay map that outlines the medical effects caused by the pollution.

If, however, you want to take your reader a little deeper into the issue, leading the reader to the source of the problem and suggesting a need for a solution, you might write a statement like this one:

> The inadequate response of the city to the toxic pollution of the Beachside landfill has resulted in serious medical effects being suffered by Beach residents.

This sentence not only states the problem, but also names the responsible party, and while the statement does not say who should take action, it suggests that action needs to be taken by someone.

To move your thesis to the next level, that of activation, you want to move your reader toward taking action, so you need to use action words. Try this statement:

> Because of the serious health concerns faced by Beachside residents, city council members must immediately adopt a responsible cleanup plan for the Beachside neighborhood.

Note the word *must* in the thesis above. Using words like *should* and *must* in the thesis is a good way to include a verb that expresses action. Now let's add an essay blueprint to the thesis statement:

> Because of the serious health concerns faced by Beachside residents, city council members must immediately adopt a responsible cleanup plan for the Beachside neighborhood. To fully understand the issue,

one must understand the history of the Beachside local landfill, the harmful effects of the toxic dumping, and the best plan for containing the pollution.

▼ DEVELOPING AN OUTLINE

Before you begin writing, you need to establish a plan, a road map of sorts, for organizing the information you've gathered through your research. In other words, you need an outline. Many students are intimidated by the task of drafting an outline while others believe developing an outline is a waste of time. Actually, spending a little time organizing your notes early in the process will help you to stay focused as you write the paper.

Consider this scenario: you have some time off and a little cash in your pocket, so you decide to take a road trip. You know your destination—New York! Do you just hop in the car and drive in the general direction of New York State based on your knowledge of North American geography? No, you get out a road map and establish a planned route. Having a plan doesn't prevent you from making changes to the route along the way, however. It simply keeps you on track so that you don't lose your way.

Similarly, drafting an outline before you begin to write your paper helps you to organize your notes in a logical order so that you are less likely to drift off topic or to leave out a vital point. Remember those topic labels you created and periodically reviewed as you took notes on your note cards? Now is the time that those topic labels become significant.

Think of your note cards as a deck of playing cards. One way to divide a standard deck of cards is by suit: hearts, spades, diamonds, and clubs. Organize your note cards in much the same way. Consider that you've carefully taken notes and assigned topic labels to your note cards. These topic labels are much like the spades or diamonds that appear at the top of the playing cards. First, divide your note cards by their respective topic labels. If you have five topic labels, then you will end up with five stacks of note cards. If you have taken your notes electronically and used folders, then similarly you will end up with five folders.

Depending upon the number of cards you have in each stack (for the purposes of the following discussion, you can substitute the word "folder"), consider each stack to be a potential paragraph. A stack with significantly more note cards than other stacks may suggest more than one paragraph's worth of material, and a stack with only a few note cards may indicate that more research is needed for this topic or that these note cards simply need to be consolidated with a more developed topic stack.

Each of your note cards reflects one idea, as discussed in Chapter 4. At this point, the reason for limiting the amount of information written on each note card should be evident, for now you can move each bit of information, trying it out in different places as you are developing the outline of the paper. Should you find a note card or two whose ideas do not reflect the topic labels you initially assigned to them, change the labels to more appropriate topics and move the note cards accordingly to different stacks, much as you would do if you were to find a spade tucked in the stack of hearts.

Once you've gotten the note cards topically arranged into groups of like ideas, decide upon a logical pattern of organization both within and between the stacks of note cards. It is difficult to tell you one particular method of organization to follow. For instance, part of your paper might explain a process, necessitating the use of chronological order, and perhaps you will need to provide definitions of key terms. You may also have to present conflicting findings of previous research, so you will need to compare and contrast. Naturally, you will need to present background information before diving into your supporting ideas. The points you will make in your paper will determine how you might best organize your ideas. To refresh your memory of organizational patterns, review the section on development with multiple strategies discussed in Chapter 1. Then, establish an appropriate pattern of organization for your paper, and arrange the note cards in that pattern.

Once you've organized your note cards in such a way that makes sense to you, transfer the ideas on those note cards (or copy and paste) onto paper in the form of an outline. Use your topic labels from your note cards to establish the topics for your online. You have a couple of options: a topic outline or a sentence outline. While both types follow the same general format, a topic outline is often the easier to construct initially because you can focus on organizing the ideas rather drafting complete thoughts. Following is the basic structure used to outline the body of your research paper:

Thesis statement and essay blueprint

Because of the serious health concerns faced by Beachside residents, city council members must immediately adopt a responsible cleanup plan for the Beachside neighborhood. To fully understand this issue, one must understand the history of the Beachside local landfill, the harmful effects of the toxic dumping, and the best plan for containing the pollution.

I. History of the landfill
  A. Burying of Materials
    1. Included garbage, industrial waste, and organic waste
    2. Taken from local naval air stations
  B. Closing of the landfill
    1. Covered by layer of earth
    2. Built homes over landfill
  C. Receiving of complaints from residents
    1. Led to testing of well water
    2. Revealed chemical pollution

II. Effects of toxic dumping
   A. Testing of groundwater
   B. Occurrence of medical problems
      1. High rate of cancer
      2. Reproductive problems
         a. Infertility
         b. Learning disabilities
         c. Low I.Q
      3. Other illnesses
         a. Skin rashes
         b. Gastrointestinal problems
         c. Nervous system disorders
III. Plan for containing pollution.
   A. Using a cover system
   B. Monitoring the waste
   C. Fencing the site

Note that the thesis statement and essay blueprint are written out completely and are separated from the main points of the outline, which are labeled as Roman numerals. While this example contains three Roman numerals, you will have as many Roman numerals as you have body paragraphs. Think of the phrase you have written by each Roman numeral as the root of the topic sentence you will write to introduce that paragraph. The capital letters (A, B, C…) represent each supporting detail that will be discussed in that body paragraph. Use as many capital letters as you need to include all of your supporting points for that main idea. Each of your supporting details should include a few concrete examples as well, which are represented by Arabic numerals (1, 2, 3…), and should you need to provide even more specific information, you can include lower-case letters (a, b, c…) to identify the next level of organization. This same pattern of organization can be used over and over again for as many body paragraphs as your paper requires.

General Rules of Thumb for Organizational Balance	For every *I*, include a *II*.
	For every *A*, include a *B*.
	For every *1*, include a *2*.
	For every *a*, include a *b*.

You can carry out each level of organization as far as necessary (you can go from A to Z!), but you don't want to have an "orphaned" main idea or supporting detail. In other words, don't create a level that has only one item.

One final point: as you fill in your outline, try your best to make sure that each level is parallel in terms of grammatical structure. For instance, in the example outline above, the Roman numeral levels are written as noun phrases, the capital letters under Roman I are written as –ing verbals, and the small letters under II. B. 2. are nouns. The important thing to remember is to be consistent at each level.

While developing an outline may take a little extra time in the beginning of the writing process, having a plan will help guide you on your research-writing journey.

Writing a Research Paper Part II— Writing a Rough Draft

Once you have arranged your ideas into an outline, you are ready to start writing. Chapter 6 will explain how to convert the information on your note cards and in your outline into a coherent rough draft.

Objectives

- explain the process of transferring your notes into your written paper;

- discuss strategies for establishing credibility as a researcher and a writer;

- demonstrate the importance and means of crediting your sources.

▼ Writing an Initial Draft

Now it's time to take all of the information you've gathered and to put it into written form. Don't feel as though you must start with the introduction paragraph, though. As Chapter 1 explained, it's more difficult to write an effective introduction if you've not yet written the body paragraphs of the paper. Consider beginning with your first main point, or Roman numeral I.

Take the stack of note cards that corresponds with the first point that you want to develop, and consider the order that you've arranged the note cards. If you planned your outline well and organized your note cards in a logical sequence, your next step is simply to transfer the information recorded on each note card into your paper, starting with the top card and working your way through the stack. Naturally, you will need to add transitional words and phrases to tie the various ideas together. In fact, you may incorporate some of your own ideas as a means of linking information gathered from different sources. If you find as you write that you need to rearrange some of the ideas, that's okay. Remember, this draft is your initial effort to consolidate your research and your own ideas into a single document. Just be certain not to leave out important details or to drift away from the main point you are trying to make in each of your paragraphs.

Components of a Well-Developed Paragraph	<ul><li>A topic sentence that clarifies the main idea of the entire paragraph and that connects the paragraph with the thesis statement and essay blueprint that you will provide in the introduction.</li><li>Clear and convincing specific details that support your general assertions made within the paragraph and that do not stray from the thesis statement and essay blueprint.</li><li>Transitional words and phrases that lead the reader from one point to the next within the paragraph and that help the reader to move from one body paragraph to the next.</li></ul>

Once the body paragraphs have been written, you will find writing the introductory and concluding paragraphs to be much easier. Consider reviewing Chapter 1 if you need more guidance on writing introductory, body, and concluding paragraphs.

▼ Establishing Your Credibility

Another consideration as you construct your research essay is to establish your credibility as both a researcher and a writer. Chapter 4 discussed the importance of evaluating your sources to determine their credibility. Avoid using primary and secondary resources whose credibility might be questioned by the reader. Using weak research only leads to writing a weak paper. Backing up your general assertions with reliable data from respected journals, Websites, books, and so forth will ensure that your paper contains information contributed and valued by experts in the field that you are discussing. In addition to using reliable source material, you must also be thorough, providing plenty of examples from your expert resources to support your general assertions.

A second means of establishing your credibility as a writer is to present all sides of your topic when your paper involves contrasting views. Let's say that you are writing a research paper on the increasingly overcrowded roads in your neighborhood. When you are passionate about a particular controversial issue, it is easy to focus on your own position as a resident and to ignore the position of the other sides, in this case, that of the developers and the city council. However, if you do not acknowledge your opposition and do not attempt to refute the points made by the opposition, your reader may perceive your research to be biased and your position to be unfair, especially if the reader is a land developer or a member of the city council! Discussing all sides of a controversial topic will strengthen both your credibility and your final written product. Chapters 9 and 10 will explain the elements and development of an argument essay in greater detail.

▼ CREDITING YOUR SOURCES

As you transfer information from your note cards to your paper, you must give credit to the sources that you are using. Every time you paraphrase, summarize, or quote researched information that is not your own, you must document your source within the text of your essay. Different manuscript styles require different elements of in-text documentation. For example, both the *American Psychological Association (APA)* and the *Modern Language Association (MLA)* require that you include the author's name in in-text citations, but APA manuscript style places greater emphasis on the year of publication while MLA style emphasizes the page on which you found the information that you are using. Following is a list of the types of bibliographic information that must be incorporated into your paper when you use ideas that are not your own:

- Author(s) or title of publication if no author is listed
- Year of publication if using APA style
- Page number(s)

In-text citations must be included for every summary, paraphrase, and direct quotation that you include in your paper. There are several ways that you can incorporate this documentation into your paper. For instance, you might choose to use a *tag line* to introduce the source. Consider the following examples of tag lines used to introduce MLA-style quotations:

According to Elizabeth Agnvall, health features editor for AARP, "The American Cancer Society recommends that people who drink alcohol limit themselves to no more than two drinks a day for men, one drink a day for women" (16).

> "The American Cancer Society recommends," states *Elizabeth Agnvall*, health features editor for AARP, "that people who drink alcohol limit themselves to no more than two drinks a day for men, one drink a day for women" (16).

> "The American Cancer Society recommends that people who drink alcohol limit themselves to no more than two drinks a day for men, one drink a day for women," *emphasizes AARP health features editor Elizabeth Agnvall* (16).

Note that the tag line can come at the beginning, middle, or end of the idea, and the *parenthetical notation* includes the page number on which the direct quotation was found. APA-style documentation for a direct quotation additionally requires the inclusion of the publication year followed by a comma as well as a lower-case *p* to indicate the page number:

> *Elizabeth Agnvall, health features editor for AARP, clarifies,* "The American Cancer Society recommends that people who drink alcohol limit themselves to no more than two drinks a day for men, one drink a day for women" (2012, p. 16).

If your source does not have an author and is listed on your bibliography page by title, use the whole title, if short, or an abbreviated version of the title for your in-text documentation. For example, let's say your source is an article entitled "Gay Bullying" taken from the web. Your direct quotation from this source would read as follows:

> The article "Gay Bullying" reports that "More than 1/3 of LBGT kids have attempted suicide."

Note that because this is an online source, no page number is included.

You can also use tag lines to introduce paraphrases and summaries in the same manner shown above. The only difference is the lack of quotation marks. While MLA style requires the page number for summaries and paraphrases just as it does for quotations, APA-style summaries and paraphrases do not require the page number, only the year of publication.

At times, you may not choose to include the name of the author or the source within the sentence itself. In this case, simply put all of the necessary documentation within the parentheses. Consider the following paraphrases of the Agnvall and "Gay Bullying" quotations previously referenced:

MLA Style:

According to the American Cancer Society, men should limit their alcohol consumption to two drinks daily and women to one. (Agnvall 16.)

Because of bullying, over1/3 of LBGT youth have tried to take their own lives. ("Gay").

APA Style:

According to the American Cancer Society, men should limit their alcohol consumption to two drinks daily and women to one. (Agnvall, 2012, p. 16).

Because of bullying, over1/3 of LBGT youth have tried to take their own lives (Gay, 2010).

Note that in the case of online sources, in-text citations will follow the formats modeled above, but there will be no page number included.

Below is an example of a paragraph taken from an MLA-style research paper about the influences on the design of the Erectheion. Note how summarizing, paraphrasing, and quoting are combined in the paragraph to support the topic sentence idea.

In addition to its complex structure, the Erectheion is noted for its ornamental design. Three features bear highlighting. First is the Ionic columns. They are regarded as the finest of the Ionic temples (Boardman 45). According to Schefold, the six columns of the east porch, just over 6.5 meters high, are the most slender in Attica (170). The six Ionic columns of the north porch are slightly larger. Their total height is 7.6 meters (Stevens and Paton 80). The shafts have twenty-four flutes with flat ridges between them (Boardman 137.) As described by Schefold, a triple plaited band can be found at the base of the columns and under the volutes (172). Reference is also made to the elegance and decoration of the molding. G. Gruber points out, "'What produced an almost magical effect was that all the meshes of the network were inlaid with bright beads and the spiral of the volutes of the springy capitals were edged with gilded strips of bronze....'" (qtd. in Schefold 172). Schefold also points out that the rosettes of the north door were inlaid with precious metals (172).

Note:

If you have a source that is quoting another source, you use the abbreviation for "quoted in" (qtd. in) to acknowledge you got it from a secondary source.

Writing a Research Paper Part III— Documenting Your Evidence

Chapter 7

As you learned in Chapter 6, when you borrow information from other sources to support your argument, you must tell the reader the source of the information. This documentation is necessary for two reasons: First, for any evidence to be considered in an argument, the source of that evidence must be held up for scrutiny. If a reader cannot locate the evidence you are citing, he or she cannot judge the validity of either its source or the evidence itself; consequently, the evidence cannot be used. Second, information is a commodity; if someone researches and publishes original information, he or she has the right to claim ownership of that information. If you borrow someone else's work and do not recognize his or her ownership, you are guilty of *plagiarism* and can be held legally accountable for stealing another writer's ideas. Remember, even if you borrow an idea but express it in your own words, you must still cite the origination of that idea. If you are unsure about when you must cite another author as you write your paper, a simple rule of thumb is *if you know you got your information from another source, you know you have to cite that source.* Chapter 7 will provide the manuscript guidelines most frequently used in research writing.

Objectives

- demonstrate appropriate formats for in-text references;

- explain the guidelines for bibliographic citations.

A number of standard methods are currently used for citing sources. The two most common are the *Modern Language Association* (MLA) system and the *American Psychological* (APA) system. Both of these will be briefly explained, but more detailed examples and explanations are available in the publication handbooks for each of these associations available in any bookstore or library.

▼ TEXTUAL REFERENCES

As you write the body of your paper, you must alert the reader whenever you include a borrowed source. This reference is called the *in-text citation*. The *APA* and *MLA* styles differ in how the in-text citations are done. For example, consider the following quotation taken from Alice Park's 2014 *Time* article on childhood obesity, page 42:

> *This is the American Nightmare – that for the first time ever a generation of children may have a shorter life expectancy at birth than their parents.*

The MLA in-text citation includes the author's name and page reference, like this one:

> Childhood obesity has become such a crisis ". . . that for the first time ever a generation of children may have a shorter life expectancy at birth than their parents" (Park 42).

Your in-text citations should be placed at the end of the material you are citing. Generally, the citation is placed at the end of the sentence. If the sentence concludes with a quotation, the citation comes after the closing quotation mark but before the final punctuation mark. If you include the author's name in the text, then only the page number is placed in the parentheses, as in the following example:

> Childhood obesity has become such a crisis Park states ". . . that for the first time ever a generation of children may have a shorter life expectancy at birth than their parents" (42).

The APA internal citation method is slightly different, requiring not only the author's name and page number, but the date of publication as well:

> Childhood obesity has become such a crisis ". . . that for the first time ever a generation of children may have a shorter life expectancy at birth than their parents" (Park, 2014, p. 42).

A variation of this citation can place the author's name and the date of publication in the text and the page number at the end:

> Park (2014) says childhood obesity has become such a crisis ". . . that for the first time ever a generation of children may have a shorter life expectancy at birth than their parents" (p. 42).

Again, remember there are other variations in the APA method, and you should refer to the *APA Publication Manual's* latest edition for an explanation of those refinements.

Should you need to quote a particularly lengthy passage that will require more than four typed lines, then you will need to indent the entire quotation ten spaces. Use your tab key to perform this function by hitting the tab key twice. Such indenting will alert your reader that you are quoting directly from a source, so quotation marks are unnecessary. Note that the tag line that is used to introduce a long quotation is generally a complete sentence followed by a colon. Also note that the end punctuation should be placed directly after the quoted material instead of after the parenthetical note. Be certain to double space the indented quotation just as you are double-spacing the entire paper. The following passage is an example of a long quotation from an MLA-style research paper on E-Business. In this example, the writer is discussing how one can research a manufacturer's website to get valuable information about a product:

> Thomas Siebel illustrates this point as he relates the story of an in-store purchase of a camera that he made without doing research on the Internet first:
>
>> In this case I didn't use the Web. I went to a camera store, and they told me which one to buy. OK, I got it home, eventually figured it out, looked at the pictures. I was pretty satisfied, but then I got on the Web, and I found out there that this camera required a very specific lens for high-contrast work. This was well known to all the photography buffs on the Web, but my salesman didn't know it. (134)

The only difference in handling the long quotation above in APA style would be the inclusion of the year along with the page number, as shown below:

> (1999, p. 134)

▼ BIBLIOGRAPHIC CITATIONS

The second element required in citing the sources of your information is the bibliography page (referred to as "References" by the APA and "Works Cited" by the MLA), which appears at the end of your document.

Guidelines for MLA Works Cited Page

1. Center the words *Works Cited* at the top of the page. Capitalize the first letter of each word and do not underline or place quotation marks around the words.

2. Arrange the entries alphabetically by the author's last name. List multiple authors in the order they appear in the source and alphabetize by the first author listed. If the author is not named, alphabetize the entry by the first word of the title (do not use *A, An,* or *The*).

3. Use the authors' full names. Only use initials if they are used in the source. The word *and* is used between two or more authors.

4. Place a period after the last author's name.

5. Capitalize all of the major words in the title.

6. Underline or italicize major titles (books, journals, newspapers) and use quotation marks around titles that appear inside the major works (articles, chapters, poems, short stories).

7. Abbreviate all months of publication except for May, June, and July.

8. Use a short form of the publisher *(Kendall* for *Kendall/Hunt Publishing Company).*

9. Indent the second line and all subsequent lines one half inch from the left margin (5-7 spaces) of a multi-line citation.

10. Double space all lines throughout the works cited page.

Guidelines for APA References Page

1. Center the word *References* at the top of the page. Capitalize the first letter of the word, but do not underline or place quotation marks around the word.

2. Alphabetize by the author's last name.

3. Use the full last name, but initials for the first and middle names.

4. Enclose the publishing date in parentheses after the name, and use a period after the parentheses.

5. Capitalize only the first word and any proper names in the title.

6. Use *p.* or *pp.* to indicate page numbers.

7. Do not abbreviate months of publication.

8. Use the full name of publishers.

9. Indent the second line of each entry one-half inch from the left margin and each subsequent line of publication information until the citation is complete.

10. Double-space all lines throughout the references page.

The following citations illustrate the most common types of sources using both the APA and the MLA formats.

Books

One author:

> **APA:** Springer, P. J. (2013). *Military robots and drones: A reference handbook*. Santa Barbara, CA: ABC-CLIO.

> **MLA:** Springer, Paul J. *Military Robots and Drones: A Reference Handbook*. Santa Barbara: ABC-CLIO, 2013. Print.

Two or more books by the same author:

> **APA:** Springer, P. J. (2010). *America's captives: Treatment of POWs from the Revolutionary War to the War on Terror*. Lawrence, KS: University Press of Kansas.

> Springer, P. J. (2013). *Military Robots and Drones: A Reference Handbook*. Santa Barbara, CA: ABC-CLIO.

> **MLA:** Springer, Paul J. *America's Captives: Treatment of POWs from the Revolutionary War to the War on Terror*. Lawrence: UP of Kansas, 2010. Print.

> ---.*Military Robots and Drones: A Reference Handbook*. Santa Barbara: ABC-CLIO, 2013. Print.

Note:

APA requires references by the same author to be listed chronologically from earliest work to most recent work. MLA simply uses three dashes and a period to signify the repeated author's name, and the works are listed alphabetically by title.

Two authors:

> **APA:** Gastman, R., & Neelon, C. (2010). *The history of American graffiti*. New York, NY: Harper.

> **MLA:** Gastman, *Roger and Caleb Neelon. The History of American Graffiti*. New York: Harper, 2010. Print.

Note:

For MLA, if you have three authors, list all three: the first name will be last name first name, and the other two names will be listed first name last name. If more than three authors, just list first name in last name first name order and then follow with et al ("and others").

A Work in an Anthology

APA: Whitman, W. (1985). The murder of President Lincoln, 14 April 1865. In J. Carey (Ed.), *Eyewitness to history* (pp. 371–375). New York, NY: Harper, 1985.

MLA: Whitman, Walt. "The Murder of President Lincoln, 14 April 1865." *Eyewitness to History.* Ed. John Carey. New York: Harper, 1985. 371–375. Print.

Note:

APA uses *p* or *pp.* to indicate page numbers, but MLA does not.

Government Publication

APA: United States Department of Health and Human Services. (2013). *Medicare & you.* Washington, D.C.: GPO.

MLA: United States. Dept. of Health and Human Services. *Medicare & You.* Washington: GPO, 2013. Print.

Brochure or Pamphlet

APA: Columbia Management. (2014). *Portfolio navigator funds: Annual report* [Brochure]. Boston, MA: Columbia Management Investment Advisors.

MLA: Columbia Management. *Portfolio Navigator Funds: Annual Report.* Boston: Columbia Management Investment Advisors, 2014.

Weekly or Monthly Magazine Article

APA: Park, A. (2014, March 3). Young kids, old bodies. *Time,* 40–44.

MLA: Park, Alice. "Young Kids, Old Bodies." *Time* 3 Mar. 2014: 40–44. Print.

Newspaper Article

APA: Gavan, B. (2013, December 4). Holiday gifts that are a little out of the ordinary. *The Florida-Times Union,* pp. E7–8.

MLA: Gavan, Barbara. "Holiday gifts that are a little out of the ordinary." *The Florida-Times Union* [Jacksonville] 4 Dec. 2013: E7–8. Print.

Personal Interview

MLA: Brown, Harold. Personal interview. 12 May 2013.

Note:

APA format does not list personal interviews in the References section. The reference should simply be included as an in-text citation.

Radio or Television Show

APA: Neumann. J. (Director). (2014, March 25). TB silent killer. [Television series episode]. In *Frontline*. Jacksonville, FL: Public Broadcasting Service, WJCT.

MLA: "TB Silent Killer." *Frontline*. Dir. Jezza Neumann. PBS. WJCT, Jacksonville, FL. 25 Mar. 2014. Television.

Film, Videocassette, or DVD

APA: Nichols, M. (Director). (2004). *Angels in America*. [DVD]. United States: HBO Films.

MLA: *Angels in America*. Dir. Mike Nichols. Perf. Al Pacino, Meryl Streep, Emma Thompson. HBO Films, 2004. DVD.

Music Recording

APA: Kazee, S. (2012). Leave. In G. Hansard (Comp.), *Once*. [CD]. New York, NY: Sony.

MLA: Kazee, Steve. "Leave." *Once*. Comp. Glen Hansard. Sony, 2012. CD.

Artwork or Photography

APA: Rubens, P. P. (1605). *The lamentation of Christ* [Painting]. Jacksonville, FL: Cummer Museum of Art and Gardens.

MLA: Rubens, Peter Paul. *The Lamentation of Christ*. 1605. Oil on copper. Cummer Museum of Art and Gardens, Jacksonville.

Note:

If the work is part of a private collection, give the name of the collection (Collection of . . .) and the location. If the collector is unknown or wants to remain anonymous, just indication Private collection and omit location.

Electronic Sources

The rapid evolution of on-line research has created a need for the formalization of procedure for citing electronic sources, though no definitive formalization exists to date. There are guidelines established by both the APA and MLA for citing most on-line sources, but in the absence of a particular format, remember you must provide enough information to allow the reader to locate the source, and you must be *consistent* in the way you cite that source throughout your document.

Nonperiodical Publication on the Web

APA: Linker, B. (2014, January 30). The great American concussion. The *Huffington Post.* Retrieved from http://www.huffingtonpost.com/beth-linker/nfl-concussions_b_4696356.html

McKirdy, E. (2014, March 26). North Korea ups stakes with latest missile launch. CNN.com. Cable News Network. Retrieved from http://www.cnn.com/2014/03/26/world/asia/north-korea-rodong-missile-launch/index.html?iref=allsearch

Gay bullying. (2010, November 7). National Youth Association. Retrieved March 26, 2014, from http://www.nyaamerica.org/2010/11/07/gay-bullyin/

MLA: Linker, Beth. "The Great American Concussion." *The Huffington Post.* TheHuffingtonPost, 30 Jan. 2014. Web. 21 Mar. 2014.

McKirdy, Euan. "North Korea ups stakes with latest missile launch." CNN.com. Cable News Network, 26 Mar. 2014. Web. 26 Mar. 2014.

"Gay Bullying." *National Youth Association.* National Youth Association, 7 Nov. 2010. Web. 26 Mar. 2014.

Note:

After the web site, you state the sponsor or publisher of the site followed by the date. In MLA, two dates appear. The first is the date of publication, and the second is the date of access. In APA, you include the date of access only when using sources in which information is likely to change over time (such as Wikipedia).

Corporate or Organizational Site

APA: General Motors. (2014, March 21). New modular Ecotec engines are more adaptable, efficient. *GM News: United States.* Retrieved March 25, 2014, from http://media.gm.com/media/us/en/gm/news.detail.html/content/Pages/news/us/en/2014/mar/ecotec/english/0319-ecotec-overview.html

MLA: "General Motors. "New Modular Ecotec Engines are More Adaptable, Efficient." *GM News: United States.* 21 Mar. 2014. Web. 25 Mar. 2014.

Online Government Publication

APA: United States Department of Health and Human Services. Centers for Disease Control and Prevention. (2014, March 17). *Stroke Signs and Symptoms.* Retrieved on March 26, 2014, from http://www.cdc.gov/stroke/signs_symptoms.htm

MLA: United States. Dept. of Health and Human Services. Centers for Disease Control and Prevention. *Stroke Signs and Symptoms.* 17 Mar. 2014. Web. 26 Mar. 2104.

Electronic Database

APA: Maney, K. (2014, January 31). Headbanger's windfall. *Newsweek,* 1. Retrieved on March 21, 2014, from http://go.galegroup.com/ps/i.do?id=GALE%7CA357248180&v=2.1&u=lincclin_fccj&it=r&p=AONE&sw=w&asid=71b5e74c936c2d4702c0683cae67311c.

MLA: Maney, Kevin. "Headbanger's Windfall." *Newsweek* 31 Jan. 2014: 1. *Academic OneFile.* Web. 21 Mar. 2014.

CD-ROM

APA: Smith, R. K. (2013). Solving the concussion problem and saving professional football. *Thomas Jefferson Law Review*, 35(2), 127-191. Retrieved on March 21, 2014, from http://www.tjeffersonlrev.org/print/35/2/ solving-concussion-problem-and-saving-professional-football

MLA: Smith, Rodney K. "Solving The Concussion Problem And Saving Professional Football." *Thomas Jefferson Law Review* 35.2 (2013): 127-191. *Academic Search Complete*. Wed. 21 Mar. 2014.

Note:

If you are working with articles that your reader can find easily, you do not need to provide database information since databases change over time, according to APA (p. 192). If however, you are using an article that might be hard for your reader to locate, then providing database information is helpful. When referencing a print article obtained via an academic database that you might access through your college library, you should include relevant citation information just as you would if you were using the original source and consider including the homepage's URL. That way, if your reader is not able to access the database that you used, then he or she can pull the original print version of the article. Again, document your retrieval dates only if the source could change. For more about citing articles retrieved from electronic databases, refer to pages 187-192 of the APA Publication Manual.

E-mail

MLA: Johnson, Steven M. "Re: Test Dates." Message to the author. 10 Feb. 2013. E-mail

Note:

If the e-mail was sent to someone else beside the author, insert the proper name instead of "the author." The in-text citation of the above model would include the following information: (Johnson). Also note that APA does not require E-mail sources to be listed on the References page. Instead, the APA in-text citation would include the following information: (S. M. Johnson, personal communication, February 10, 2013)

Tweet

MLA: Brad Pitt (BradPittsPage). "Pleading the 5th Amendment is like saying, 'I did it! But I'm not telling.'" 21 Mar. 2014, 7:24 a.m. Tweet.

Note:

In the parentheses, include the twitter name if known and different from real name. Also note that APA does not require Twitter sources to be listed on the References page. Instead, the APA in-text citation would include the following information: (B. Pitt, Tweet, March 21, 2014).

Digital File

APA: Peckham, P. H., Thrope, G., Woloszko, J., Habasevich, R., Scherer, M., & Kantor, C. (1996, April). Technology transfer of neuro-prosthetic devices [PDF]. *Journal of Rehabilitation Research and Development* 33.2, 173-183. Retrieved February 12, 2014, from http://www.rehab.research.va.gov/jour/96/33/2/pdf/peckham2.pdf

MLA: Peckham, P. Hunter, et al. "Technology transfer of neuroprosthetic devices." *Journal of Rehabilitation Research and Development* 33.2 (April 1996): 173-183. PDF File.

To learn how to cite other types of sources not listed in this chapter, consult the *MLA Handbook for Writers of Research Papers* or the *Publication Manual of the American Psychological Association*, either of which can be found in your local bookstore, library, or online. Finally, you will note that many databases and sites offer automated citations. These are not always accurate. Make sure you review these carefully to see they are in accord with the appropriate documentation guide before using such citations.

Chapter 8

Writing a Research Paper Part IV— Writing the Final Draft

Writing a final draft is a lot like putting together an unfinished piece of furniture. Let's say that you've purchased a kitchen table that is "in the raw"; in other words, you are responsible for the assembly and finishing of the table. Once you've constructed the table, it becomes a functional piece, but you probably wouldn't leave it in its unfinished condition. You will want to check that the table is balanced so that it does not rock from side to side. The rough spots will also need to be sanded, and the surface will need a coat of stain and a finishing coat of varnish. Writing a final draft of your research paper is a very similar process. You want to transform your rough draft into a polished final product. Once the initial draft is done, set it aside for a day or two. You want to approach the rough draft with fresh eyes when you begin to revise and to check for accuracy. Chapter 8 will guide you in refining your paper.

Objectives

- ◆ provide guidelines for checking documentation;

- ◆ explain the process for reviewing for accuracy and bias;

- ◆ discuss strategies for improving readability;

- ◆ identify common grammatical and mechanical errors.

▼ CHECKING YOUR DOCUMENTATION

When checking your documentation, you have three objectives that you want to fulfill: ensuring all researched material has been documented, checking that the documentation is correct, and making sure that the format of the documentation has been done according to the appropriate guidelines.

Your first objective is to ensure that you have documented all researched material in your paper. As you have learned, whether you have quoted, paraphrased, or summarized material in your paper from an outside source, you must document that information to avoid plagiarism. Documentation informs your reader that the information is not from your own knowledge and lets the reader know where the original material can be found for verification and further exploration.

When writing your final draft, then, first make sure you have provided in-text documentation for each quotation, paraphrase, or summary in your paper. If you have omitted such documentation, use the appropriate bibliography and/or note card to include the required information. In particular, look at those places in your paragraphs where you may have several sources intertwined with your own writing. For example, in a paragraph, you might have a paraphrased section followed by your own explanation, followed by another paraphrase. Make certain you have documented both paraphrases and not just the second one. In reviewing your documentation, also verify that you have placed your in-text references in the appropriate place. Your in-text references need to be located after you have completely stated each piece of researched material. With regard to your *Works Cited* or *References* page, make sure you have included all of the sources used in your paper.

In checking your documentation, next make sure of the accuracy of your references and entries. For your in-text references, verify that you have identified the correct source of each quotation, paraphrase, or summary. Also, confirm that you have listed the appropriate page reference if required. Next, check your *Works Cited* or *References* page for correctness. For book entries, see that the authors' names, the titles of the books, the publishing and copyright information are accurate. For periodical and newspaper entries, also verify the accuracy of the titles of the articles, the names of the periodicals and newspapers, the dates of the articles, and the page references indicated. Similarly, for online sources, verify the accuracy of author names, titles of articles, names of the web sites, the sponsors of the web sites, the posting dates. No matter what type of source you may have listed on your *Works Cited* or *References* page, check for the accuracy of all information. Use your bibliography cards or original computer listings to verify all entries.

Finally, in this checking of documentation, review each of your in-text references and each of your Works Cited or References entries for correctness of format. No matter which association's guidelines you are using to document your paper, you must follow them accurately. Part of the learning experience in writing a research paper is adhering to appropriate guidelines. Thus, make sure you have provided all the information required for each reference or entry, you have listed the information in the order specified, and you have used the correct punctuation marks. Refer to the models in this text or by those provided in the appropriate association's handbook to review the correctness of your documentation.

When reviewing your paper, make sure you have used quotation marks appropriately. Quotation marks should appear before and after any short passages you have taken directly, word for word, from another source. Also, if a passage you are quoting has words or phrases already in quotation marks, make sure you have used single quotation marks to indicate the quotation within a quotation.

With regard to your Works Cited or References page, check to see that you have double-spaced all lines and that you have indented five spaces the second and subsequent lines of an entry. Also, check your use of quotation marks and italics or underlining. Titles of chapters, essays, short stories, and magazine articles should appear in quotation marks. Names of books, magazines, and pamphlets should be italicized or underlined. An easy rule of thumb to remember is if a work appears as part of a larger work, the smaller work goes in quotation marks, and the larger work gets italicized or underlined.

▼ REVIEWING AND REVISING FOR ACCURACY AND BIAS

As you write your final draft, you particularly want to review all of your researched material in the paper for accuracy. Accuracy means that you have presented all the researched information correctly and that you have not misinterpreted any of that information.

If you are going to convince your reader to accept your position or argument, you must present accurate information. One piece of misinformation will cast doubt on the remainder of the information in your paper, and you will have a nearly impossible job of convincing your reader to accept your premise.

Also, accuracy is important from a legal and ethical standpoint. Throughout the research process, you have learned how important it is to take the appropriate steps to avoid plagiarism by avoiding using someone else's words unless quoting and by providing proper documentation. However, just as important, you do not want to misrepresent another person. From an ethical stance, you do not want to provide false information, and you certainly do not want to be legally liable for attributing false information to an authority or expert.

As a starting point, review your quotations. Make sure that each quotation that you have used has been worded exactly as in the original. Verify the wording in your paper against the wording on your note card or against the original source. Be certain you have not changed or left out any words. If you have omitted any words, make sure you have indicated this omission with ellipses marks and that you have not changed the meaning of the original quotation.

Next, review your paraphrased passages. It is extremely important to check that you have not misinterpreted the original source of your paraphrase. Read over each paraphrased section carefully. Verify that you have correctly transferred your information from your note card to the paper. If you made any wording changes in your paper from the note card, make sure the idea has not been changed in any way. If you are unsure of the accuracy of your paraphrase, take the time to review your original source to make sure you have not misunderstood the original meaning.

Your third step is to review the accuracy of your researched material as you have presented it in your paper within your own explanations and comments. Look at every quotation and paraphrased section and review how you have incorporated each within your paragraphs. Does the piece of researched information truly support the assertion that you make? Does the piece of researched information provide the correct example to illustrate your point?

REVISING FOR SENTENCE STYLE AND WORDINESS

When you wrote your rough draft, your main concern was to get your ideas down on paper in an organized fashion. As you write your final draft, you now can concentrate on its readability. You want your reader to concentrate on your ideas and not be hampered by how you expressed them. Thus, you want to ensure that your paper is understandable to your reader, that it reads coherently, and that it is free of any unnecessary wording.

Following are the major areas you should look out for as you revise for sentence structure, word choice, and wordiness.

Sentence Structure

With regard to sentence structure, look for places in your draft where you may have written a long, cluttered sentence or a passage containing short, choppy sentences. In the first situation, divide that long sentence into two or more shorter, clearer ones. In the second situation, combine the short, choppy sentences into a longer, more coherent sentence by using coordinating or subordinating conjunctions, or use transition words to improve the flow between the sentences.

Note the revision below. A long, awkward sentence has been rewritten into several sentences, making this passage more readable and understandable:

Original

Although there is much speculation as to the inner plan of the Erectheion and the uses to which it was put, everyone agrees this building was a marvel of Ionic architecture of the late fifth century B.C., contrasting, with its asymmetrical appearance and complex design, the austerity and symmetry of the Parthenon.

Revision

Although there is much speculation as to the inner plan of the Erectheion and the uses to which it was put, everyone agrees this building was a marvel of Ionic architecture of the late fifth century B.C. With its asymmetrical appearance and complex design, the Erectheion contrasts with the austerity and symmetry of the Parthenon.

In contrast, you might find a passage in your rough draft that is composed of a series of short, choppy sentences. In this situation, combine those sentences into a more coherent unit.

Original

For years the Native Americans lived off the land of America. They became efficient farmers and taught their offspring the ways to cultivate the land. After the General Allotment Act was passed, Native Americans could no longer provide for themselves adequately. They started to sell their land. Native American tribes quickly realized that their sovereignty was in jeopardy.

Revision

For years the Native Americans lived off the land of America, becoming efficient farmers and teaching their offspring the ways to cultivate the land. After the General Allotment Act was passed, Native Americans could no longer provide for themselves adequately and eventually they started to sell their land. Native American tribes quickly realized that their sovereignty was in jeopardy.

Word Choice

As you revise your rough draft, make sure you correct misused words, remove repetitive wording, and eliminate pretentious language.

First, be attentive to your word choices. Have you used the correct word to convey the appropriate meaning? Many words have meanings that are similar but each is more appropriate in certain contexts. For example, you have written, "Having fallen on his quadruple jump, the Olympic skater could sympathize with his competitor when he had the same mishap." In revising, you should notice that "sympathize" is not the correct word choice. The sentence should read, "The Olympic skater could empathize . . . ."

In addition, revise for repetitive wording, instances in a sentence or a group of sentences wherein you have used the same word over and over instead of using a synonym. "Any modifications in surgical procedures resulting from modifications in healthcare policy have been beneficial to patients." To avoid the repetitive use of the word *modifications*, you could change the first *modifications* to the word *changes*.

Pretentious wording occurs when your vocabulary choices become pompous-sounding. In such cases, your readers are more taken by your words than your ideas. For example, you could have written, "By wearing protective clothing, the explorers avoided the deleterious effects of insect and snake bites." Although the word *deleterious* is a perfectly fine and appropriate word here, this idea can be more clearly expressed with the word *harmful.*

Wordiness

Revise your rough draft to remove any unnecessary wording. Wordiness usually results from using redundant expressions or using wordy expressions or phrasing.

Redundant expressions occur when the second word in an expression repeats the first. Some common redundancies are "revert back," "repeat again," "advance forward," and "final completion." In each case, one of the words (*back, again, forward,* and *final*) is unnecessary because the other embodies the action or idea of the unnecessary one. Refer to any college handbook for a list of redundant expressions to help you locate them in your paper.

In revising for wordy expressions, look for certain structures that lead to wordiness. Sentences that begin with "There is" or "There are" usually can be written more simply and more straightforwardly. For example, "There are a number of everyday products that can lead to brain disorders in children." This idea would be better expressed by writing, "A number of everyday products can lead to brain disorders in children."

Two other types of phrasings to avoid are passive constructions and unnecessary subordinate or dependent clauses. A passive construction occurs when the doer of the action is not the subject of the sentence, but the one acted upon is. For example, "The training exercise was conducted by the United States Army" is a passive construction. The preferred, and less wordy, active construction would read, "The United States Army conducted the training exercise." Unnecessary subordinate clauses result from your using a subordinate clause when a simple adjective, prepositional phrase, or participial phrase would have expressed the idea more concisely and clearly. The following sentence, "Texting, which is a convenient way to stay in touch with friends and family who live distant, has become the preferred means of communication over e-mail," could be simplified to read, "Texting, a convenient way to stay in touch with distant friends and family, has become the preferred means of communication over e-mail."

Take this sentence as another example: "The large urn, which was made of oak, was discovered by the archaeologist, who was digging at the excavation site." As you write your final draft, you might rewrite this sentence as, "While digging at the excavation site, the archaeologist discovered the large, oaken urn."

Finally, wordiness also results from certain phrases that are a very lengthy way of saying a very simple idea. For example, "due to the fact that" just means "because," "at this point in time" means "now," and "provided that" means "if." Generally, such expressions consist of "filler" words. Your handbook again should provide a list of such wordy expressions, so review this list as you revise your paper.

Editing for Grammatical and Mechanical Errors

No matter how well supported and well documented your research paper is and no matter how well organized your material is presented, if your paper is filled with grammatical and mechanical errors, you may not be able to convince your reader to adopt your position. The reader will feel that if you are sloppy in your writing, you were also sloppy in your research, and your reader just might not be able to understand your points because your writing errors prevent clarity of idea.

To make sure writing errors do not take away from all the hard work you have put into planning, researching, and writing your paper, make sure you edit your rough draft for any grammatical and mechanical errors as the last step in preparing your final version. Reread your rough draft sentence by sentence, looking for writing errors. Use your college handbook as a reference to help you locate and correct errors. Because of the many types of grammatical and mechanical errors that can occur, we cannot discuss all of them here, but listed below are some of the major types of errors you should avoid.

Sentence Structure Errors

Make sure all of your ideas are written in complete sentences. Be on the lookout for run-on sentences, comma splices, and fragments. All three types of errors are a reflection of poor logic as they show an inadequacy in recognizing a complete thought. Run-on sentences and comma splices occur when you have too many complete thoughts joined together improperly. A run-on results when two complete ideas are run together with no punctuation or no conjunction joining them. A comma splice results when two complete ideas are separated by a comma only. Fragments occur when you have not expressed a complete thought.

Comma splices are particularly troublesome. Review your paper to make sure you have not linked two sentences with a comma. For example, take this following sentence from a research paper dealing with early literacy: "We must continue to demand this level of proficiency for all children in early learning environments, we must turn our attention to other emerging literacy skills that need similar improvement to bring children to a full state of readiness." The comma between *environments* and *we* creates a comma splice as there are two complete thoughts here. As you know, comma splices can be corrected in a variety of ways with the simplest being using a period instead of a comma.

Comma splices are also apt to occur with the use of conjunctive adverbs, such as *however, in addition, nevertheless, therefore,* and *consequently.* When these words are used to join two sentences, the proper punctuation is to place a semicolon before the conjunctive adverb. A comma in front of such words results in a comma splice. The following is an example of a comma splice: "Research has led to the development of many beneficial treatments to keep symptoms in check, however, no cure has yet been discovered." This sentence needs to be corrected by placing a semicolon in front of *however*: "Research has led to the development of many beneficial treatments to keep symptoms in check; *however,* no cure has yet been discovered." When reviewing for sentence structure errors, pay close attention to those sentences in which you have used conjunctive adverbs.

Also, be mindful of fragments. Fragments can especially occur when you are giving examples. Again from the paper on early literacy, take this example: "Investments in high-quality early literacy programs result in economic benefits to both individuals and society. For example, increased achievement scores, improved behavior, and less grade retention." The group of words that begins with *For example* is not a complete thought. One way to correct a fragment is to add the missing sentence elements to make it a complete thought. This fragment could be corrected to read, "For example, increased achievement scores, improved behavior, and less grade retention are just a few of the results observed in this study."

Mixed Construction

A mixed construction is a type of sentence error that occurs when you begin your sentence with one type of structural pattern and shift to a new one in the middle of the sentence, creating a very awkward construction. This situation generally occurs when you begin a sentence with a preposition and follow it with a gerund (an –ing verb used as a noun). An example of a mixed construction is as follows: "By understanding the early learning strategies that help children develop literacy skills will help parents to be more effective in teaching critical literacy skills to their young children." This sentence's structural pattern changes after the word *skills*. The sentence begins with a preposition phrase, so after the word *skills*, a subject is expected, not a verb. Such a construction can be corrected in one of two ways:

By understanding the early learning strategies that help children develop literacy skills, parents will be more effective in teaching critical literacy skills to their young children.

or

Understanding the early learning strategies that help children develop literacy skills will help parents to be more effective in teaching critical literacy skills to their young children.

Punctuation Errors

Punctuation errors can easily occur when punctuation marks are used with quotation marks. Remember that periods and commas that come after the quoted material should fall within the quotation marks. Question marks and exclamation points should come within the quotations if they are part of the quotation itself. Here are some examples:

> "The evidence is extremely convincing that in a man with usual risk and no symptoms, the PSA test causes more harm than benefit," states Dr. Reid Blackwater, president of the American Academy of Family Physicians.
>
> David Griffith, AAA travel consultant, points out, "From the gourmet dining to the complimentary umbrella I was given when I went onshore on a rainy day, I was pampered the entire trip."
>
> Bettye Stevenson, writer for *National Science*, questioned, "Will laser dental surgery ever become inexpensive enough to become a viable procedure?"

Question marks and exclamation points fall outside of the quotation marks if the sentence you are writing is a question or an emphatic statement, and not the quotation itself. Consider the following example:

> Did Florida Senator Rubio say, "I do not believe that human activity is causing these dramatic changes to our climate the way these scientists are portraying it"?

When reviewing the use of punctuation marks with quotations, also check for the punctuation introducing your quotations. If your quotation flows naturally as part of your sentence, make sure you have separated your sentence from the quotation with a comma. If you have a complete thought before you present your quotation, then you should use a colon. Using the quotation from Dr. Blackwater noted above, consider the following option:

> Dr. Reid Blackwater, president of the American Academy of Family Physicians, made this statement regarding PSA screening: "The evidence is extremely convincing that in a man with usual risk and no symptoms, the PSA test causes more harm than benefit."

Agreement Errors

Agreement errors fall into two categories: subject-verb errors and pronoun-antecedent errors. These types of errors occur when you do not have the proper agreement in person and number, either the verb does not agree with the subject or a pronoun does not agree with its antecedent. Your handbook will review the various rules for each type of error, and you should edit your paper using these rules.

However, watch out for three frequently occurring agreement errors. The first error involves subject-verb agreement. When writing a sentence that contains one or more prepositional phrases between the subject and verb, be especially careful that you have made your verb agree with the subject. Remember that in the present tense, a singular verb must be used with a singular, third-person subject. Consider this sentence:

> The *result* of the recent studies in early literacy developments *has* been that more child care centers are being transformed into early learning centers with a greater focus on early literacy acquisition.

Note that the correct verb is *has* and not *have* because of the singular subject *result*. The subject should not be confused with either the words *studies* or *developments*. Edit your paper carefully for subject-verb agreement errors.

Frequently, pronoun-antecedent errors occur with the use of indefinite pronouns, such as *everybody* and *everyone*. Indefinite pronouns are considered singular, and when they are the antecedents, they require the use of singular pronouns. For example, take this following sentence:

> *Everybody* undergoing this type of surgery found that *their* recovery period was shorter than *they* expected.

Although this sentence sounds correct and may be acceptable in conversation, in formal writing this construction is incorrect. Since *everybody* is singular, the pronouns *they* and *their* are incorrect. The sentence should read like this one:

> *Everybody* undergoing this type of surgery found that *his or her* recovery period was shorter than *he or she* expected.

Note the use of both the masculine and feminine pronouns to avoid the use of sexist language. Because of having to use both gender pronouns in singular constructions like this one, the easier way to correct this type of sentence is to avoid the use of the word *Everybody*, and in its place use a plural noun. For example, another way to correct this sentence is to write the following:

> All *patients* undergoing this type of surgery found that *their* recovery period was shorter than *they* expected.

A similar type of error can occur with the use of singular nouns, such as *person, student,* and *scientist,* which are preceded with indefinite adjectives. Consider this example:

> *Any person* who considers this experimental surgery should consult *their* doctor about the risks before undergoing such surgery.

As with the previous example, an agreement error occurs here because *person* is singular and *their* is plural. A correct version would read as such:

> *Any person* who considers this experimental surgery should consult *his or her* doctor about the risks before undergoing such surgery.

Again, to avoid having to use this dual-gender reference, correct such an agreement error by rewording your sentence so the antecedent is made plural:

> *All persons* who consider this experimental surgery should consult their doctor about the risks before undergoing such surgery.

This type of error easily occurs when you use such similar phrasing as *each person, every person,* and *no person.* Review your research paper carefully for such constructions.

Pronoun Reference Errors

A pronoun reference error occurs when you use a pronoun that has an unclear or vague antecedent. Make sure you consult your handbook for the various types of pronoun reference errors. One particular pronoun reference error that is very easy to overlook and deserves highlighting here is the vague use of the pronouns *this* and *that.* These pronouns should be used to refer to a particular object, not to a complete idea. Look at this passage:

> Food suppliers need to display nutritional information in a manner that is more comprehensive to the public. *This* would ensure that consumers understand what they are putting into their bodies and reinforce the importance of watching what they eat.

The highlighted *This* is used incorrectly. It is being used to refer to the idea of the previous sentence. To correct a vague pronoun reference error, include a noun after the *this* or *that* pronoun. In this case, your second sentence should read this way:

> *This approach* would ensure that consumers understand what they are putting into their bodies and reinforce the importance of watching what they eat.

Carefully review your paper for any places you may have used either *this* or *that* by itself, particularly at the beginning of a sentence. If you have used the pronoun to refer to the previous sentence, add to the sentence as suggested.

▼ CHECKING THE FORMAT OF YOUR PAPER, INCLUDING HEADING AND TITLE

Your last step in completing the final draft of your research paper is to review the format of your paper. Make sure you have numbered all of the pages consecutively, from your first page through your Works Cited page. Each number should appear in the upper right hand corner of the page, one-half inch from the top and flush with the margin. MLA style requires your last name before each page number, such as *Williams 5*. APA style is slightly different. Instead of your name, a one-word or two-word header that reflects the paper's title accompanies the page number at the top of each page.

Next, verify that you have used one-inch margins throughout the paper and have double-spaced all lines. Check to see that you have indented all first words of paragraphs five spaces and have indented long quotations ten spaces from the left margin.

The MLA format does not require a title page. Therefore, the heading and title of your paper should appear on the first page. Type your heading one inch from the top and flush with the left margin. Next, include the following information: your name, your instructor's name, the course number, and the date of the paper. Each item should be on a separate line and doubled-spaced. (Please note that if your instructor does require a title page, follow the specifications you are given.) Place the title of your research paper two lines below the date and in the center of the page. Make sure you do not underline the title or place in quotation marks. Do *not* type your title in all capitals. Capitalize the first word and last words of the title as well as all of the major words. Do not capitalize articles (a, an, the), prepositions (in, of, to, etc.), and coordinating conjunctions (and, but, for, or, so, nor, yet) when these words appear within the title.

APA, on the other hand, does require a title page, which includes several components: the page header, the running head, the title of the paper, your name, and school. The page header consists of a phrase that is lifted from your paper's title and the page number, starting with page one. This page header is placed in the upper right-hand corner and is included on every page of the paper. The running head is an abbreviated version of the title, and it should appear two spaces below the page header, beginning at the left-hand side of the page. The title of your paper should be centered on the page. Your name and school name appear directly below the title, double-spaced and centered on the page. Please note that the format described in this paragraph and shown in the APA model paper is the recommended format for manuscripts submitted for publication. For papers submitted for class assignments, your professor may suggest alternative information for the title page.

Once you have finalized the format, your research paper is completed and ready for submission. By following all of the guidelines in this textbook for writing a research paper, you will have produced a well-written, well-researched, well-developed and well-documented paper. You should be proud that you have created a document that will enhance your readers' lives because of the information you have shared or that will cause them to rethink their position on some issue because of your convincing arguments.

Following are two sample research papers, one using MLA manuscript style, and one using the APA documentation format.

MLA Example

Cherie Brunelle

Professor Perniciaro

ENC 1102

15 November 2013

Nightmare Bacteria

An army of potentially lethal bacteria is slowly creeping its way into today's healthy society and causing a myriad of health issues and diseases that modern medicine is finding difficult to battle. Bacteria that cause infections and illness in humans and animals are treated with drugs called antibiotics, but due to the overuse of these drugs, genetically modified strains of bacteria now exist. The mutated, multidrug-resistant bacteria, commonly called superbugs, have serious effects on human and animal health. The nightmare bacteria render many antibiotics ineffective and can cause life-threatening or deadly infections. There is a looming fear that the health and well-being enjoyed today will eventually be replaced by a post-antibiotic state in which infectious diseases will no longer be curable due to the lack of usable antibiotics.

Antibiotic resistance to bacteria, its major causes and consequences, and identification of areas in which action is needed are interwoven problems that require attention. The causes of antibiotic resistance are complex and the consequences affect many levels of society. Factors contributing to the creation of these superbugs are the widespread misuse and overuse of antibiotics in humans and food-producing animals. The lack of new antibiotics to fight infections caused by the misuse of the drugs is a major concern for medical professionals and public health specialists. Immediate attention to the serious threat of nightmare bacteria is necessary.

Bacteria are miniscule, single-celled organisms that can be found everywhere but seen only under a powerful microscope. Some bacteria are beneficial, such as those that aid in the process of fermentation and decomposition, but bacteria that cause infections are dangerous and require antibiotic or antimicrobial intervention. Antibiotics are medicines made from natural substances such as mold or bacteria that inhibit or attack and kill the growth of other bacteria (Salyers and Whitt 2). Antimicrobials, made by a chemical process, are synthetic forms of antibiotics and function in the same manner. Antibiotics and antimicrobials are often praised as being the most important drug discoveries in the history of medicine (Aminov 2). Armstrong, Coon, and Piller of the National Center to Infectious Diseases state that these drugs' ability to control infectious diseases caused by bacteria, such as pneumonia, influenza, tuberculosis, and syphilis, contributed to a drastic increase of human life expectancy since the early 1900s. They point out that infectious diseases in the United States claimed 797 out of every 100,000 lives in 1900 but by 1980 the number of deaths had declined to 36 per 100,000. The introduction and mass distribution of antibiotics is responsible for the increase of life expectancy in the United States.

The discovery of three drugs laid the foundation for the modern antibiotic era. In 1910, the first antimicrobials, Salvarsan and its less toxic brother, Neosalvarsan, were mass produced and sold by a drug company for human use. The drugs were the outcome of a scientific collaboration spanning the years between 1904 and 1910 by scientists Paul Ehrlich, Alfred Bertheim, and Sahachiro Hata. By 1910, the venereal disease syphilis had reached endemic proportions and Salvarsan was the much needed cure for the deadly syphilis bacteria. Salvarsan and Neosalvarsan were the most frequently prescribed drugs until 1945 when the first antibiotic, Penicillin, was mass produced (Aminov). Penicillin was manufactured and used to treat WWII soldiers with bacterial infections, which developed in their battle wounds. Subsequently, it has been the predominant antibiotic to cure infections and diseases that once threatened lives and has earned the name "miracle drug" because of the speed in which it controls infections. Since WWII, hundreds of different types of antibiotics have been created to treat various infections.

In addition to human use, antibiotics are also commonly used to treat infections in animals. Low doses of antibiotics are also routinely added to the feed and water of livestock, poultry, and fish to promote growth as well as to prevent and control disease. The Food and Drug Administration (FDA) approved the guidelines for use of antibiotics in food animals over 50 years ago as a benefit to animal welfare and continues to update the regulations in order to provide consumers with the safest food possible. All testing criteria for meat and poultry, the specific amount of time between administration of an antibiotic and when an animal can be slaughtered for food use, and acceptable drug residue amounts for human consumption are outlined under FDA Title 21 Code of Federal Regulations of the Federal Food, Drug, and Cosmetic Act.

The amount of antibiotic medicine used annually is staggering. According to an FDA report of April 2013, in 2011, 29.9 million pounds of antibiotics were sold for use on US industrial farms, and 7.7 million pounds were sold for human illness ("FDA Hopes"). It is important to note that the antibiotics used to treat sick people are the same ones given to animals. Using the same kinds of antibiotics weakens the defense mechanisms of both humans and animals due to the evolution of the antibiotic and the organism it attacks. Every time low doses of antibiotics are used, some of the "bad" bacteria are killed, as well as some of the "good" ones. The bacterium that is left over genetically mutates and develops resistance. When resistance to an antibiotic develops, there is no cure and a nightmare bacteria is unleashed which could potentially kill people and animals.

In her article "Antibiotic-Related Illness in U.S. Tops 2 Million Annually," Whitney McKnight brings to light the very serious problem of an antibiotic crisis and the risks to the general public. She states, "Each year in the United States, more than 2 million people contract drug-resistant infections and 23,000 die" as reported by the Centers for Disease Control and Prevention (CDC). In summarizing the CDC report entitled *Antibiotic Resistance Threats in the United States, 2013*, McKnight writes that the CDC ranks nearly two dozen antibiotic-resistant bacteria into three public health threat levels. The first level is "urgent" and includes carbapenem-resistant Enterobacteriaceae (CRE), which typically strikes hospital patients and has become resistant to almost all existing antibiotics. *Neisseria gonorrhoeae,* which causes the venereal disease gonorrhea, is showing signs of drug resistance. The second level is "serious" and contains many multidrug-resistant bacteria which the CDC considers "significant" threats that will only get worse. The lowest threat level, "concerning," contains a list of bacteria which are still treatable with several kinds of antibiotics. In McKnight's article, she outlines what the CDC believes are the four most important actions to fight antibiotic resistance.

Brunelle 3

These actions include the prevention of infection, the tracking of infections, the improvement in antibiotic use, and the research and development of new antibiotics. At the media briefing for this CDC report, Dr. Thomas Frieden, Director, CDC, stated, "If we're not careful, the medicine chest will be empty when we go there to look for a life-saving antibiotic for a deadly infection. But if we act now, we can preserve these medications while we work on the development of new medications" (qtd. in McKnight).

While the FDA and CDC freely admit that antibiotic resistance is a major concern and publish facts and statistics in regard to the use of antibiotics, they are reluctant to acknowledge that bacteria can move from an animal host to a human host or vice versa. Tom Laskawy, on the other hand, does not shy away from the subject in his article "Finally, a Smoking Gun Connecting Livestock Antibiotics and Superbugs." Laskawy dives head first into what seems to be the major conflict of dealing with the mutating bacteria problem. He asserts that the deadly bacteria are due to the overuse and misuse of antibiotics in farm animals and claims the farming industry is ignoring or avoiding any responsibility in the making of the superbugs. He further states that "until scientists trace a particular bug from animals to humans and show precisely how it achieved resistance and moved from farm to consumer, there's no smoking gun" and the farming industry will continue to shirk responsibility.

Laskawy proceeds to write about the scientific journey of a strain of methicillin-resistant *Staphylococcus aureus* (MRSA) called ST398 or pig MRSA. The superbug ST398 began as a strain of semi-resistant staph bacteria in a human, infected a pig, and became resistant to antibiotics. ST398 then moved back into human hosts and made them ill. The mutated organism then forged a path into a hospital setting, moved on to another country, appeared in meat purchased by consumers, and then caused infections in people who had no connection with the farm of origination. ST398 is the smoking gun Laskawy thought agricultural farmers needed in order to realize the dangers of antibiotic use in animals, but the reaction from the National Pork Board (NPB), in Laskawy's opinion, was a disappointment. Paul Sundberg, Vice-President of Science and Technology NPB, is quoted in the article as saying the assessment of ST398 is "an interesting finding with no human health implications."

The story of ST398 is feared to be the first of many superbugs unless livestock, poultry, and fish farmers work with government agencies such as the FDA and CDC to curb the use of antibiotics. This particular strain of MRSA is the direct result of misuse and overuse of antibiotics in animals and humans, which is the crux of the superbug conundrum, and Tom Laskawy successfully connects the relationship. In his words, "Ladies and gentlemen, we now have a smoking gun" and ignorance will only exacerbate the antibiotic resistance problem. The existence of ST398 is the basis on which judicious use of antibiotics in food-producing animals should be limited to ensuring animal health. Furthermore, it presents excellent reason to halt the use of the same kinds of drugs in animals and humans, and lends credence to the need for development and approval of new antibiotics.

Before a new antibiotic can be approved and then sold, it goes through laboratory and human testing. The drugs that are in these phases form the pharmaceutical pipeline. In the article "Who's Trying to Fix the Pipeline Problem," Emma Schwartz states that "The problem is clear: There aren't enough antibiotics." According to Schwartz, there has been a steady decline of antibiotic development since 1980 and, consequently, severe illness, loss of limbs and life are on the rise. The main reasons for the decline are due to the difficulty in finding new drugs that can be tolerated without side effects, the low return of investment for drug companies, and the regulatory hurdles set forth by the FDA.

Antibiotics are naturally occurring substances in soil which are increasingly difficult to find. The pace of research has been reduced due to the lack of availability of new substances to test and digging deeper into the earth to find them is a time-consuming and expensive endeavor. Pharmaceutical companies do not have the financial ability to fund the process of discovery and are finding it impossible to fund development because of financial and government roadblocks (Schwartz). Antibiotics yield a negative financial return of investment for drug companies, even with federal government grants. The average cost of bringing a new antibiotic to market is over $800 million (Salyers and Whitt 117) and government grants only average $200 million. Schwartz explains that drug trials, a costly portion of development, are lengthy due to the stages regulated by the FDA to test safety and drug effectiveness. Helen Boucher, an infectious disease specialist at the Tufts Medical Center, stresses that "The lack of a robust research and development pipeline is a huge problem for patients today and for the future . . ." (qtd. in Schwartz). The end result of these hurdles is that only a handful of big companies are involved in development of new antibiotics and the drugs cannot come fast enough to combat the problems of a world full of superbugs.

Preserving the effectiveness of antibiotic drugs is vital to protecting human and animal health. Antibiotics should be used judiciously in humans and animals because overuse contributes to the emergence, persistence, and spread of resistant bacteria. Government statistics prove that there is a correlation between antibiotic use and resistance. With the spread of deadly antibiotic-resistant bacteria, medical professionals, health specialists, pharmaceutical companies, and government agencies need to work together to curtail and eradicate these superbugs before a health nightmare becomes a reality.

Works Cited

Aminov, Rustam I. "A Brief History of the Antibiotic Era: Lessons Learned and Challenges

for the Future." *Frontiers in Microbiology*. Frontiers Media, 8 Dec. 2010. Web. 7 Nov.

2013..

Armstrong, Gregory L., Laura A. Conn, and Robert W. Pinner. "Trends in Infectious Disease

Mortality in the United States During the 20th Century." *JAMA* 281.1 (1999): 61–66.

Web. 12 Nov. 2013.

"FDA Hopes to Curb Antibiotic Use on Farms." *CNN.com*. Cable News Network, 12 Dec.

2013. Web. 7 Nov. 2013.

Laskawy. "Finally, a Smoking Gun Connecting Livestock Antibiotics and Superbugs."

Grist.Org. Grist Magazine, 24 Feb. 2012. Web. 13 Nov. 2013.

Brunelle 5

McKnight, Whitney. "Antibiotic-Related Illness in U.S. Tops 2 Million Annually." *Internal*

   Medicine News 1 Oct. 2013: 14. *Academic OneFile*. Web. 6 Nov. 2013.

Salyers, Abigail A., and Dixie D. Whitt. *Revenge of the Microbes: How Bacterial Resistance*

   is Undermining the Antibiotic Miracle. Washington D.C.: ASM Press, 2005. Print.

Schwartz, Emma. "Who's Trying to Fix the Pipeline Problem?" *Frontline. PBS.org.* WGBH

   Educational Foundation, 22 Oct. 2013. Web. 7 Nov. 2013.

United States. Dept. of Health and Human Resources. Food and Drug Administration.

   Federal Food, Drug, and Cosmetic Act. 5 Dec. 2011. Web. 9 Nov. 2013.

APA Example

Challenges of Educating the Digital Brain

Bowen S. Barrs

Florida State College at Jacksonville

Educating the Digital Brain 2

Abstract

Digital media has profound effects on social behavior and cognitive development of students born between 1980 and 2000. Dubbed the *digital natives*, these students exhibit a change in mental and social activities due to a lifetime immersed in digital media. Many medical and mental health experts disagree on how digital media affects cognitive development. In this report, these controversies are discussed regarding the nature of maintaining focus in a techno-world of distractions. Areas of concern for teachers of digital natives include the following: memory, attention span, social behavior, critical thinking, and multitasking. In an effort to include not only expert analysis but also common public opinion, a short survey was conducted that asked questions regarding perceived changes in memory and attention spans. Ultimately, after reviewing the expert opinions coupled with the survey, it is apparent that technology combined with traditional education is imperative to enhance the educational needs of digitally immersed students.

Keywords: cognitive development, digital media, digital natives, critical thinking, multitasking, educational technology

Challenges of Educating the Digital Brain

The first digitally immersed children are now in their early thirties. These individuals, born after 1980, have always had digital technology as part of their world. Mediated experiences are as natural as the air they breathe. Students in classrooms today, kindergarten through college, are all digital natives. Because of this, there is much discussion, research, and controversy surrounding the use of digital technology in education. Marc Prensky, author of "Digital Natives, Digital Immigrants" (2001) wrote, "Our students have changed radically. Today's students are no longer the people our educational system was designed to teach" (p. 1). In contrast, the article "The 'Digital Natives' Debate: A Critical Review of the Evidence" from the *British Journal of Technology* suggested that critical research is lacking and no such distinctive divide exists: "Education may be under challenge to change, but it is not clear that it is being rejected" (Bennett, Maton, & Kervin, 2008, p. 783). Although compelling arguments warn of the dangers of people's heavy dependence on technology for collecting and deciphering information, a balanced perspective on how best to approach the cognitive shift of digital natives in and outside of the classroom is advantageous in creating a productive learning environment for the wired generation.

Literature Review

The Digital Brain

Prensky (2001) wrote in "Digital Natives, Digital Immigrants" that today's older folk were "socialized" differently from their kids, and are now in the process of learning a new language. And a language learned later in life, scientists tell us, goes into a different part of the brain (p. 2). Additionally, he expressed the seriousness of the problem that educators will face in dealing with digital natives: "Immigrant instructors, who speak an outdated language . . . are struggling to teach a population that speaks an entirely new language" (p. 2).

Peter Etchells, an experimental psychologist at the University of Bristol, reacted differently in an article for *Wired Magazine*:

> Anyone who does any research in neuroscience or psychology knows that everything changes the brain—that's the foundation of how we learn. Saying that using Facebook is changing our brains—of course it is. It's not interesting to say that. It's interesting to go beyond that simplistic argument and say what's going on—are there good points or bad points? (Cheshire, 2013, para. 11)

Reviewing the pros and cons of the effects of digital media on the brain revealed that some scientists, psychologists, and educators support the theories that children born into a digital world have brains that operate differently. There seems little doubt that many areas of the brain are greatly affected by immersion into digital media, but the extent of that change is still entrenched in controversy.

Memory

Studies documented in the article "Google Effects on Memory" (Sparrow, Liu, & Wegner, 2011) demonstrated the shift in the brain's retention of facts to the retention of where these facts are stored on the computer. The Internet's effects on memory are still largely unexplored, but results of the experiments had led Sparrow et al. to conclude that the Internet has become people's primary external storage system. Michael Rich, an associate professor at Harvard Medical School commented on this notion in an article for the *New York Times*: "Their brains are rewarded not for staying on task but for jumping to the next thing. . . . The worry is we're raising a generation of kids in front of screens whose brains are going to be wired differently" (Ritchel, 2010, para. 7).

Attention Spans

Most professors and students in the high school and college environment would agree that attention spans in teens and young adults during a classroom lecture seem shortened amidst the wealth of digital distractions. MIT Associate Professor David Jones, interviewed for the PBS documentary Digital Nation (Dretzin, 2010), sees his students as highly intelligent people who are easily distracted by their computers. For example, Jones was concerned that after distributing a midterm with obvious questions in which he predicted his students would score 100%, the mean score was about 75%. He surmised that "it's not that the students are dumb, it's not they're not trying, I think they're trying in a way that's not as effective as it could be because they're distracted by everything else" (Detzin, 2010).

According to Taylor (2012), ". . . attention is the gateway to thinking" (para. 6). Without it, other aspects of thinking including reasoning, decision-making, memory, and learning cannot occur at all. He further mentions that attention is a "malleable quality" and "most directly influenced by the environment in which it is used" (para. 7). Taylor said some studies, contrary to conventional thoughts, show that text only readers find presentations more informative and engaging than text filled with ads and hyperlinks.

Social Behavior

In a Pew Research study conducted by Lenhart, Ling, Campbell, and Kristen (2010), the researchers reported that texting has become the preferred mode of communication for teens: "One in three teens sends more than 100 text messages a day" (p. 2). This form of communication creates tension for teens at home because parents see the "attachment to their phones [as] an area of conflict and regulation" (p. 4). The conflict bleeds over into their schools where cell phones are seen as a "disruptive force that must be managed and often excluded from the school and the classroom" (p. 4). With a smart phone's access to the Internet, social media has become an enticing digital playground for teens' social interaction that erodes their ability to focus on one task at a time, whether that is conversing at the family dinner table or sitting in a desk during a class lecture.

Similar to the study mentioned above, Fox and Rainie (2014) conducted a Pew Study that analyzed how the Internet is viewed in terms of social interaction. The report notes that there were no significant differences in this opinion across a wide range of demographics such as age, sex, or income.

> There is considerable debate about whether online communication . . . has strengthened or weakened relationships. Internet users' own verdict is overwhelmingly positive when it comes to their own ties to family and friends: 67% of Internet users say their online communication with family and friends has generally strengthened those relationships, while 18% say it generally weakens those relationships. (para. 7)

Overall, the report signified that people are comfortable with using the World Wide Web as a means of emotional connection to others. Instead of the Web serving as a means of apprehension or fear, most avid Internet users see it as a tool to successfully connect with the people in their lives.

Critical Thinking

Reading on the web consists of quickly scanning information and searching for hyperlinks to other relevant information. The setup of a webpage encourages Internet users to explore in a nonlinear approach of consuming information. Carr (2008) noted in "Is Google Making Us Stupid?" that digital media is not just a passive channel of information:

> "What the Net seems to be doing is chipping away my capacity for concentration and contemplation. My mind now expects to take in information the way the Net distributes it: in a swiftly moving stream of particles" (para. 4). What Carr alluded to is that the way in which Internet users collect and process information on the Web alters their cognitive ability to sustain focus for long periods of time on one piece of information. Via Google, Internet users become accustomed to accessing information in snippets rather than practicing the skill of analyzing longer pieces of text.

> Inevitably, the skill of reading longer texts in order to strengthen one's vocabulary and critical thinking skills has faded among the digital natives. Researcher Patricia Greenfield noted that "students today have more visual literacy and less print literacy. Many students do not

read for pleasure and have not for decades" (Wolpert, 2009, para. 9). This increase in visual literacy, however, does not correlate to a skilled ability to multitask and obtain a deeper understanding of information (para. 13).

Multitasking

Juggling more than one task at a time is especially prevalent in teens and young adults. In school, these digitally wired learners are constantly checking e-mail and social media, surfing the internet, and texting. In *Digital Nation* (2010), MIT students regularly claim to be excellent and efficient at multitasking, but the research negates this perception. Professor Sherry Turkle, director of the MIT Initiative on Technology and Self, commented in the documentary that a multitasking learning environment serves no good (7:10). In support of Turkle's statement, Professor Clifford Nass, who studies multitasking at Stanford University, found that the students he tested think that their ability to multitask is much higher than the actual results; however, when he timed the students, the tasks assigned took longer and were done with less efficiency. After reporting these results, Nass is left with no other conclusion than to see multitasking efficiency as a myth (8:20).

Method

In an effort to further analyze how my technological affluent peers perceive their ability to concentrate amidst a barrage of digital distractions, I posted a survey on Facebook and asked two questions about perceptions of cognitive changes in attention span and memory due to the Internet:

   1) Do you feel your attention span has been affected by using the Internet?
   2) Do you feel your memory has been affected by using the Internet?

The questions were available for 24 hours before tabulating the results. The participants were from my list of 225 Facebook friends. The participants were 49 females and 29 males. The participants ranged in age from 23 to 61 years. Only 1 participant was in the 55 or older age category, and 16 participants were in the 45 to 55 age category. The largest response of 40 participants came from the 35 to 45 age category. Seventeen participants were in the 25 to 35 age category, and 4 participants were in the 18 to 25 age category.

Results

Participants agreed that their attention span was relatively short, but the reason for it was divided by age. Those 23 to 35 years of age acknowledged that their attention spans were short but not really changed much from the past. Those participants who were older than 35 seemed to believe with certainty that the Internet and digital technology were responsible for a decline in their attention spans. This response would make sense because participants older than 35 are definitely adapters of the technology and not native to it.

Educating the Digital Brain 6

In response to the second question, there was again a division along age lines. Older people felt they should attempt to keep remembering information. Worries on aging made one respondent state, "If you don't use it, you lose it!" Trust issues with the Internet and the fear that electronically stored information could disappear were reasons offered for not wanting to rely on the web. Many of these respondents did not think their use of the web affected memory as much as phones and computers themselves. Speed dial and the calendar applications were mentioned as technologies that have become a necessity rather than a convenience. The younger digital natives in the 18 to 25 age category acknowledged a lack of remembering dates, times, and historical events. Several students expressed frustration with recall-type tests that are strictly memory-driven. Most of these respondents did not feel the necessity to remember things that can easily be accessed through their phones or computers. No fears about Internet use or a loss of information were expressed. The responses to these questions show a divide in perception between those born into digital reliance and those who adapted to it. Adapters clearly have more skepticism and worry about the negative effects of technology on their cognitive processes. The digital natives think little about using technology and have always relied on it in lieu of retaining information.

Discussion

Technological advances are creating changes in society at a rate never experienced in the history of humankind. The digital world is changing much faster than researchers can possibly study it. Humans are adapting and utilizing technology far beyond what was imaginable 25 years ago when the World Wide Web was born. People are forever melded with their digital devices now that entire generations have been raised in a mediated world of hyper reality. How people recognize and deal with the digital world will be critical for future generations. Changes must be made now to ensure positive outcomes for students.

Simply allowing students to access the Internet in school does nothing in regard to using technology as a teaching tool; it merely becomes a distraction. Engaging students with technology can create a learning environment that is positive for both pupil and educator. A balanced relationship between classic teaching principals and innovation can be accomplished. Reading and writing are essential in developing critical thinking, but today's students will be required to have vast amounts of technical skills for future employment. Using what they already know and capitalizing on these skills can be very powerful teaching tools. Social media, interactive gaming, and virtual reality programs have opened educational opportunities never before imagined. Social networks can be used to interact within groups, obtain instantaneous feedback, receive assistance with projects, and form social bonds that stretch across the globe. These technologies can enhance the learning experience and keep students engaged and excited to learn.

Throughout history naysayers have warned of dire problems concerning every new technological advancement in society. Oftentimes people forget familiar technology once rankled many in its infancy. Human beings are in the adolescent phase of the digital world. It is turbulent, unpredictable, emotional, and rapidly growing. In time, society will find a balance and succeed in incorporating technology into the fabric of our history. The importance of embracing technology in a positive manner is imperative. Society can be enhanced rather than diminished by digital media. People should use technology to build upon our foundations of education. Social media and digital learning environments can be used with conventional teaching methods to actively engage students in a way that encourages group cooperation and critical thinking skills.

References

Bennett, S., Maton, K., & Kervin, L. (2008). The "digital natives" debate: A critical review of the evidence. *British Journal of Educational Technology*, 39 (5), 775–786. doi:10.1111/j.1467-8535.2007.00793.x

Carr, N. (2008, July 1). Is Google making us stupid? What the Internet is doing to our brains. *The Atlantic*. Retrieved from http://www.theatlantic.com/magazine/archive/2008/07/is-google-making-us-stupid/306868/

Cheshire, T. (2013, December 10). Distracted? How hyperstimulation is making you smarter. *Wired Magazine*. Retrieved from http://www.wired.co.uk/magazine/archive/2013/12/features/hyperstimulation

Dretzin, R. (Producer & Director). (2010). *Digital nation: Life on the virtual frontier.* [Documentary]. Retrieved from http://www.pbs.org/wgbh/pages/frontline/digitalnation/

Fox, S., & Rainie, L. (2014, February 27). The web at 25 in the U.S.: Summary of findings. In Pew Research Center. Retrieved from http://www.pewinternet.org/2014/02/27/summary-of-findings-3/

Lenhart, A., Ling, R., Campbell, S., & Kristen, P. (2010, April 20). Teens and mobile phones. In Pew Research Center. Retrieved from http://www.pewinternet.org/2010/04/20/teens-and-mobile-phones/

Prensky, M. (2001). Digital natives, digital immigrants. *On the Horizon*, 9(5), 1–6. Retrieved from http://www.marcprensky.com/writing/Prensky%20-%20Digital%20Natives,%20Digital%20Immigrants%20-%20Part1.pdf

Richtel, M. (2010, November 21). Growing up digital, wired for distraction. *The New York Times*. Retrieved from http://www.nytimes.com

Sparrow, B., Liu, J., & Wegner, D. (2011). Google effects on memory: cognitive consequences of having information at our fingertips. *Science*, 333, 776–778. doi: 10.1126/science.1207745

Taylor, J. (2012, December 4). How technology is changing the way children think and focus. [Blog post]. Retrieved from http://www.psychologytoday.com/blog/the-power-prime/201212/how-technology-is-changing-the-way-children-think-and-focus

Wolpert, S. (2009, January 27). Is technology producing a decline in critical thinking and analysis? In UCLA Newsroom. Retrieved from http://newsroom.ucla.edu/portal/ucla/is-technology-producing-a-decline-79127.aspx

Chapter 9

Understanding the Elements of Argument

Every waking day you are required to make thousands of choices, often without your being consciously aware that you are doing so. You make these choices as part of your routine, but also in reaction to the changing environment around you and to decisions you may have made earlier. Imagine that you are in the grocery store, perusing the cereal selections on aisle four. Which cereal will you buy? Will the authority of Olympic Gold Medalist Evan Strong convince you to buy a box of Wheaties? Will the one-half gram of fat listed on the side of the box sway your choice? Will the catchy slogan influence your selection? After all, we all want to eat the breakfast of champions, right? As a consumer and as a writer, you should understand the elements of persuading a targeted audience. Chapter 9 will explain the elements of argument.

Objectives

- differentiate between induction and deduction;

- explore the role of semantics and authority in an argument;

- examine the use of statistical evidence in an argument;

- explain eight commonly encountered logical fallacies.

▼ INDUCTION AND DEDUCTION—THINKING LOGICALLY

As we already mentioned, you are required to make choices constantly as you follow your daily routine. While you may not be aware of this process, every action you take requires a choice. Your day is a complicated web of your decisions, reactions, and a constant awareness of the decisions of others. Interestingly, though, there are only two processes you use to make your choices—*induction* and *deduction.*

INDUCTION

When you wake up in the morning, one of the first choices you have to make is what to wear. In making that choice, you might have to consider a number of criteria. What activities do you intend to do today? What is the weather forecast? What did you wear yesterday? What's clean? Whom will you have to impress? Once you have gathered the answers to these questions, you might then make the appropriate choice of clothing. However, even the best answers may be only educated guesses. A twenty percent chance of rain usually means no rain, but weather, not weather forecasters, makes the final determination. When you make your choice after getting all the information, you cannot be absolutely sure you've made the right one, even though all the evidence seems to suggest it. This process of gathering information, analyzing it, and using it to make a final decision is called *induction.*

If you have served on a jury, you are quite familiar with the inductive process. As a juror, you are charged with listening to all the evidence before making your decision of guilt or innocence. You also are aware that evidence is sometimes contradictory and may be unreliable. Your final decision is, at best, merely "beyond a reasonable doubt." The absolute certainty we would all like to have in an inductive decision, particularly in one as important as a jury verdict, is probably not attainable. Even if the defendant pleads guilty, can you be certain she is not covering up for her son or daughter, or is insane, or has been coerced to make that plea? An inductive process leads us to an *inductive leap* where we must overcome all but reasonable doubt to reach a decision.

Research is another area in which you will follow the inductive process. In doing your research about the causes of the Russian invasion of Ukraine, you will need to look at the historical background of the region, and you will have to examine the perspectives and opinions of numerous experts and political figures. After gathering this information, you will draw an inductive conclusion about the origins of the conflict. Of course, your conclusion will only be as good as the evidence upon which it is based. For example, when the Gallup pollsters predict the winner of the presidential election, they do so only after taking a wide sampling of potential voters all across America. Their predictions, read by millions of people, are respected only so long as their predictions continue to be reasonably accurate. So, what do the pollsters do to insure the continued success of their predictions? The answer lies in their ability to answer these three questions:

1. Is the sample (evidence) large enough?

2. Is the sample (evidence) representative of the total population being served?

3. Is the sample (evidence) accessible?

The number of people that Gallup polls is based on several factors. First, the sample must be large enough to support the conclusion. A sample of ten voters may not be sufficient to support a prediction about the outcome of a state or national election. Size is not the key issue, however; a more important factor in determining how large the sample must be is found in the second question:

Is the sample (evidence) representative of the total population being polled?

If you want to find out how many male students between the ages of 18 and 20 at a local college will binge drink during homecoming weekend, your sample size will consist only of that population group and can be relatively small. If, however, you want to find out how many students at the college will binge drink, you must be sure to include all sexes and all age groups. Consequently, because you have a larger representative group to sample, your sample size will have to be larger. The third question, though, has to be answered:

Is the sample (evidence) accessible?

Too many times, people make claims about research or evidence that cannot be verified. How many times have you heard, "I can't tell you the source, but I know this to be a fact . . ."? Evidence, if it is to be considered in your inductive process, must be available for all to see. If it is not available, that evidence cannot be part of the final conclusion.

Induction, then, is the process of gathering evidence, analyzing it, and drawing a logical conclusion. Remember, though, that evidence is seldom complete, and at some point you must make an inductive leap based on your best analysis of the evidence to reach your conclusion. It might be helpful to remember Occam's Razor as you begin your final analysis: *Given all the evidence, the simplest conclusion is usually the best conclusion.* It may be more fun to generate conspiracy theories and deal in extraterrestrial fantasies, but ultimately good conclusions come from a careful reading of the known facts at hand.

DEDUCTION

Another way you reach your decisions is through the process of deduction. Unlike induction, which starts *with* the process of gathering information, deduction starts with a known broad conclusion and applies it to a specific situation. For example, it is a generally known fact that mammals are animals that breathe air through their lungs. If you are sightseeing on the Intracoastal Waterway in Florida, you are likely to see dolphins leaping out of the water alongside your boat, and while you may consider them to be like any other fish, you will notice that they surface frequently and breathe through a hole in the top of their heads. Your reasoning process about the dolphins' breathing might look something like this:

- Mammals breathe through their lungs;

- Dolphins are mammals;

- Dolphins breathe through their lungs.

You use this kind of reasoning in many ways. Look at how you might teach your child about riding safely in the car:

- Kelly, when we are in the car, we always wear our seatbelt;

- We are in the car;

- Therefore, you will fasten your seatbelt.

The three-part construct used in both these examples is called the *syllogism*. The syllogism consists of two premises and a conclusion, and can be very effective in leading you to an appropriate conclusion. While a jury's verdict may be derived from an inductive process, the premise that controls reaching the final verdict may be a deductive one:

- If the evidence supports a guilty verdict, we must convict;

- The evidence does support a guilty verdict;

- Then, we must convict.

The Syllogism

The first statement of the syllogism is called the *major premise*. The major premise must be true, and it usually has broad applications. For example, you might state that *dogs bark*. Certainly, it's conceivable that there are mute dogs, and you might even find a dog or two which have learned to howl to music or chatter in seemingly human voices. Generally, though, barking is attributed to all dogs, and the premise is probably true as stated.

The second line of the syllogism is called the *minor premise*. The minor premise focuses the major premise to a specific situation. For instance, I might state that my pet Trixie is a dog. The major and minor premises would look like this:

- All dogs bark;

- Trixie is a dog.

If both of these premises are true, what can you deduce to be a logical conclusion about Trixie? Certainly, the only logical conclusion is that Trixie barks.

Let's look at another situation. Your instructor tells you when he was a student, he and the other students in the class all met together on the weekend and studied for the midterm exam. As a result, his entire class passed the test. He then reminds the class the midterm exam is next week. What is the basic syllogism evident in the instructor's story?

- Students who study together on weekends pass their exams;
- You should get together this weekend to study for the midterm;
- Then, you will . . .

Is it effective? Is it logical? Remember, quite often, deductive arguments may be effective, even while being illogical. As in inductive reasoning, you must ask yourself three key questions before you can be assured your conclusion is logical:

- Are the premises true?
- Is the language ambiguous?
- Is the syllogism correctly constructed?

Are the premises true?

If either or both of the premises are not true, your conclusion cannot be true. For example, if you accept the following major premise as true:

- Taking a life is murder;

then, you leave yourself open to the following minor premise:

- Killing an enemy in war is taking a life.

The conclusion from these premises is

- Killing an enemy in war is murder.

If this conclusion were true, all soldiers who did so in past wars would have to be tried as murderers since, by this argument, they committed murder. The truth is, society distinguishes between taking a life on the battlefield, or in self-defense, or in the carrying out of a death penalty, or even in some medical situations, and the major premise is not true as it is written. Look at another possible version of the major premise:

- The illegal taking of another person's life is murder.

Is this major premise more defensible? Can it be applied to a specific situation to form a logical syllogism? Look at this example.

- The illegal taking of another person's life is murder;
- The perpetrator illegally took the bank manager's life in carrying out his crime;
- Therefore, the perpetrator is guilty of murder.

Is the language ambiguous?

Another problem to look for in a deductive syllogism is any language that may have a double meaning. A commercial kitchen supplier that states:

> "Incorporating a built-in Sub-Zero refrigerator system into your restaurant's kitchen design will make you a *cool dude*"

is playing on our fondness for ambiguous language. The effect of such language can be entertaining, but in a logical argument the effect can be serious. If a word or phrase can have more than one meaning or is open for multiple interpretations, so can the deductive conclusion, leaving your syllogism in question. Look at the debates raging over what constitutes "life" and what the authors of the constitution meant when they guaranteed the "right to bear arms" or forbade "cruel and inhuman punishment."

Is the syllogism correctly constructed?

Look at the following claim:

- All dogs bark;
- All roosters crow;
- Therefore, roosters don't bark.

There may be truth in each of the premises, but they do not lead the reader to a logical deductive conclusion because the minor premise is not related to the major premise. If the minor premise affirmed that the subject was a dog,

- All dogs bark;
- Lassie *is* a dog.

or if the minor premise denies the action,

- All dogs bark;
- Lassie *doesn't* bark.

then your syllogism will lead to a logical conclusion:

> Therefore, Lassie barks
>
> or
>
> Therefore, Lassie isn't a dog.

In the minor premise, the noun is referred to as the *antecedent,* and the action is called the *consequent.* Remember, you can reach a logical deductive conclusion by affirming the antecedent or by denying the consequent.

Look at this major premise:

A syllogism must have a major and minor premise.

What is a minor premise that affirms the antecedent? There are a number of possible minor premises. Look at this one:

- A syllogism must have a major and minor premise;
- *That example is a syllogism;*
- Therefore, it has a major and minor premise.

What would be a good example of a minor premise that denies the consequent?

- A syllogism must have a major and minor premise;
- *That example does not have a minor premise;*
- Therefore, it is not a syllogism.

If the form is correct, if your premises are true, and if your language is unambiguous, your deductive conclusion will be reliable.

A Final Note

Whether you use induction or deduction, the reliability of your conclusion will be based on how thorough you are in ensuring the quality of the evidence. The most reliable arguments are those in which the evidence is supportable and in which truth, not emotion, is the ultimate goal. In the next sections, we want to look at a few issues that may affect the integrity of your argument, including a breakdown in the inductive or deductive processes.

Semantics

You have always been aware that words carry a great deal of power and can dramatically affect or change any situation. During a volatile period in world history, the U.S. press and media outlets reported former Russian Premier Nikita Kruschev's Cold War challenge to America, "We will bury you!" The American response was dramatic, with national newspapers calling for an increase in arms spending and greater economic sanctions against the Russian menace. Unfortunately, the translation of Mr. Kruschev's statement was a literal one; for someone more familiar with the Russian language, the translation would more correctly have been, "We will leave you in the dust," a considerably less aggressive challenge based more on economic competition than on physical threat. The importance of correctly understanding what someone else says cannot be understated in considering a logical discussion or argument. Members of a jury listen carefully to the evidence presented by the witnesses, but their decisions are based ultimately on what sense they make of the testimony; if they incorrectly interpreted what the witness said, the jury's final verdict may be flawed. How do you know what someone means when he or she says something?

First, you need to be aware that words carry different meanings. Many words have two levels of interpretation—the *denotative* and the *connotative*. The denotative meaning is the literal definition of the word. If you tell your best friend you like her black Labrador retriever, there is little doubt of what the word "black" means, since black Labrador retrievers are named for their color. The denotative meaning does not require much interpretation on your part. However, if you tell your business associate that your lawn care business will end the calendar year in the "black," then "black" takes on a connotative meaning, one that goes beyond the literal meaning and one that often assumes symbolic value. In this statement, "black" connotes that the business has been profitable that year. Perhaps celebration is in order, or it's time to buy a new weed whacker for the crew! Wearing a "black" tie to work and attending a "black" tie affair mean different things, depending on whether you simply take the word at its denotative level or look at it from a more complex connotative one.

Look at this excerpt from an acceptance speech someone might give for being chosen for a new position:

> We climb ladders all our lives. Sometimes the ascent is swift, and the rungs seem close together; at other times, the rungs make us stretch and pull, and the ascent seems painfully slow. But, each reach for that next level makes us stronger, and, with patient fortitude, our climb to success will pass through any glass ceilings or insurmountable obstacles—on life's ladder, even the sky is not a limit.

Is the language of the speaker denotative or connotative? Is he or she literally climbing a ladder? Is the "glass ceiling" really a roof? Obviously, this speaker is counting on the audience's ability to go beyond the literal denotative meaning and understand the symbolic significance of the lifelong struggle.

Writers and speakers must also be aware that being understood requires a good understanding of the audience—the person or group whom you want to understand your meaning. Getting to know your audience may require you to do some research and thinking *before* you make a statement. The words you choose to describe your most recent Saturday night on the town may differ considerably depending on whether your audience is your mom or your classmates. A potential witness may describe his or her version of an incident one way if he or she is not being charged with a crime, but he or she may find a different choice of words if he or she is a litigant. We might call people who blow up the enemy's transportation infrastructure "freedom fighters," but the nation that is protecting their transportation systems might call those individuals "traitors" or "terrorists." When you listen to your city's current mayor as she launches her reelection campaign, she may speak of herself as "conservative" in her spending habits; you might call her a "cheapskate" or a "pinchpenny." Audiences bring their own attitudes and expectations to a discussion, and good writers and speakers construct their arguments using language that is appropriate to address the views of particular audiences.

APPROPRIATE AUTHORITY

Another consideration in sorting through your evidence is whether the source of the information is truly knowledgeable about the subject and, if so, to what degree. Most lawyers spend a considerable amount of time at a trial establishing the credibility of their witnesses. In a famous case that was broadcast nationally and involved O.J. Simpson, a renowned football star, the forensic witnesses who testified about the evidence (the DNA, the autopsy reports, the weapon, and so forth) were first questioned extensively about their background and expertise. Questions were asked about their degrees or training, the number of similar investigations with which they had been involved, the number of years they had been in their current positions, and their previous opportunities to testify. In many cases, experts with similar credentials were presenting totally different interpretations of the evidence, thus making the jurors' perception of their credibility as authorities more important than the actual evidence.

When you see a nationally known actor or athlete promoting a product on TV or in the newspaper, you might ask yourself whether you consider that person an authority on the product. More than likely, the only expertise that that celebrity has about the product is the salary he or she got for doing the promotion. The premise of such advertisement is that if we like the person promoting the product, we will like the product. Unfortunately, that premise has very weak logical foundations.

Another factor to consider in looking at the authority behind your evidence is the *bias* that the expert might have. If you ask your local Trek Bicycle dealer which company—Trek or Schwinn—makes a better road bike, the shop owner's answer should come as no surprise. Many experts do have biases that influence their judgment, and in weighing your evidence, it is important to be aware of those biases as you consider the reliability of the evidence.

Finally, don't forget that experts might deliberately choose to present erroneous or incomplete evidence if it is in their best interest to do so. It would be nice if everyone were honest and each person considered the general good to be more important than his or her personal concerns. The fact is, though, people will act in their own self-interest, particularly when their personal or professional survival is at stake. If you were to ask the CEOs who were responsible for the California Savings and Loan scandal, which cost citizens billions of dollars in lost savings, about the extent of their involvement, they would probably deny being aware of the problems that brought about the financial disaster. Certainly, the threat of long prison terms might affect their ability to recall key bits of information.

STATISTICS

People who claim numbers don't lie probably have never taken a statistics course. Research often requires quantitative support, and numbers can have a major impact on any conclusions derived from the research. The amount of your insurance payments on your life or your health or your health is based on the statistical averages of the claims for your age group, for the type of your pre-existing health conditions, and for the region in which you are located. Averages have a tremendous influence on what your academic grades are, where new chain restaurants and stores are built, and what movies are brought to your area theaters, but how do companies and researchers determine averages? How do they determine what the average moviegoer in Walla Walla, Washington, wants to see in the local theater?

You should be aware that when you look at an average in your evidence, there are three ways the average may have been calculated: the *mean, median,* or *mode.*

Mean

The mean is the average derived from adding the values of all the items in your survey and dividing by the number of items. For example, if your test scores for the term are 78, 95, 86, 95, and 0 (you failed to show up), the total value for these tests would be 78+95+86+95+0 = 354. If you divide that value by the number of tests (5), your *mean* test value for the term is 70.8. Whew! That looks like a grade of C!

Median

The median average is the value of the middle number when all the items are arranged in order. Using these same test scores, and arranging them in ascending (or descending) order, the scores are 0, 78, 86, 95, 95. The middle number for these five scores is 86, which becomes the *median* value. If you have an even number of test items, you simply find the mean of the two middle numbers. Notice that with these scores, the median average is considerably higher than the mean average for the same scores. In fact, you got yourself a solid B!

Mode

The mode average is simply the value in a list of items that occurs most frequently. Look at the five test scores again. Which value occurs most often? The only score that appears more than once is 95, and that is the *mode* value. Congratulations! You have yourself an A!

You can see, then, that three different methods for finding the average may give you three very different values. If you are going to tell your parents what your average is, you probably will compute the mode. If you don't want to embarrass your girlfriend or boyfriend whose average score is 86, you might choose the median. If you want to challenge the professor about the difficulty of his tests, you might use the mean score, arguing that the class averages are well below the school average. Unfortunately, individuals often use averages in their arguments or evidence, but they fail to reveal how those averages were computed. Even worse, averages computed as the mean might be compared with other averages computed as a mode, making the comparison unfair and unreliable.

Another factor in considering statistics is that many statistics are meaningless. If you read that 35 percent of all females have broken their nails in the last five years, you certainly have to wonder how such a statistic was determined as well as why it's important. When Los Angeles says its rat population exceeds the entire human population of India, the same question about how that statistic was derived must be raised. Do you know how many times a week on the average you think about going grocery shopping? Or how many times a year you go to the movies? You can guess, but is that an accurate guess and, if not, does it have any value in a logical discussion?

Keep in mind, too, that individuals being questioned in a study don't always tell the truth. National averages about sexual practices among teenagers are derived from responses of teenagers who might be engaging in more wishful thinking than in actual fact. Is a teenager really going to tell a stranger how many sexual experiences he or she has in an average month?

When you consider statistical information, always ask these questions about the data before you weigh their value in your argument:

Key Questions	• Where did the data originate? • How were the data computed? • Do the statistical data apply to the situation being studied? • Is the statistic meaningful?

Good statistical evidence can be invaluable in any discussion or argument—the challenge for you is knowing whether the evidence is good. Ultimately, you have to make that decision.

▼ LOGICAL FALLACIES

Earlier, you learned about how we reach decisions through induction or through deduction, and you were given a number of criteria to use in determining if the evidence used in making those decisions was reliable. If the processes break down, or if some of the criteria are omitted or distorted, then the process can be flawed and the conclusion could be proven to be inaccurate. Such breakdowns in the logical process are called *fallacies*. There are more possible fallacies than we can discuss in this chapter, but it is important that you become familiar with some of the most frequently occurring fallacies and that you be able to recognize them when you encounter them in your research or discussions. We will look at eight of the most common fallacies, but you should be reminded that there are many more, and the more fallacies you can recognize, the better you will feel about the logical decisions you make. We will briefly discuss *post hoc (ergo propter hoc), ad hominem, non sequitur, either/or, hasty generalization, false analogy, red herring,* and *bandwagon*.

POST HOC ERGO PROPTER HOC

The *post hoc* fallacy literally translates, "After this, therefore because of this." Because we like to know why things happen, quite often we look at whatever occurred immediately prior to the incident as a probable cause. For example, if you see your little brother playing with frogs after a hard rain, and a few hours later he develops a case of warts on the back of his hand, you may be inclined to assume that because the play date with the frogs happened just a few hours prior to the outbreak of warts, the frogs somehow caused the warts. With no other evidence to support your conclusion, you are probably guilty of a post hoc fallacy. Just because something happens prior to something else is not sufficient reason in itself to conclude the first event caused the second. In reality, most instances may have multiple causes, and those causes may have cumulatively led up to the incident. Of course, if you see your dog Trixie pick up one of the frogs in her mouth, and then she begins to foam at the mouth shortly thereafter, you probably have sufficient evidence to conclude that the frog caused your dog's mouth to foam. If, however, Trixie began to roll over and kick her legs in the air just prior to foaming at the mouth, your causal assumption may once again be post hoc.

AD HOMINEM

Ad hominem means "to the person." When an argument deteriorates to the point that one of the people involved quits debating the issues and instead attacks the other person, he or she is resorting to the ad hominem fallacy. Consider the following example:

> Discussing the Defense of Marriage Act with the likes of Senator Smithers is nonsensical since he is famous for his widespread philandering during the past ten years that he has been in office!

Name-calling is a favorite tactic among children, but it also is not uncommon in public debate and argument. Avoid the ad hominem trap by keeping the issues in focus, not the person debating the issue.

NON SEQUITUR

Non sequitur means, "It does not follow." Just because your best friend is the president of the Student Government Association doesn't automatically make her a candidate for the "Outstanding Student" award. A good mother may not necessarily be a good den mother for the neighborhood Cub Scout troop. Similarly, just because a local community activist has been an effective advocate for the arts program at your local high school, that alone may not predict whether he will be a good elected school board member. The non sequitur *predicts* a condition based on existing conditions, which are perceived as being similar. You must always ask yourself in making such predictions whether the conditions are, indeed, related. We have elected many media personalities to public office based not on their political skills, but on their popularity and public image, and we may judge somebody in one area based on what we know about them in an entirely different set of circumstances. You may hear someone say, "I don't see how he could have done that; he's always been a good neighbor." Being a good neighbor may have little connection to a whether a person is an embezzler at work.

EITHER/OR

The either/or fallacy is a fallacy of limited choice. In most real situations, you often have many alternatives, and using those alternatives often gives you greater opportunity to reach a solution in an argumentative situation. Sometimes, though, a person unnecessarily limits his or her options. For example, in a disagreement with your spouse, you might in anger blurt out, "Either you quit smoking, or I am leaving you for good!" Whereas you might have worked out the problem through a wider examination of the alternatives, now you are limited to only two alternatives, and a confrontation is almost certain. A hot topic in the news is climate change, and one related either/or assertion that you may have heard before is that power companies can either stop burning coal or destroy the earth. While burning coal has its problems, there are many more possibilities than this claim allows. Power companies can burn less coal and increase the use of alternative energy sources, or companies can explore cleaner methods for burning coal. Destroying the earth is not necessarily an end-all ultimatum. By limiting yourself to only two options, you may be losing the opportunity to enjoy more possibilities. Don't accept someone's simplistic assertion that "either you're part of the problem or you're part of the solution." The real problem probably stems from that person's inability to recognize the either/or fallacy.

HASTY GENERALIZATION

The hasty generalization is another inductive fallacy in which a conclusion is drawn from too little evidence. In many cases, prejudice is a result of hasty generalizations—assumptions about groups based on limited interaction. If you receive poor service and find a hair in your scrambled eggs at the local franchise of a national pancake house, those experiences provide insufficient evidence to conclude that poor service and hair in the food are the norm, and no one should eat at that pancake house restaurant chain again. Similarly, if a colleague of yours tells you that his car was recently rear-ended by a sixteen-year-old driver, and he argues that all teen drivers should be banned from the highways because they are incompetent, you should recognize that such a broad condemnation of a group based on a single incident is a hasty generalization. Such logic is both faulty and, perhaps, dangerous in that it promotes stereotypical thinking. Similarly, if you are served a cold hamburger at the local fast food restaurant, that is insufficient evidence to conclude the cold burger is the norm, and no one should eat at that place again. Hasty generalizations are easy traps to fall into because we often have only limited experiences with certain groups. However, a logical person is aware of the need for sufficient evidence in any inductive process; if you continue to get bad service and find non-food-related items in your meals, and you begin to hear others making the same complaints about the service and the food from other restaurants in the same chain, then you have a better basis to draw a broader conclusion.

FALSE ANALOGY

In a recent debate over whether a school system should adopt a district-wide school dress code, several students interviewed complained the schools were "just like prisons." Anyone who has visited a prison knows that a public school and a prison are quite different, and, though they are both institutions with institutional policies, the differences are too substantial to make the comparison a fair one. Sometimes in our eagerness to explain something, we try to compare it to something else. It may be helpful to imagine the brain as a vast computer with electrical connections continuously firing as data are taken in and assessed. Analogies can give us a different perspective in trying to understand difficult issues. However, a false analogy may do more to create misunderstanding than to alleviate it. To state that raising children is just like raising a garden is a gross over-simplification. When a person argues that "taking away my gun is like taking away my life," the comparison has emotional impact, but is obviously logically faulty. Teenagers often make the same argument when they lose their smart phone privileges. The same can be said for the anti-gun lobbyists who argue that playing with toy guns is no different from playing with the real thing. A logical analogy draws a realistic comparison based on fact, not emotion.

RED HERRING

Dog trainers often put their dogs through their final tests by dragging a smelly object through the woods for the dogs to track. Along that path, they might use a fish (a red herring) to lay a counter trail to see if the dog will be distracted by the stronger fish scent. Any deliberate attempt to lead someone away from an issue in order to avoid that issue is known as a red herring. Listen carefully to the candidates' speeches and interviews during the next election. If a candidate, when asked about his or her policy on a specific issue, such as climate change, responds, "Well, you know that's not the real issue; the *real* issue is whether we want to ensure that we are supporting our children's education . . ." he or she is probably committing a red herring fallacy. The real issue was the one presented in the question—climate change; the candidate either doesn't know the answer, or doesn't want to take a position for or against it, or simply wants to redirect the conversation to his or her preferred platform topic—in either case, the intent of the answer is to distract the audience from the question.

BANDWAGON

If you buy your child a Sony PlayStation because everyone else seems to be buying one for his or her children, you may be acting in response to the bandwagon fallacy. We like to consider ourselves as part of the favored group and don't like to feel we are being "left behind." Advertisers and politicians take advantage of that social reality and try to convince us to "get on the bandwagon" and join the rest of our neighbors and friends. Children, of course, are very vulnerable to such pressure; adults, however, can also be influenced, even to the point of acting illogically. In Suzanne Collins' *The Hunger Games Trilogy*, the Games and the competitors themselves are celebrated at a great feast, where the citizens of the Capitol engage in a purging practice that allows them to gorge on incredible amounts of food throughout the evening. Katniss Everdeen, the heroine of the trilogy, is encouraged to join in this experience, to "get on the bandwagon" so that she can continue to partake in this unhealthy yet commonly practiced and widely accepted feasting activity. She, of course, is repulsed by this nonsensical disregard for the precious food, which the families in her district sorely lack. Such silliness to "keep up with the Joneses" may explain why people begin buying particular smart phones or participating in risky uses of social media just because everyone else seems to be doing it. Certainly, if you are sitting in your classroom or office and you notice everyone else running for the exits, you may not be acting illogically to do the same and ask why later. However, doing things that may not be in our best interest or buying things we can't afford because others are doing so may do little more than create bigger problems for us; being on the bandwagon may not be the best way to go.

BEGGING THE QUESTION

Sometimes we are so sure about an argument that we can't wait to state our opinion. Unfortunately, this rush to judgment often ignores evidence that might lead to a different conclusion. When we assume something to be true *before* we have looked at all the evidence, we are committing the fallacy of *begging the question.*

Perhaps you have watched an episode or two of the reality show *TruTV*, which broadcasts live trials. During an episode, you may see a lawyer make an opening statement to the jury in which he or she argues that the defendant is a thief. This view might be a valid conclusion *after* the trial but begs the question when it is stated before the evidence is presented and before the jury has had the opportunity to draw its own conclusion. Certainly, the defendant's lawyer would immediately rise up in righteous indignation and shout, "Your honor, I object! The prosecutor is begging the question."

On a personal level, you may sometimes conclude there is no hope in trying to do something because you believe you have no chance to get it done. Such reasoning begs the question unless you have ample evidence to suggest it is, indeed, an impossible task. Next time you hear yourself saying, "There's no reason to study for this exam; I won't pass it anyway," stop and remember you are begging the question. Don't fail a test because your conclusion was based on fallacious thinking.

You can see, then, that good thinking is a deliberate process in which a person tries to make intelligent choices based on a careful analysis of the evidence. In the next chapter you will be learning how to construct argumentative papers. Remember, a good argument is no better than the evidence that backs it up. As you write, be aware of the logic you are using to make your case. A perfectly written argument may pass the grammarian's scrutiny but fail to pass the critical test of sound reasoning. In short, *think* before you *write!*

Chapter 10

Writing an Argument Paper

Students often mistakenly associate the concept of argumentation with an unpleasant altercation of some sort. While arguing certainly can lead to fighting, fisticuffs are not usually the end result of a lesson on argument, at least not in a freshman writing class. Rather, the study of argument is an exercise in the use of logic and evidence to make a point. Developing an argument in either oral or written form can prove very useful when you need to establish your position on a particular issue and to convince others to adopt your way of thinking. Chapter 10 will guide you in writing a well-developed argument paper.

Objectives

- discuss the selection of an argumentative topic;

- explain the significance of considering the paper's audience;

- provide strategies for refining the thesis statement and essay blueprint;

- emphasize the importance of establishing credibility as a writer and as a researcher;

- suggest ways of incorporating supporting evidence into the paper;

- delineate organizational patterns appropriate for argumentative papers;

- recommend ways of addressing opposing viewpoints.

▼ SELECTING A TOPIC

When you are trying to find a topic for writing an argumentative paper, choose a topic that is both debatable and interesting to you. Think about controversial issues in the news or something you heard about on the radio or read in the school newspaper. What are some topics about which you feel passionately: Today's health care policies? Teachers' carrying guns in public schools? Genetically altered foods? The use of drones? Whatever topic you choose needs to reflect controversy.

For example, let's say that you've decided to write about the effects of energy drinks on users of such products. A topic such as this one lends itself to a value argument, or one that establishes a positive or negative impression of the topic at hand. One approach might be to discuss the dangers associated with the use of energy drinks. On the other hand, you might argue that energy drinks can increase mental and physical performance. There are certainly proponents for both sides of this energy drink debate.

Another type of argument is one of policy, calling for a change. Let's say that you decide to write about the increasing number of fatal accidents occurring with motorcyclists. One approach might be to argue in favor of requiring motorcyclists to wear helmets. One possible solution might be to reenact the mandatory helmet in your state. Of course, such a recommendation would most certainly affect current law, not to mention aggravate a lot of motorcyclists.

▼ CONSIDERING YOUR AUDIENCE

Once you've selected your topic, identified your position, and considered other points of view, you must consider your audience. Who will be reading your paper? How hard will you have to work to convince your reader to buy into your point of view? In most cases, the members of your audience will fall into one of three categories: those who favor your position, those who are neutral, and those who oppose your stance.

Think about this situation: You are about to complete your first semester in college, and you are writing letters to get more money to cover next semester's expenses. Several people appear on your list. First is your very rich Great-Uncle Harry, who considers you to be his favorite among all of your cousins. Next is the college's Dean of Student Success, who helped you to resolve a financial aid issue at the beginning of the term. Last is your dear old dad, whose emergencies-only Visa card balance was filled with pizzas and road trips during that first term. Obviously, Great-Uncle Harry will require very little coaxing to contribute financially to semester number two, but the Dean may require a little more hard data in your favor if you are to gain a little extra attention for your financial aid needs. Your father, however, will require significantly more convincing. You will have to acknowledge your overspending on the Visa card and make a case that persuades him that you will not repeat the financial performance of your first term.

Other considerations to take into account when identifying your target audience are the level of education of your readers and their level of expertise regarding your topic.

Questions about Reader Composition	• What are the wants and needs of your intended audience? • How much do they need defined for them? Are they already experts? Is the paper too simple or too difficult? • Are the readers partially convinced already? Are they fence riders, or are they staunchly opposed? • Is there a chance that your audience will consider your paper's tone or position to be offensive?

Taking the time to analyze your paper's audience before you begin to write and making an effort to meet your readers' needs will help you to write an effective argumentative essay.

▼ CONSTRUCTING AND REFINING THE THESIS STATEMENT AND ESSAY BLUEPRINT

At this point, you've probably read about your topic in a variety of sources and collected quite a few notes on your topic. You also should have a clear idea of the direction your paper is headed and the points you will need to discuss in the paper. Before you begin writing, though, you need to spend a little time refining your thesis statement and essay blueprint.

Again, to review, in Chapter 1, we defined the thesis statement as the one sentence in the introduction that lets your reader know the controlling or main idea of the entire essay. We also discussed that the thesis statement is often followed or preceded by a sentence that serves as an "essay blueprint," a sentence that helps the reader to see the paper's organizational plan. Also remember that the thesis should not be written as a question, nor should it begin with phrases such as, "In this paper, I will address . . . " or, "This essay will be about . . . ."

Another point to remember is that thesis statements can be written on three levels of action, depending on the reaction you are seeking from your reader: stimulation, motivation, and activation. Using words like *should* and *must* in the thesis is a good way to include a verb that expresses action and helps you to inspire your reader to take action. Chapter 5 reviews this thesis-writing strategy.

The main point to remember about writing a good thesis statement for an argument paper is the following: The statement must be arguable, and it must make a value judgment or call for a change in policy, something with which your reader can agree or disagree.

For example, let's say that you've decided to write about the effects of fast-food restaurants on society. Consider the following thesis statement:

Energy drinks have permeated our lives as a means to increase mental acuity and physical performance.

Most people would probably agree with such a statement. It's difficult to go anywhere in the world, much less the United States, and not spot Red Bull, Monster, Five-Hour Energy drinks in vending machines or convenience stores. While you might be able to write a sound informative paper on this topic, it wouldn't be an argumentative paper. Your thesis statement must be arguable. Try this one:

Energy drinks are a dangerous means of increasing mental and physical performance.

Note that this statement becomes arguable simply by adding one word: dangerous. While you may feel that energy drinks are hazardous to your health, and many medical doctors and nutritionists would probably back up your assertions, the CEOs of energy drink companies and many users would more than likely disagree with your view. Such a statement makes a value judgment. When you make a value judgment, you've opened the door to debate.

To create an essay blueprint for this thesis, you might try something like the following:

Energy drinks are a dangerous means of increasing mental and physical performance. Excessive use of such drinks can lead to dehydration and loss of fluids; cause such side effects as irritability, anxiety, and insomnia; and result in long term effects of heart diseases.

To try something different, let's say that you decide to write an argumentative essay on motorcycle fatalities. Consider this thesis statement:

The number of motorcycle fatalities on the roads today is increasing.

Yes, this sentence is arguable, but what is the point? The argument will be answered simply "yes" or "no." Once the data are provided, there is nowhere else to go with this argument. Consider making this topic an argument of policy. Try this thesis statement:

Because of the increasing number of motorcycle fatalities on the roads today, the State should reinstate the mandatory helmet law for motorcyclists.

This thesis statement gives your paper some direction. You've stated a problem, which you will now have to prove exists by providing logical reasons and then using evidence to back up your assertions. You've also suggested a policy change in the form of a solution to the problem.

Let's add an essay blueprint to the thesis:

> Because of the increasing number of motorcycle fatalities on the roads today, the State should reinstate the mandatory helmet law for motorcyclists. Since the repeal of the State's mandatory law more motorcyclists are riding without helmets. Reinstating the mandatory helmet law will reduce the number of fatal accidents due to head trauma and will have a positive impact on rising insurance and medical expenses.

Again, adding an essay blueprint to your thesis statement gives the paper a little more direction and lets your reader know the points you intend to make in the paper. The development of these ideas will be discussed later in this chapter.

▼ ESTABLISHING YOUR CREDIBILITY

While Chapter 6 discussed at length the importance of using credible sources, it is important to review those points as you prepare to write an argumentative paper. Remember, your goal is to present yourself not only as a credible writer, but also as a credible researcher.

Questions About References	• Does the author have an agenda or bias that might skew the information provided in the article? • Does the author have extensive background or expertise that lends credibility to the source? • Is the publication a reputable one? Does it carry a bias or slanted perspective? Are you using multiple sources?

Once you've determined that you have found a variety of solid, reliable sources, be sure to include plenty of evidence from your sources to support your argument and to address opposing views. Be thorough in your presentation of information, providing sufficient examples to support your general assertions. Also, attempt to establish common ground with your audience, and demonstrate fairness, presenting all sides of the topic if there are contrasting views. Acknowledge the arguments of the opposing side, and then refute those arguments using evidence from your source material. Strategies for incorporating evidence into your paper and addressing opposing views will be discussed next.

SUPPORTING EVIDENCE

In the 1980s, an advertisement campaign for the fast-food chain Wendy's used the slogan, "Where's the beef?" This slogan conveyed the meaning that if you wanted a quality hamburger sandwich, you needed more than the bun, the toppings, and the condiments—you needed meat! This same philosophy holds for an argument essay. If you want to write a "quality" argument, you need more than the structure of an essay: you need the "meat"—the *EVIDENCE*. If you are going to convince your readers to accept your thesis and believe each of your points in support of your thesis, you need evidence to show that your points are valid. Your evidence is key to changing your reader's opinion.

In researching your argument topic, look for four types of evidence: facts, examples, statistics, and testimony. Let's say that you are writing an argument paper on motorcycle fatalities. You want to convince your readers that the State should reinstate the mandatory helmet for all motorcyclists. The following discussion will show how the four types of evidence could be used.

Facts

Facts are verifiable pieces of evidence. Facts can be useful to describe a particular situation or to show the need for action. In showing the need for this reinstatement, you can describe the current helmet law in your state and point out when the previous mandatory helmet law was repealed.

The most important consideration in using facts is to make sure your facts are accurate. Your reader may become suspect of all your evidence if you provide one piece of inaccurate information. Only use credible sources to supply your facts. In the case of your state's motorcycle helmet laws, you could actually refer to your state's statutes.

Example

Examples are illustrations that show that your point is true. Many times examples take the form of brief narratives. Examples are very helpful in getting your reader to visualize or "experience" the reality of your point. For instance, you want to show not wearing a helmet can lead to a fatal motorcycle accident. You can prove this point by stating names of motorcycle riders and describing the fatal accidents in which they involved.

In using examples fairly and ethically, you want to make sure your examples are relevant and typical. It would not be relevant to give examples of helmetless bicycle riders who were involved in fatal accidents. Also, it would not be fair to give an example of an accident involving a helmetless motorcycle rider whose fatal accident had nothing to do with a head injury. Many times people try to skew the truth with examples by giving extraordinary cases that do not happen very often and trying to pass them off as common occurrences. If there were only one fatal accident in your state involving a motorcyclist not wearing a helmet, it would not be fair to use this one example to prove that going helmetless results in a fatal accident. In this situation, the example would be an extraordinary case. A good way to show that your examples are typical is to combine them with statistics.

Statistics

Statistics are numerical data used to show the enormity of a problem or the trend of a situation. They can be used very effectively to show your reader the severity or importance of your argument. For example, you can use statistics to show how problematic riding a motorcyle without a helmet can be by stating how many fatal accidents helmetless motorcyle riders are involved in each year. You can argue that your solution needs to be enacted now by using statistics to show that the trend for the past five years has been a steady increase in the number of accidents involving motorcyclists not wearing helmets.

In using statistics, you can make your data have more impact for your reader by translating large numbers into more meaningful units. Instead of just stating that motorcyclists are involved in 2900 accidents a month, you can point out that this statistic translates to one motorcyle accident every fifteen minutes.

Because statistics can be used deceptively, make sure you use a source for the statistics. Your source should explain who performed the study, how the numbers were determined, and what size sample was used, if appropriate. Saying one in three motorcycle fatalities in your state results from a helmetless rider would be misleading if only three accidents were used for your sample. A good source for statistics for motorcycle accidents and fatalities would be the Department of Transportation.

Testimony

Testimony means you use the words of an authority to support your assertions. The key to using testimony is quoting an authority in the relevant profession. Many times, advertisers use the testimony of celebrities to promote products. If you want to convince me to buy a certain camera, I want the endorsement of a famous photographer, not that of a famous actor.

Testimony provides credibility to your assertion. You cannot be an expert in all areas. You need someone to verify that your statement is true. For example, one of the arguments you might give for the mandatory helmet law is the severity of head trauma and brain injuries resulting from accidents in which motorcyclists are not wearing helmets. To support this assertion, you need the testimony of experts to verify this statement. You should use the words of a noted medical doctor who specializes in head/brain injuries to convince your reader that you are correct in your argument.

For testimony to be as effective as possible, make sure your expert is truly recognized in his or her field as an expert. If it is a person with whom your reader may not be familiar, provide that person's credentials. Finally, make sure your expert does not hold a bias or vested interest that might affect the objectivity of his or her research or position.

▼ ORGANIZING YOUR ESSAY

As with any essay, your argument essay will need an introduction, body, and conclusion. Your introduction should identify the issue you are addressing. Begin with an appropriate attention grabber, such as examples, statistics, or a descriptive narrative. Your opener should capture your audience's attention as well as introduce the issue. Also, provide in the introduction any background or historical information that would be helpful for your audience to understand the issue. Conclude your introduction with your thesis and essay blueprint.

After your introduction, you are ready for the body of your argument essay. In the body, you present your arguments for your position and your supporting evidence. In keeping our analogy of a hamburger sandwich, you would find it very difficult (as well as messy) to eat such a sandwich without the bun. Likewise, your reader will find it very difficult to follow your argument without a logical structure holding the evidence together. An argument paper can be organized in a variety of ways. You need to select the pattern that best presents your argument. No matter what pattern you select, you need to present and refute the arguments of your opposition.

If your argument essay addresses a question of value, organize your essay by placing your reasons in emphatic order, from the most important reason to the least or the least important reason to the most. For example, let's say you want to argue that energy drinks are a dangerous way to increase mental and physical performance. Your three reasons for your position are the following:

I. Energy drinks can lead to dehydration and fluid loss.

II. Energy drinks can cause such side effects irritability, anxiety, and insomnia.

III. Energy drinks can result in the long-term effects of heart diseases.

Each one of these reasons serves as one of your body paragraphs. If you feel your argument about heart diseases is your strongest argument, then your essay, as outlined above, would be organized from your least important argument to your most. You will have decided to win over your readers by hitting them with your most powerful argument last. If you believe it would be better to convince your readers by starting with your strongest reason, then you will reverse the order of your three reasons as listed.

No matter which arrangement you select, you will still need to address your opposition. You can address your opposition's views before your arguments or you can address them after you present your side. Another approach is to address your opponent's points as you present your reasons. After you state the opposition's view, you refute it by giving one of your reasons. For example, your opponent argues that energy drinks boost physical performance. You can counter that argument with your first point that such drinks, though, build up caffeine in the body leading to dehydration and fluid loss during exercise.

Determine, based on your audience, which emphatic order to use and where to place your opposition's arguments. Is your audience favorable to your viewpoint? Is your audience neutral? Are you writing to an audience that opposes your position? If you are addressing a favorable audience, begin with your reasons, starting with your least important, and then ending with your opponent's points. In this situation, you are trying to strengthen your audience's agreement with your position, so you do not want to endanger that support by beginning with your opposition. However, if you were writing to an audience who opposes your viewpoint, tackle your opponent's arguments first and then present your reasons, starting with your strongest one. In this case, you want to remove your audience's objections first, so they will be more open to your arguments.

Two of the most common patterns for organizing the body of an argument essay that advocates a change in policy are Problem/Causes/Solution and Problem/Effects/Solution. In the first pattern, you begin by describing the situation as it currently exists and show that there is a problem that needs remedy. Then, you state the causes for the current problem. You should present several causes, each being a separate paragraph. Finally, you offer your solutions that will solve for the causes. As previously mentioned, you need to address any issues or concerns those who disagree with you might contend. You can place your opponents' arguments in one of three positions in your essay. You could address them before you begin your points, you could address them as you discuss each of your points, or you could respond to them after you present your side of the argument. With the problem/cause/solution format, you could present your opponents' side before you discuss your causes, you could discuss any opposition argument while you are discussing a particular cause or solution, or you could handle your opposition after you state your solutions.

The second typical pattern is similar except after describing the current problem, you state the various effects this problem has caused, with each effect being a separate paragraph. Then, you offer the solutions that will solve for the effects. The inclusion of your opposition's arguments parallels that of the previous pattern, either before you state the effects, while you state each effect or solution, or after arguing your solutions.

Using the problem/cause/solution pattern, you could arrange your paper on the motorcycle fatalities as follows:

Problem:	The number of motorcycle fatalities on the roads today is increasing.
Causes:	Since the revocation of the State's mandatory helmet law, a large percentage of motorcyclists ride without helmets
	When involved in accidents, helmetless motorcycles experience greater fatal head injuries and serious brain damage.
Solution:	The State should reinstate the mandatory helmet law for motorcyclists.
Opposition/Rebuttal:	A mandatory helmet law infringes on the personal liberty of the motorcyclist.

| Rebuttal: | Wearing a helmet may be an inconvenience, but doing so protects the life of the motorcyclist. |

Using the problem/effect/solution pattern, you could arrange your paper on the helmet law and motorcycle fatalities as follows:

Problem:	Since the revocation of the State's mandatory helmet law, a large percentage of motorcyclists are riding without helmets.
Effects:	An increasing number of accidents involving fatalities and serious brain damage have been the result of motorcyclists not wearing helmets.
	Since State law has exempted motorcyclists from wearing helmets, State citizens have experienced a negative impact on medical and insurance expenses.
Solution:	The State should reinstate the mandatory helmet law for motorcyclists.
Opposition/Rebuttal:	A mandatory helmet law infringes on the personal liberty of the motorcyclist.
Rebuttal:	Wearing a helmet may be an inconvenience, but doing so protects the life of the motorcyclist.

As with any essay, end with your concluding paragraph. Your conclusion should fulfill two purposes: reaffirm your position and direct your audience as to what to do next. First, restate your position on the issue. If your argument paper is relatively lengthy, also summarize the main arguments. Second, let your audience know what steps you would like them to take. You have just convinced your audience to accept your position, now what? You might have some type of call to action for them to undertake, or you might just want them to reconsider their position. How much you can expect from your audience will depend on who your audience is and how favorable your audience was to your position when you started. Use examples, a descriptive narrative, or a quotation to reinforce your position in your conclusion and to leave your readers with the greatest impact.

ADDRESSING OPPOSING VIEWPOINTS

In the previous section, you were introduced to several methods of organizing your argument essay and were shown that your argument is strengthened by your willingness to address the opposing point of view. Keep in mind that when you engage an audience in argument, you are speaking to three major groups: those who agree with you, those who disagree, and those who have not formulated an opinion. If your purpose is to increase the number of people who agree with you, the members of your target audience are those who oppose your point of view or those who have no opinion—not those who already take your side of the argument. Your opposition will, of course, have reasons for believing the way they do, and these reasons are the issues with which you must contend if you reasonably expect to convince them. You can address these opposing arguments in a number of ways, but first remember that no one likes to be insulted. To state that someone's arguments have no merit, or that the person is foolish for believing a particular point of view, will probably do little more than anger the opposition and make them refuse to listen to you any further. When you refute another person's point of view, you must present a reasonable argument for doing so, *and* you must present your refutation in a respectful manner.

One way to counter an argument effectively is by showing that the data used to support the opposition are flawed. For example, if you are arguing that energy drinks contain excessive amounts of caffeine, and the opposition has data that says one energy drink contains no more caffeine than a cup of coffee, you probably can find data that refutes that contention. Oftentimes, arguments are supported by unsupported or flawed data, and if you can find credible evidence that challenges these data, your argument will certainly be stronger.

A second way to challenge an opposing view is to challenge the logical process that led to that view. In Chapter 9, you learned about induction and deduction and about how these processes of drawing logical conclusions can be compromised. When a person has a breakdown in either induction or deduction, he or she has committed a *fallacy*. For example, if someone argues that because he drinks energy drinks he has improved his athletic performance. You can counter this assertion by showing the flaw in this reasoning. The energy drink was in all probability not the cause of his improved athletic performance. The argument doesn't address the likelihood that his hours of practice, or his time spent in the training room exercising, or the advice he received from his coach was responsible for his success.

A third way to address the opposing point of view is to concede that the opposition's argument is true, but then point out that your argument has greater merit. Yes, energy drinks do increase physical performance. However, that effect is short-lived and once it is, the user is dealing with irritability, anxiety, and insomnia.

Finally, you might be able to question the source of the opposition's claim. Obviously, if the CEO of an energy drink company claims that a regular intake of energy drinks does not cause any health risks, you can certainly question the objectivity of the evidence. Similarly, the tobacco industry had an apparent bias in publishing data in the last few decades that claimed smoking was not harmful. When there is an apparent bias such as in these cases, you certainly have an opportunity to question the validity of the opposition's evidence, and an even greater opportunity to present countering evidence that is from more objective sources.

However you decide to address the opposition's argument, remember that your own argument will be greatly enhanced by your doing so. If done respectfully and with attention to the evidence, you will find you have a much greater opportunity to win others to your point of view.

A Final Note: Remember that any evidence you present in your argument *must* be cited; that is, you must follow a standard format of identifying the source of the evidence. Chapter 7 provides you with the most common formats for citing evidence. Your evidence has little credibility unless you follow these formats and identify the person and publication from which your evidence was taken. Evidence must be "known" to your audience—that is, your audience needs to be able to find your evidence and decide for himself or herself if the facts you present are credible. If your reader is confident in the accuracy of your research, then the reliability of your argument will be greatly enhanced.

Following is a sample of an MLA-style argumentative research paper.

McKinney 1

Casey McKinney

Professor Nielsen

ENC 1102

15 April 2014

Eyewitness Memory: Not Enough for Conviction

Many people do not know how easily memory can become distorted. They also do not think about the effect of a distorted memory on the life of another person. The Innocent Project reported that out of the first 130 people proven innocent by DNA after conviction, about 78% were wrongfully convicted based on the statements of eyewitnesses (*Eyewitness Identification*). Eyewitnesses mistook innocent people for the criminals, and because of that, the innocent people had to spend time in prison for something they had not done. Anyone could be mistaken for a criminal at one point in time, and if eyewitness memory is considered reliable, anyone could go to jail for a crime they did not commit. One problem is the standard lineup procedure can cause witnesses to point out innocent people as the criminals just because they look similar to the actual criminals. Also, memory can become distorted easily, which could cause eyewitnesses to think innocent people are really the criminals. Both of these problems can lead to someone spending time in prison for a crime they did not commit. Therefore, eyewitness memory should not be considered reliable enough for conviction. It should be backed up by other evidence such as DNA.

The standard lineup procedure has flaws that can lead to wrongful convictions. According to the Justice Project's report *Eyewitness Identification*, eyewitnesses often compare the people in a lineup to decide which one looks most like the criminal. If the criminal is not in the lineup, the person who looks most like the criminal is going to get chosen as the perpetrator. This association could lead to innocent people, like a family member, a close friend, or even you, getting sent to jail just for having a likeness to a criminal. Likeness between people is common. People have similar facial structures, skin tone, and hair as others in their community. In big cities, people are bound to have at least two or three other people that look similar to them. If one of those other people did something wrong, that innocent person could get included in a lineup and chosen as the criminal. If other evidence were required, that person identified could be proven innocent, but if all that were required is eyewitness identification, then that innocent person could spend the rest of his/her life in prison for something that he/she did not do.

Selecting the wrong person in a lineup can also lead to that innocent person's face being permanently ingrained into the eyewitness's memory as the criminal. Such a scenario is what happened to Jennifer Thompson-Cannino. Thompson-Cannino, Cotton, and Torneo in their book *Picking Cotton* write about how she picked Ronald Cotton as her attacker out of a lineup, and even though he was proven innocent she still continued to see his face in her memory as her attacker. She backed up her claim with all she had, and when he was proven innocent, she could not understand where she went wrong. She swore it was he, and his face was the one in her memory, but her memory had changed and tricked her (236). Because Jennifer's eyewitness identification was enough, Ronald Cotton had to spend eleven years in prison for a crime that he never committed.

Memory is fragile. As Englehardt points out it can change and become distorted just by talking to different people. In her paper, she writes about the influence of others on people's memories. She describes how people change their biases based on to whom they are telling their stories. She explains how when people change their biases, their memory of the event changes with it. According to Engelhardt, the more people the witnesses talk to, the more their biases change, and the more their memories change. When people witness crimes, they tend to tell a lot of people. They usually have to talk to a few police officers, and maybe even some detectives. People also usually tell their friends and family about what they witnessed. The more people they tell, the more their memory is in danger of becoming distorted. Once their memory is distorted, their testimony should no longer be considered reliable enough for conviction. They are no longer able to recall that event with accuracy. Details become fuzzy or even change. After such distortion happens, they might end up picking out innocent people as the criminals. Because of this fragility of memory, the *New York Times* in its editorial "A Check on Bad Eyewitness Identifications" reports that the Oregon Supreme Court has shifted the "burden of proof" to the prosecution when it comes to eyewitness testimony. In a decision based on two cases, the court said that witnesses should be handled like evidence. The court thinks that witnesses should be handled like they could become contaminated easily. The court knows how easily police officers can cloud witnesses' memories just by proceeding in a certain way. A few simple words can cause witnesses' memories to become contaminated and distorted. Because of the easy manipulation of memory, if the justice system were to rely just on witnesses' memories then a lot of innocent people, even a friend, or family member, could be put in jail for something that they never did. If eyewitness memory were to be backed up by DNA, then those people could be proven innocent.

If it were required that eyewitness testimony be backed up by other evidence, what would happen if there was only eyewitness testimony? Those who believe eyewitness testimony is sufficient for conviction argue that the justice system should not just let the criminals roam free because the police do not have any other evidence on them. The public's safety is more important than the slight possibility of one innocent person being thrown in jail. People might get robbed, raped, or even murdered because most criminals usually do not change their ways. Should public safety be put in danger just because eyewitnesses' memories might be unreliable? Should the community be put in danger just because one innocent person might go to jail?

Eyewitness Identification makes the point of how the public's safety would be in more danger if the courts put innocent people in prison. This situation would leave the actual criminals free to roam the streets. If justice system put innocent people in prison, then the police would no longer be looking for the criminals. With no one looking for them, the criminals could continue doing whatever they would please. The public would still be in danger, but they would not be aware that they were in danger. They would have their guard down and be more likely to get hurt than if they were cautious because they knew that a criminal was still at large. If police were to spend a little more time investigating, they would probably find more evidence. Then, they could put away the right people and assure the community that it was safe.

Safety is the most important priority when placing criminals in jail. In order to provide that safety, the justice system must put the right person in jail. Anyone could be wrongfully accused and convicted if eyewitness testimony were considered reliable enough. That means that a friend, a family member, or even you could end up in jail for a crime you never committed. Imagine being in jail and having no hope of ever being free again because you were mistakenly identified as the criminal. If it were required that eyewitness testimony be backed up by other evidence, innocent people would not end up in jail for something that they never did.

McKinney 4

Works Cited

"A Check on Bad Eyewitness Identifications." Editorial. *New York Times.* New York Times, 5 Dec. 2012. Web. 9 Mar. 2014.

Engelhardt, Laura. "The Problem with Eyewitness Testimony: a talk by Barbara Tversky, Professor of Psychology and George Fisher, Professor of Law." *Stanford Journal of Legal Studies.* N.p, n.d. Web. 9 Mar. 2014.

Eyewitness Identification: A Policy Review. The Justice Project, n.d. Web. 9 Mar. 2014. <http://www.psychology.iastate.edu/~glwells/The_JusticeProject_Eyewitness_Identification_A_Policy_Review.pdf>.

Thompson-Cannino, Jennifer, Ronald Cotton, and Erin Torneo. *Picking Cotton.* New York: St. Martin's, 2009. Print.

Chapter 11

Writing a Critique

Imagine that you are in the museum cafe, hungry as usual. Perhaps you are in the gourmet flatbread line, waiting for the server to put that cheesy slice of fresh basil and tomato flatbread on a plate for you. As her spatula slides under one of the flatbread slices, you realize that her trajectory is all wrong. A little panicky, you quickly clarify, "No, not that one! The slice next to it!" The server rolls her eyes and sighs heavily, but she does retract the spatula from the first slice and slides the one you've identified onto a paper plate, making you smile. Sure, there was nothing really wrong with the first flatbread slice, but you had already determined that the second slice, *your* slice, was better. You may not have realized it, but all along, you were critiquing those flatbread slices, and your brief evaluation of the two slices established that one just *looked* better than the other. Maybe the slice you chose appeared slightly larger or cheesier, or perhaps it had a few more tomato slices on it. Whatever the reason, you've decided that that slice meets your requirements.

With everywhere you go, everything you do, everyone you meet, you are constantly evaluating the places, experiences, and people that you encounter on a daily basis. In an academic setting, such evaluations are often called critiques, reaction papers, or reviews. Disciplines such as the humanities, the social and behavioral sciences, and the natural and physical sciences have particular organizational formats and manuscript styles that writers are expected to follow when writing evaluative papers. As you continue to explore different disciplines throughout your college experience, you will be required to write different kinds of papers for these courses. Chapter 11 will guide you in determining the right approach for developing such evaluative papers for a variety of disciplines.

Objectives

♦   discuss the common types of critiques;

♦   explain the organization and development of a purposeful criteria;

♦   demonstrate the use of outside sources;

♦   provide examples of the various types of critiques.

▼ SELECTING AN APPROPRIATE TYPE OF CRITIQUE

As you begin this chapter, you may be thinking that your next writing assignment will involve criticizing something, or picking out its bad qualities. Unfortunately, the term *criticism* is frequently associated with solely negative comments. In fact, students often mistakenly think of criticism or a critique as a paper that focuses on only the negative aspects of a particular subject. However, criticism can provide a positive, praising response. A critique takes a closer look at both the positive and perhaps the not-so-positive elements of the subject that is being analyzed. The key component to critiquing, or criticizing, is actually the analysis: breaking the subject into its parts and examining each part for the purpose of judging the whole. Essentially, a critique, sometimes called a review, makes an assessment of the whole, and this assessment is then supported with specific examples.

As a student, you may be asked to critique or review any number of things, such as a work of art, a restaurant, a film, a book, a journal article, a research report, or even a car. In some instances, your task may be to compare or to synthesize the ideas found in two or more similar works, such as two poems or several research articles. Whatever your assignment might be, you must select the appropriate type of critique to fulfill your writing goal.

Three common types of critiques are the evaluation, the reaction, and the review. Sometimes the definitions of these three classifications are blurred, and different texts may explain each one a little differently, but generally, an *evaluation* essay makes a purposeful judgment, a *reaction* essay summarizes and indicates your agreement or disagreement with the subject at hand based on personal experience, and a *review* essay summarizes and possibly synthesizes ideas from one or more sources and then evaluates those ideas. All three types of critiques will include your opinion, and like the argumentative essay discussed in the previous chapter, you must back up your assertions with specific examples. Examples of each of these critiques will be discussed later in this chapter. For now, let's explore the process for developing a critique.

▼ ESTABLISHING YOUR CRITERIA

When you are critiquing something, you are determining its value, and oftentimes you are comparing it to similar things. For example, if you are evaluating a car, such as the Mazda Miata, you would do well to compare it to other convertible utility vehicles in its class. However, to state simply that all convertible sports cars, including the Miata, have a manual-shift option and convertible rooftops leads the reader to ask, "So what? Why do I care?" At this point, it becomes necessary to reveal your purpose and establish your criteria to the reader; otherwise, your reader may feel that you are simply stating the obvious.

So why would you evaluate a convertible sportscar? Is it to convince your audience that a particular convertible is safer? Faster? More economical? More luxurious? Your purpose dictates the criteria that you will establish, and your criteria will be the basis for your final judgment. If your focal point is economy, then your evaluation of the Miata may be very different than if your main interest is safety, speed, or luxury.

Once you have established your purpose, consider the background information your reader will need to know in order to understand your position regarding convertibles in general and the Miata specifically. Depending upon your audience, you may need to go as far as defining what makes a convertible what it is.

Next, you must consider the characteristics or criteria you will include in your critique. Perhaps performance, crash results, fuel economy, luxury options, and purchase price are all significant to the evaluation of the Miata model as compared with other convertibles. At times, one characteristic may conflict with another. Perhaps the Miata has performed well in fuel economy tests, but its purchase price is rather high compared with other convertibles. If fuel efficiency and price and maintenance costs are all a priority, you will have to establish which characteristics outweigh the other in your evaluation.

Once you have identified the characteristics to be evaluated, provide specific examples to support your opinion of each characteristic, establishing whether the Miata successfully or unsuccessfully meets the criteria.

▼ CONSTRUCTING A THESIS STATEMENT

Whether your essay is an evaluation, a reaction, or a review, establish a clear thesis statement and essay blueprint early in the paper so that your reader has a clear understanding of your paper's purpose.

In the introductory paragraph, you should begin by introducing the title and source of your essay's focus. For example, in your evaluation of a convertible sports car, you will want to identify the particular makes and models that you intend to evaluate. Next, you should write a thesis statement that alerts your reader to your overall purpose for evaluating the Miata. The essay blueprint that follows the thesis statement should briefly identify the criteria you will use to make your evaluation. Try this one:

> If you are considering the purchase of a convertible sports car, the Miata is a convertible model that deserves serious consideration. Its cost, fuel economy, and performance are primary factors that separate the Miata from other convertibles in its class.

▼ DEVELOPING THE CRITIQUE

Once again, whether your critique is an evaluation, a reaction, or a review, you need to establish your credibility, and you should provide your audience with the necessary background information needed to understand your critique. In most cases, a summary or description of the work you are critiquing is appropriate, clearly delineating the main idea and the supporting points of the work. This information should appear in a paragraph immediately following your introductory paragraph.

In the next paragraph, you will want to establish the criteria by which you will evaluate the work you are analyzing. Clear explanation of your evaluation benchmarks will help your reader to understand your overall evaluation of the work under analysis.

In the following paragraph, you will relate your opinions about the work to your audience, and you must be certain to support your general assertions by providing evidence. Such evidence should include specific examples from the original source or sources. Judging the work point by point may require more than one paragraph.

Your conclusion paragraph should include your overall stance toward or dominant impression of the work you are evaluating. Remind your audience of the work's strengths and weaknesses, and restate your thesis as concretely as possible.

Using Outside Sources

Although you may very well be an expert in the area that you are critiquing, adding the views of other individuals recognized for their expertise in the field of the work that you are critiquing only makes your argument that much stronger.

In this instance, you will want to use the expert opinions of others to support your own views, not to take the place of your own assertions and supporting details. It is best to paraphrase and summarize the thoughts of other critics before including these ideas in your own paper; however, quoting your sources directly is certainly appropriate if it is done sparingly.

Remember, any idea that is not your own, whether it is paraphrased, summarized, or quoted, must be credited to the appropriate source. Also, you want to be sure to document your sources accurately. You may wish to review Chapter 7 on crediting your sources.

Managing Personal Opinion

Although a critique is based on opinion, you want to ensure that two things occur: first, that you support your general assertions with specific examples from the source that you are critiquing, and second, that you clearly delineate where your opinions begin and end, and where someone else's ideas begin and end. Furthermore, you need to consider your audience and be aware of your biases going into the analysis.

Student Critiques

Following are more in-depth explanations of the different types of critiques and sample student essays that model the three types discussed in this chapter: the evaluation, the reaction, and the review.

Evaluation Essay

The evaluation essay is a paper that makes a purposeful judgment by clearly defining the criteria on which you will base your judgment and demonstrating whether the subject being evaluated succeeds or fails to meet those criteria. Ultimately, when you are writing an evaluative essay, your goal is to present your opinion regarding each criterion and then to support that opinion with substantive evidence. Upon addressing all of your criteria, each main point that leads to your final judgment should be made clear to the reader.

One discipline in which instructors frequently assign evaluation essays is the humanities. You might be asked to critique a work of art, a piece of music, or even a film.

Points in Evaluating Works of Art

- initial reaction to or dominant impression of the painting
- the size, the materials used, and the title
- the colors and brushstrokes
- the use of light and shadow
- the subject of the work and its arrangement
- the theme of the piece

Consider the following evaluation essay on American painter Thomas Benton's work *Cradling Wheat.*

An Analysis of Thomas Benton's Painting *Cradling Wheat*

The theme of the American prairie and man's interconnectedness with nature, the land, and his country are exhibited in *Cradling Wheat,* a painting by regionalist painter Thomas H. Benton. Benton grew up in the Midwestern United States and was greatly influenced by the prairie landscape and the lifestyle it offered. Through his brushstrokes, use of color, and choice of subjects, Benton effectively captures the spirit of the distinctive Missouri landscape and a local activity in an idealized, picturesque way.

Cradling Wheat, an oil and tempera painting on canvas mounted on a panel 31" x 38", is not very large, yet the artist creates a feeling of the expansiveness that pervades the prairie. He accomplishes this effect through the use of fluid, curvilinear lines. The clouds, the horizon lines, the contours of the earth all respond to the same broad, rhythmic sweep within the painting, mirroring the rolling topography of the prairie. Benton's smooth brushstrokes and lines also create a sense of motion across the canvas. Thus, the painting is far from static. The people, the land, even the sky are all dynamic.

Benton creates a feeling of warmth for this study of the local land and its features through his use of color. The hue intensity of the yellows, pale greens, pale browns, and pale blue—the colors dominating the painting—is of medium saturation, giving the painting a bright yet soft light. Deep, rich greens and blues provide sharp contrast in delineating the people in the painting, as well as dividing the painting into three distinct horizontal parts.

While the sky does lend to the feeling of open spaces in the painting, the rolling land and the men working the land are the emphasis of the painting's composition. In fact, the people cover half the painting. The dark green trees that stretch toward the sky seem to bend in the wind toward the center of the painting while the sheaves of wheat on the lower sides of the painting also lean toward the center, drawing the viewer's eyes toward the center of the painting where the men are working in the wheat fields. Interestingly, these laborers are idealized, almost caricature-like. They appear earth-bound, for they are located at the bottom of the painting and are all looking toward the ground as they toil in the wheat field. None of the individuals is facing the viewer, creating a sense of anonymity—their identity is not as important as their interconnectedness with the land. One critic explains that Benton was "at heart a fabulist, intent on converting most of his scenes, however commonplace, into kind of an instant folklore, an effect he most often achieved through a subtle distortion of forms crowded into sinuously writhing, rather hermetic compositions" (Hassrick 161).

Through his use of lines, hues, and arrangement of subjects, Benton succeeds in delineating a truly American theme through the image of the Midwestern prairie in his painting *Cradling Wheat*. According to Matthew Baigell, Benton's goal was to provide Americans with a democratic art easily accessible to the average citizen (100). This painting certainly serves as an effective example of Benton's celebration of the common man and the provincialism of the Midwestern prairie region.

Works Cited

Baigell, Matthew. *Thomas Hart Benton*. New York: Abrams, 1975.

Hassrick, Royal B. *History of Western American Art*. New York: Exeter, 1987.

Film is another art form for which you might be asked to write an evaluation essay. Note that film critiques are often called *reviews*. Good films not only contain the elements of a good piece of fiction. They also fulfill visual and aural qualities. A film critique involves an analysis and evaluation based on most, if not all, of the following criteria:

- theme
- conflict, setting, and plot structure
- symbolism and characterization
- camera angles, movement, and framing
- lighting
- special effects and music
- acting and dialogue
- point of view

The following essay serves as a good model of an evaluation essay for a film.

Ah! What Might Have Been!
A Review of *The Remains of the Day*
by Gerald Pine

The Remains of the Day explores the British class system, circa the 1930s to the 1950s, through the characters of Stevens, the butler; Miss Kenton, the housekeeper; and Lord Darlington. Stevens (Anthony Hopkins) is so steeped in the tradition of service that he is blind to the larger world and to the failings of Lord Darlington, and insulated from his own humanity. His interaction with the news of the day is that he irons the newspaper for Darlington; he does not see Darlington's flirting with Nazism as immoral; and he stoically resists the advances of Miss Kenton (Emma Thompson).

Critic Anthony Lane says, "I have an unfortunate and incurable problem with regard to this tale: having been drenched in P.G. Wodehouse from the early age; I find it impossible to take the master-slave relationship entirely seriously. It can't just sit there and stagnate, but needs to be enlivened by subtle transactions of power" (114). This statement intimates that one cannot appreciate tragedy because one once read a comedy. The strength of the *Remains of the Day* is that its filmic qualities and its superb acting make the situation sympathetic, even to viewers reared in a more democratic milieu. The downside of tradition is that its dead hand does cause class relationships to "just sit there and stagnate."

One of the early scenes has Stevens offering stirrup cups to the riders of the hunt, as they gather before Darlington Hall. The camera pans from the horsemen high astride their mounts to groundling Stevens proffering the cup to one rider, who is engaged in conversation over Steven's head. The cup is held up; the rider's hand descends, but only in a conversational gesture; the cup is held patiently, but the hand again ignores it. Finally, even the camera proves to have less patience than the butler and moves on to more interesting matters. This bit of business is a symbol of the life of service—Milton had it right.

Darlington Hall, itself, is a character in the film. The way the camera lovingly sweeps through its magnificent rooms gives the concept of service a believability: it would be almost an honor to slave amid such beauty, and to have responsibility there would be heavenly. The preparing of a banquet becomes an incredibly complex ballet, and the file of jingling call bells in the servants' quarter a symphony. The butler and housekeeper marshall dozens, if not hundreds, to the serving of every whim of the "swells."

We learn that Stevens, himself, is the son of a butler. His father, however, who enters the film as an elderly man looking for work, is not on Stevens' level: he is a boisterous man with a Cockney accent; Stevens is the soul of propriety with an accent more aristocratic than Lord Darlington's. (In one scene Miss Kenton tries to beard Stevens in his den and catches him reading a sentimental novel. He justifies himself by telling her that he reads to improve his use of the English language.) But the fact that Stevens' father served before him makes Stevens a more sympathetic character; the man knows of no other life.

Anthony Hopkins is cast in a very difficult role. Stevens is so stoic a character that he is given almost nothing to do that would delineate a human being. Hopkins must use little more than a slight softening about the eyes to indicate repressed passion, a slight opening of the lips (the ghost of a gasp, so to speak) to indicate a blow to his very soul. His walk in the 20-years-later scenes is a very subtle mimicry of his father's lumbering pace.

Only upon leaving Darlington Hall on his quest for Miss Kenton, now divorced from her West-County husband and looking for work, does Stevens become human. He allows some pub denizens to follow their own path of logic into believing that his life of service involved his possibly having been an advisor to prime ministers, and he denies ever having had any involvement with the now described Lord Darlington, who after the war lost a suit for slander against a newspaper that had called him a collaborator. Later, he regains his honor somewhat by admitting to one of them that he had indeed been a butler, served Lord D., and found him to have been a fine gentleman. The man is incredulous.

When Stevens meets Miss Kenton again, he is unable to give life to something that had never been born. It is almost as if her having had an actual life away from Darlington Hall puts her beyond his ken. Her daughter is now with child, and she says she has decided to stay in the West Country to be near her. Stevens, of course, cannot leave the Hall, and he cannot offer anything so passionate as a proposal of marriage. The scenes at the end are close to painful to watch; Miss Kenton obviously yearns for the man's love, and he is just as obviously yearning to offer it, but the years of service to others have created, as John Simon calls him, a "self-castrated character" (62). The bus pulls out; her outstretched hand is pulled from his outstretched fingers; and she rides off with tears in her eyes. His upper lip is stiff enough to survive, and he returns to Darlington Hall—now owned by an American. Somehow, he will now have to justify to himself that he is in service to an other-than-noble man—that he is a man's gentleman, not a gentleman's gentleman.

Works Cited

Lane, Anthony. "In Which They Serve." *The New Yorker* 15 Nov 1993: 114–117.

Simon, John. "Remains' to Be Seen." *National Review* 13 December 1993: 61–63.

A third type of evaluation assignment that you might encounter in a humanities course is a music critique. Following are some of the musical qualities to consider as criteria when evaluating a piece of music:

- historical context, if appropriate
- theme and title
- structure and style
- tempo and rhythm
- tone, dynamics, and texture of the melody line
- tone, dynamics, and texture of the harmony lines

The following evaluation essay demonstrates how one writer critiques musical composer Gustav Holst's classical work, *The Planets*.

The Role of Man and Nature in Gustav Holst's *The Planets*

Gustav Holst's *The Planets,* composed between 1914 and 1916, is a suite of seven orchestral tone-poems suggested by astrological significance rather than Greek gods, bearing the titles "Mars, the Bringer of War," "Venus, the Bringer of Peace," "Mercury, the Winged Messenger," "Jupiter, the Bringer of Jollity," "Saturn, the Bringer of Old Age," "Uranus, the Magician," and "Neptune, the Mystic" (Groves 332). Through his use of tempo, tone, dynamics, and texture of the harmonic and melodic voices, Holst effectively creates a sense of man's personal mystical experience with nature as reflected in the night skies.

According to music critic and historian William W. Austin, two of the chief devices found in Holst's music are "five-and seven-beat measures" and "bass lines descending through an octave with ominous even motion, usually quarter notes" (94). While the first device is difficult to hear without actually seeing the music, the complex rhythms and counter-rhythms are indeed difficult to pin down to something as simple as a duple or a triple. The second quality, however, is quite evident in the first movement, "Mars." In this piece the tempo is quick, forceful. The dynamics steadily change early in the piece, for the piece begins almost pianissimo but rapidly barrels toward fortissimo and maintains that strong level of sound throughout the piece. The melody line is polyphonic,—each voice controls the melody from moment to moment, but the real drive comes from the lower voices, trumpets, and horns while the middle and higher woodwind and string voices run up and down the scale, swelling from decrescendos into great crescendos. A lot of drama is established through the tone color of the piece. The tones are dark, forceful, perhaps depicting the power, majesty, and vastness of nature as seen in the night sky, particularly in the planet Mars.

A second piece from *The Planets* that has a significantly different mood is "Saturn." This movement evokes a profound peacefulness. It begins pianissimo, and with a slow, deliberate tempo set by the tones of solitarily plucked harp strings, it gradually moves into piano, shifting from major to minor chords and back again. Little by little, it gradually grows to a level of fortissimo, and while the bass line sets a steady cadence, the middle and high voices drift into a somewhat ethereal "tinkling" of eighth notes, which gradually fades back to pianissimo, with the plucking of harp strings. The strings, particularly the violins, take over the polyphonic melody for the remainder of the movement, once again running fluidly up and down the scale, creating a mystical, ethereal feeling. The tone quality of the piece is rich, but not harsh or demanding like "Mars." Once again, the focus is on the heavenly bodies that make up the light in the night sky.

A third piece that captures a rather mystical mood is the appropriately titled "Neptune, the Mystic." The tone color of this movement is dream-like, ethereal. The sounds are soft and pleasant, yet haunting at times because of the inclusion of female voices softly singing, creating an effect of their being far away, much like the planets themselves. Lots of harp and tinkling percussion are accompanied by long, flowing phrases by the strings. The polytonality also creates a sense of the mystical as the major chords from one instrument or the human voices are gently combined with the minor chords from another instrument. There is not a clearly defined rhythm to this piece—it seems almost to float along. Even the melody line is not really clear—there isn't much of a tune to whistle or hum. The dynamics do not go through a dramatic change like the remainder of *The Planets* movements. It begins very softly and gently, and it ends the same way, tapering away into no sound at all—as though has been and always will be—a sense of permanence or eternity, much like man's regard for the heavens.

As these three movements demonstrate, the composer, through his music, has successfully communicated man's sense of awe regarding the power and grandeur of nature and the humble and fleeting role of man in relation to the immensity and longevity of the world.

Works Cited

Austin, William W. *Music in the Twentieth Century from Debussy to Stravinsky*. New York: W.W. Norton, 1966.

Grove's Dictionary of Music and Musicians, 5th ed. Vol. 4. Ed. Eric Blom. New York, St. Martin's Press, 1973.

Note that papers written for the humanities require MLA manuscript style, as demonstrated in the three evaluation essays above. For simplification's sake, though, title page information, pagination headings, and separate pagination for the Works Cited page have been omitted from the sample papers. Please follow the correct format as described in Chapter 8 for "Writing the Final Draft."

Other disciplines that may require you to write an evaluation essay are the social and behavioral sciences. Following is a slightly different graduate-level essay that evaluates a qualitative research study in the behavioral science field.

Rachel and Her Children: Qualitative Inquiry or Research?

In his book *Rachel and Her Children: Homeless Families in America*, Kozol (1988) presents a disturbing yet powerful account of what it means to be a member of a homeless family in the city of New York. The aim of this paper is to determine whether Kozol's work falls into the category of qualitative inquiry or qualitative research. First, the fundamental elements of the work will be examined. Next, qualities that reflect both qualitative research and qualitative inquiry will be addressed and evaluated accordingly. Finally, conclusions will follow.

Fundamental Elements

The three fundamental elements of the book include the purpose for the study, the study's intended audience, and the methodology.

Purpose of the Study

Early in the book, Kozol establishes that the focus of his book is twofold: first, to focus on the way that ". . . homelessness creates an underclass, enhances the underclass that may already have existed, and, combining newly poor and always-poor together in one common form of penury, assigns the children of them all to an imperiled life," (p. 20) and second, to focus on "the creation of an institution that makes healthy people ill, normal people clinically depressed, and those who may already be unwell a great deal worse" (pp. 21–22). Toward the book's end, Kozol clarifies that his goal in writing the book is to bring to light the sad but very real atrocities faced by homeless families in America today: "The purpose of this book is to attest to [the sad realities'] existence, to give witness to the toll they take upon the children of the dispossessed, and to pay tribute to the dignity, the courage, and the strength with which so many parents manage to hold up beneath the truly terrifying problems they confront" (p. 185).

Audience for the Work

Rather than writing an esoteric piece of research for a small group of academicians or fellow researchers, Kozol seeks to write for a much wider audience: the American public, policy makers—anyone concerned with our society's present and future, for Kozol is compelled to reveal that homelessness, specifically in New York City, has become ". . . an institution, one of our own invention, which will mass-produce pathologies, addictions, violence, dependencies, perhaps even a longing for retaliation, for self-vindication, on a scale that will transcend, by far, whatever deviant behaviors we may try to write into [the homeless'] past. It is the present we must deal with, and the future we must fear" (p. 21). Through a direct call to action, Kozol urges his audience to become involved. In fact, Kozol provides an address for a nonprofit organization created expressly to give emergency assistance to families known by the author to be in urgent need so that his audience can make donations. This book's purpose reaches beyond being a report on the state of affairs for the homeless. This inclusion carries Kozol's work to a level of activating his audience.

Methodology

Kozol's investigation is an ethnographic study that uses multimethods and triangulation to corroborate data collected through extensive interviews and observations of homeless families and their advocates, primarily at the Martinique Hotel in New York City, and through the examination of city documents. He describes his book as ". . . a description of a journey that began for me a few days before Christmas 1985 and has continued to the present time" (p. 194). According to Scheirer (1997), one's research method follows one's research question, and Kozol's method is no different. He opens with foreshadowed problems in the form of a series of questions, moving from general to specific:

1. Where are the homeless?

2. How many are homeless in America?

3. Why are they without homes?

4. What distinguishes housing from other basic needs of life, and why, of many essentials, is it the first to go?

5. Is homelessness a temporary crisis?

6. Why focus on New York?

7. What is the route a family takes when it is dispossessed in New York City?

8. What is the breakdown of the costs in New York City?

9. What forms of support do homeless families regularly receive?

10. What are the chances of getting out of the hotel and into a real home?

11. Who are the people in these buildings? Are they alcoholics, mentally ill people, prostitutes, drug addicts, or drug dealers?

Analysis

This analysis of the book attempts to identify the elements of Kozol's work that classify it as qualitative research as well as the characteristics that mark it as qualitative inquiry.

Qualitative Research or Qualitative Inquiry?

While recent class discussion determined Kozol's work to be qualitative inquiry rather than qualitative research, an argument can be made for both possibilities. First, let us examine the work's qualitative research characteristics. According to Bogdan and Biklen (1992), qualitative research looks at the particular, the specific, the individual. This focus is indeed reflected by Kozol's work, in which he focuses on a specific issue and particular individuals through case studies developed through interviews and observation. Furthermore, qualitative research has no hypothesis that would threaten to bias what is seen in observation, and Kozol's work offers no such hypothesis. His effort involves a more emergent design, unfolding as he gathers more information and develops grounded theory regarding the cycle experienced by homeless families in New York City.

McMillan and Schumacher (1993) describe ethnography as ". . . interactive research, which requires relatively extensive time in a site to systematically observe, interview, and record processes as they occur naturally at the selected location. Ethnographic interviews of individuals who have had similar experiences focus on what the experience means to them" (p. 405). Moreover, the authors explain that ethnographic research is based on a "naturalistic-phenomenological philosophy of human behavior. An ethnographer seeks to understand people's constructions—their thoughts and meanings, feelings, beliefs, and actions as they occur in their natural context" (p. 407). Kozol captures these elements in all of his stories about each individual and their families. One example of the book's meeting these goals involves Kozol's ability to capture the above qualities in the experience of Rachel—the woman after whom the book is titled.

After a lengthy description of how her life came to be the way it is, Rachel says to Kozol, "A lot of women do not want to sell their bodies. This is something that good women do not want to do. I will sell mine. I will. I will solicit. I will prostitute if it will feed [my children]."

Kozol then asks Rachel, "'Would you do it?'"

She replies, "'Ain't no "would I?" I would do it. . . . Yes. I did'" (p. 70).

Further evidence indicates that Kozol's work continues to follow the process involved with qualitative research. As mentioned before, Kozol's investigation is an ethnographic study that uses triangulation and multimethods to corroborate data. While ethnographic interviews and participant observation are the primary methods of data collection reported in the book, artifact collection also weighs heavily in Kozol's findings, as reflected in the book's notes section. Also, the author establishes foreshadowed problems and clearly delineates the process of arriving at his ultimate purpose for his book's discussion of the problems created by homelessness, which is reflected in the topical narrowing of the previously listed questions, and which leads to the data collection strategies that he chooses to employ. For example, interviews, participant observation, and document collection are logical means for gathering information about the process a dispossessed family in New York City undergoes or about the homeless people who reside in the temporary shelters of run-down New York City hotels.

To gather his data, Kozol assumes the primary role of interviewer, taking notes and making sound recordings of what people tell him as well as what he observes during his multiple visits to the Martinique Hotel and other homeless shelters as well as public locales in New York City. He interviews not only homeless people, but also city employees and government officials responsible for helping the homeless. His interviews with the homeless are presented much like mini case studies, focusing on understanding one phenomenon: the underclass created and perpetuated by homelessness, and providing descriptions and analysis of themes voiced by Kozol's homeless participants.

Finally, according to Scheirer (1997), researchers are seeking to recognize, understand, and ultimately accept what is out there and to determine the best way to react to it—to "go with the flow and do the best that we can." Kozol's work also aligns itself with this idea, for the author presents his data, makes his case, and then offers the reader with two challenges: emergency relief for the homeless and an answer to the conditions that have forced the homeless into the streets. Furthermore, he concludes with recommendations and suggestions made by the homeless women and men and their advocates whose stories he has shared in his book.

Qualitative Inquiry?

While much of Kozol's book does qualify as research, much of it does not follow the constraints and standards of qualitative research. Howe and Eisenhart (1990) have attempted to focus the required elements of qualitative research into five standards: fit between research questions and data collection and analysis techniques; effective application of specific data collection and analysis techniques; alertness to and coherence of background assumptions; overall warrant; and value constraints. One of the problems with the book's fitting into the category of qualitative research is that it does not meet all five standards. Regarding the first standard, Kozol's data collection and analysis techniques do indeed "fit" the research questions that Kozol asks. Interviewing, observing, and then using documents to corroborate all of the information gathered are logical and effective means for answering the aforementioned questions. However, whether or not Kozol's measures for selecting participants meet Howe and Eisenhart's standard of effective application of specific data collection and analysis techniques is certainly debatable since the selection of participants often was a result of happenstance. Furthermore, while Kozol's background assumptions based on his previous research fall in line with alertness to and coherence of background assumptions, he really does not incorporate a review of the literature, another standard required by Howe and Eisenhart. Even so, Kozol does establish overall warrant—the data he presents discounts much of what city government policy and city officials have dictated regarding issues that surround the plight of homeless families. Finally, Kozol also meets the internal and external value constraints established by Howe and Eisenhart, for he is ethical in his research, going out of his way to protect the safety of his participants, and he presents sound experiences that lead to further understanding of the problems associated with homeless families, reporting his findings in such a way that all who need to read it are able to do so quite easily.

Other elements of Kozol's work also cause the book to lean more toward inquiry rather than research. One obvious characteristic about the work that separates it from typical research is that the presentation of the data doesn't follow the regimented format of research; in other words, it doesn't really discuss the methodology at length; it tells individual stories and makes references within the text to sources without formal documentation. For example, bibliography and notes are arranged as the author sees fit rather than in strict APA style. Moreover, while the author does make reference to the helpful contributions of one particular individual's research skills in gathering needed information, Kozol himself doesn't refer to his book as a "study" or as "research." In fact, critics on the book's cover refer to Kozol as an "author" as opposed to a "researcher." Also, rather than using formal academic language, Kozol refers to his observation/interview sessions as "visits."

Other qualities about the book make Kozol's work seem a little too unfocused to be classified as research. For example, the author's primary site is the Martinique Hotel, but he also explores other sites and interviews a variety of people at sites other than the Martinique. He even includes a chapter describing a visit to his friend Elizabeth's place in Boston during which the two of them share ideas about the overwhelming "data" that Kozol has collected in New York City thus far. His "case studies" are also loosely constructed and, as suggested before, do not always result from purposeful sampling; thus, the reliability and validity of the data are indeed questionable. Kozol selects interviewees based on timing, serendipity, and the recommendations of other participants as well as unnamed sources, not based on careful sampling. Finally, Kozol becomes emotionally involved with the participants. He even admits to being warned by advocates of the homeless not to romanticize the homeless people whom he describes in detail in the book and yet finding himself perhaps having done that very thing.

Evaluation

The aim of my evaluation of Kozol's work is to determine four elements: the degree to which the author's work furthers the understanding of homeless families, the effectiveness with which the author engages the reader and clarifies the data, potential improvements for the study regarding its purpose and audience, and elements to adopt or adapt for future research.

Researcher's Success in Furthering Understanding

Kozol has successfully furthered my understanding of the plight of homeless people. Attending an urban college campus, I come into contact with homeless people and welfare mothers on the brink of homelessness every semester—they are enrolled in classes along with me. I have listened to their stories and know how difficult—practically impossible—"the system" makes it for these people to get ahead. After having read Kozol's book, though, I have experienced an awakening—one that has been none too pleasant. I tried to begin reading this book three times, and each time, I found it too upsetting to continue. Finally, I was leaving town on business, and this book was the only one I had picked up for this assignment. So I read it . . . and I literally cried through every chapter. I am sure that I gave more money to the homeless I encountered on the streets than I spent on my own meals while on that business trip. I cannot even think about this book without becoming angry, and I am actively pursuing personal involvement in local homeless issues. Yes, Kozol's book does meet the research requirement of furthering the reader's understanding of the research topic.

Engaging & Clarifying Approaches to Reporting

One technique the author uses to engage the reader in order to clarify the horrors faced by the homeless is to tell vignettes, sharing with the reader little stories about his personal encounters with and discoveries about particular individuals and their families. He then juxtaposes these situations with a barrage of statistical information regarding the city's and government's handling of the homeless situation, oftentimes revealing information that seems painfully repetitive, creating such feelings within the reader as, "Yes! This is inefficient! Yes! This is wrong! Yes! This is an inhuman system! How can one individual (a "have") treat another individual (a "have not", often with little dependent "have nots" in tow) in this manner?" This back-and-forth handling of the data is powerfully disconcerting, and yet Kozol maintains the text's readability. In fact, Kozol presents the details and facts in such a way that the total illogic of this vicious cycle that so many homeless families suffer at the mercy of "the system" becomes quite evident to the reader.

Kozol also gets the reader emotionally involved by presenting heart-wrenching accounts of homeless families—not merely single men and women, but mothers and fathers, struggling to keep their children healthy and their families whole.

Potential Improvements for the Study's Purpose & Audience

The style in which the book is written is an effective means of reaching a wide audience, and for a topic such as this one, a large audience is a good thing. Because this book, which focuses on personal accounts, isn't written in a formal research style with a lot of jargon, the average American is more likely to read it, and a lot of people need to read this book. If, however, improving the study as it relates to its audience and purpose were to involve making it more academic in nature, following more closely the guidelines of qualitative research and APA style, Kozol would need to regard himself as a researcher and to regard his book as a study. Also, he would need to fine-tune his research methodology, giving more careful attention to the selection of participants and the reliability and validity of his data collection.

Overall, though, the book effectively depicts the tragic and seemingly endless cycle that condemns the majority of the homeless to absolute destitution.

Elements of the Effort, in the Methodology, and in the Writing Up to Adopt or Adapt

Kozol's book harbors several elements that make his work effective. First of all, Kozol shares with his audience his initial research questions and allows the reader to follow his thought processes in narrowing his topic to the end result, enabling the reader to understand where the author started and how he ended up with his ultimate purpose or goal for writing the book. Also, his varied methods of collecting data are a part of the methodology that seems imperative to adopt in a future qualitative research project. Last, but probably most significant, Kozol's ability to capture the raw nature of the lifestyle of his participants through his case studies, or vignettes, and to juxtapose these scenarios with statistical data leads to real emotional involvement on the part of his audience. Such graphic imagery lends a sense of realism that simply cannot be communicated through mere statistical information alone.

Conclusion

After having explored this book from both a research perspective and an inquiry perspective, Rachel's Children has proven to be an example of qualitative inquiry. While it contains many of the characteristics of research, it probably did not begin as a formal research project, and it just has too many gaps to qualify as research. Even so, it is a marvelously informative and powerfully touching account of the circumstances of many of America's homeless.

References

Bogdan, R. C., & Biklen, S. K. (1992). *Qualitative research for education: An introduction to theory and methods* (2nd ed.). Boston: Allyn & Bacon.

Borg, W. R., & Gall, M. D. (1989). *Educational research: An introduction* (5th ed.). New York: Longman.

Eisner, E. W. (1991). *The enlightened eye: Qualitative inquiry and the enhancement of educational practice.* New York: Macmillan Publishing Company.

Howe, K., & Eisenhart, M. (1990). Standards for qualitative (and quantitative) research: A prolegomenon. *Educational Researcher, 19* (4), 2-9.

Kozol, J. (1988). *Rachel and her children: Homeless families.* New York: Fawcett Columbine.

McMillan, J. H., & Schumacher, S. (1993). *Research in education: A conceptual introduction* (3rd ed.). New York: Harper Collins.

Scheirer, E. A. (1997, February 13). Class Lecture. In *Research in Educational Leadership: Methodologies in Qualitative Research.* Jacksonville: University of North Florida.

Note that papers written for the social and behavioral sciences require the use of APA manuscript style. Please follow the correct format for title page information, pagination headings, and separate pagination for the References page as described in Chapter 8.

Reaction Essay

A reaction essay requires a different strategy from an evaluation essay. Writing a reaction essay generally involves your summarizing or describing in detail a written, drawn, sculpted, filmed, or performed piece of work such as an article, a painting, a sculpture, a video, a play, or a speech, and then reacting to that work, indicating qualities that you like or dislike, or perhaps identifying points with which you agree or disagree, based on your own experience and subjective reaction.

If you recall, Chapter 2 discussed the process of summarizing as rewriting the main ideas of someone else's work in your own words. Providing a summary or a description of the work to which you are reacting is the first step in writing a reaction paper. Perhaps your assignment is to react to an opinion article on campaign finance reform that appeared in a recent issue of a popular news magazine. Following the steps to writing a clear summary, you should identify the author's main points and then provide your reaction to each point, one by one.

Instructors from a number of disciplines will require that you write reaction essays. Consider the following example of a student's reaction to a piece of abstract art.

Art Analysis:
A Reflection of the Self
by Chris Weed

Our class attended an art exhibit at the Williams' Center on January 13, 2000. It was an exhibit of mostly ceramics and stoneware, ranging from the abstract to pieces that were representational in their meaning. My attention was drawn to a particular piece by Toshiko Takaeyu called *Ka-Hua*; I found this work to be the most intriguing in the exhibit.

The piece in question was a large, roughly spherical ball of clay or stone with two uneven halves of disparate coloration. The top half was an earthen-hued light beige, while the bottom half was dark, nearly black. This blackness extended to the top half in the form of some feathery shapes that seemed to suggest birds, as well as some spikes that intruded the light half like great spires of darkness. Though I did not touch the sphere, it appeared to be of a rough, matted texture.

At first, my feelings towards this piece were mainly of curiosity because of the size of the sphere. However, as I examined it closer, I began to see some meaning in the abstractness of the shapes and rough symmetry of the division of color. In my mind, the feathery shapes began to resemble birds above the darkness, which seemed to represent the depths of the oceans or perhaps the earth, with spikes like mountains ascending into the heavens. It was at once peaceful and somewhat disconcerting, as I started to imagine the dark and the light to be at war with each other, melding at times in shades of gray. I began to think of the sphere as a possible representation of balance, of a sort of yin and yang. Considering the nationality of the artist and the fact that the yin and yang have been an integral part of Eastern philosophy, *Ka-Hua* became even more meaningful. Perhaps Takaeyu used the medium of art to make a statement on Eastern philosophy in an abstract and visual manner.

As I reflected on the possible deeper purposes of this piece, I was reminded of how much I take to heart balance in my own life, endeavoring to be neither too harshly analytical nor too creatively impulsive, neither too serious nor too hedonistic. I strive to be in balance with nature and centered within myself. Just by looking at the art work, I felt a bit less alone and more at peace, knowing that there are others who perhaps share my beliefs. Gaining insight into the piece seemed to lessen the feeling of insignificance that one can be afflicted with if he thinks of himself as one of so many, as a mere speck of that sphere that represents our entire world.

In general, I feel that abstract works of art are just that—abstract—and that discerning the artist's meaning is a task for those more schooled in analysis than I. Yet it was rewarding to discover a piece that held some resonance for me, whether or not my interpretation corresponded with the artist's intentions. Perhaps the ultimate intention of true artists is to provoke inner reflection within their audience. Indeed, when we look at works like Takaeyu's Ka-Hua, it is almost as if we are peering into a mirror, subjecting ourselves to self-examination. To find greater meaning in art, we must have a reference base to draw upon and enough introspection to explore our feelings on something that we do not wholly understand, but are intrigued by anyway. Perhaps self-discovery, then, is the underlying purpose behind any work of art or art analysis.

Note how this reaction essay differs from the previous evaluation essay models. While the student provides a vivid description of the artwork, he does not establish specific criteria and then attempt to prove whether the piece meets those criteria. Rather, he explores his initial and subsequent reactions to the piece.

The next student essay is a reaction to a magazine advertisement.

Fact vs. Fiction
by Celena Soto

What you don't know can indeed hurt you. Thanks to extensive studies over the years, our society does not have this problem when it comes to cigarette smoking. Through medical research, people have been informed of the consequences of smoking; they are advised not to start or to quit if they have already acquired this habit. However, these warnings go unheeded, for the number of smokers has not dramatically decreased over the years. Smokers suffer many consequences: some of the minor ones include yellow teeth, bad breath, foul-smelling hair, and premature wrinkling. Other more serious effects of smoking involve emphysema, heart disease, and lung cancer. Despite knowing these facts, many normal, level-headed individuals actually choose to pick up their first cigarette because of the way in which tobacco manufacturers glamorize smoking as a cool, sexy, and trend-setting habit.

This image is most definitely propagated in magazine ads by giving false generalizations of the way people are or, at least, should be. Found in predominantly female magazines such as *Cosmopolitan* and *Glamour,* ads for Virginia Slims cigarettes provide prime examples of this marketing strategy by sporting the slogan "It's a Woman Thing." These ads target an audience largely consisting of young women in their twenties and even in their teens. This particular ad was taken from the May 1997 issue of *Seventeen,* a popular magazine among adolescent girls. Every ad features a slim, beautiful, sophisticated woman acting as a spokesperson for all women. This exaggerated portrayal of women contributes to the idea of logical fallacies, invalid ideas that are used to convince an audience of a particular viewpoint.

At least three logical fallacies—bandwagon, false analogy, and red herring—can be identified in the Virginia Slims ad.

The bandwagon fallacy is commonly used in everyday life to convince an individual to do something because everyone else already is. For example, a child tries to convince his mother to buy a certain pair of shoes for him because "all his classmates have them." Specifically, the bandwagon fallacy argues that "everybody else is doing it, so you should, too." It appeals to the human desire to fit in, to belong. With this concept in mind, the Virginia Slims ad paints a picture of an elegant lady strapping on a black sandal while standing amid several different black shoes strewn about the floor. Although we can only see the bottom half of the woman, it is enough for us to deduce that she is slim, attractive, and fashionable. She could very well be the type of woman whose example most females would want to follow.

Along with this carefully conveyed image comes the caption, "Why do we own 15 pairs of black shoes? Why not?" The use of the pronoun "we" gives the reader the idea that she is on the same level as the seemingly perfect woman in the picture; moreover, the word "we" suggests that those women who are smart and attractive follow this type of behavior. Granted, not every woman is as attractive as the model is, but undoubtedly most women would like to be. In summation, the ad says that this intelligent and sophisticated woman smokes Virginia Slims, and if the viewers want to be as admirable as the model is, then they must smoke these cigarettes too. In other words, the audience must do as she does, and become what she is. The image is false because, obviously, smoking Virginia Slims cigarettes does not transform one's personality, nor does it change one's popularity. Nevertheless, the bandwagon appeal is very effective in producing desired results which is why it is the basis of the Virginia Slim ads.

Just as prevalent as the bandwagon fallacy, yet not as well-known, is the false analogy, the second fallacy found in this cigarette ad. False analogy is an assumption that because two things are similar in some ways, they are also alike in others. Revealing this fallacy, the ad uses women as the conjunction between two separate matters: owning many pairs of black shoes and smoking Virginia Slims cigarettes. "Why do we [includes woman in picture who smokes Virginia Slims and the female reader] own 15 pair of black shoes?" Well, "why not?" Then the clincher, "It's a Woman Thing," implies that this situation is the norm for any woman. Getting the reader to connect with the woman in the picture makes it easier for the reader to relate to the Virginia Slims cigarettes. The ad apparently implies that just as it is common for women to possess various pairs of black shoes, so also is it natural for women to smoke Virginia Slims. Yet the correlation is invalid: owning many pairs of black shoes has nothing to do with a woman's preference of cigarettes. This illogical comparison between two unrelated matters forms the false analogy.

The third fallacy that can be extracted from this Virginia Slims ad is known as a red herring. This fallacy is defined as avoiding the real issue by drawing attention to one that is irrelevant. The red herring is used in ads to convince people to overlook the bad or harmful elements of a product. In this ad, the product, Virginia Slims cigarettes, is potentially fatal. Many people have now become aware of this fact, leaving cigarette companies with the challenging task of successfully advertising their product. The advertisers must make the audience forget about the bad effects of smoking by promising them helpful results in their lives.

This concept can easily be applied to the cigarette ad in question. About two-thirds of the page is covered with the picture of a slender woman in fashionable attire, preparing for a night on the town. This image along with the caption attracts the reader's focus and makes her believe that she too can be like the model. The reader forgets about the harm that cigarettes can do to her body. She sees only that the Virginia Slims will gain her popularity, as the ad depicts. The fact that the woman is not even holding a cigarette in her hand actually makes this picture completely irrelevant to the product. Even so, the ad works in diverting the attention of the viewer from the real and dangerous issues of smoking. As further evidence that this ad is an example of a red herring fallacy, the careful reader will observe that the only connection that can be made between the picture and the Virginia Slims cigarettes is a woman. This association, which is not even valid, clearly illustrates a red herring.

Like most cigarette ads, the one for Virginia Slims contains a number of logical fallacies hidden in its context and picture. Three fallacies in particular—bandwagon, false analogy, and red herring—are the most apparent ones. They also have a significant connection with one another: each of the three fallacies is a way to distract the reader from thinking of the real dangers of the product, and there are many. Studies show that, sadly, these cigarette ads, which portray numerous fictitious ideas, actually do their job. Despite all the knowledge society now possesses about smoking, the number of smokers remains high. People continue to neglect their ethics, values, and physical health by smoking. Hopefully, more people in the future will heed the warnings about smoking. Perhaps, then, they will be able to think for themselves and discern the false from the true components in such misleading cigarette advertisements as the Virginia Slims one.

Note that the student focuses on the logical fallacies that appear in the ad, addressing each one in a separate paragraph. Again, she does not establish criteria and then evaluate whether or not the ad meets those criteria. Instead, she does a point-by-point analysis and reacts subjectively to each one.

Review Essay

A third type of critique, the review, is a paper that also requires a brief summary of the work or works being analyzed, yet it differs from the reaction paper because it is less subjective, less reactionary. Such papers are often written in the social and behavioral sciences as well as in the natural and physical sciences.

Following is a sample book review written for a social science class.

Shifting Paradigms: A Review of J.A. Barker's
Paradigms: The Business of Discovering the Future

Barker, J.A. (1992). Paradigms: *The business of discovering the future*. Harper Business.

SUMMARY

In his book *Paradigms: The Business of Discovering the Future*, Barker explains that the last twenty to thirty years have involved turbulent change in which the basic ways that we do things—our fundamental rules (or paradigms)—have been and are constantly being altered and revised, a phenomenon which futurists have termed *paradigm shift*. The author further asserts that in order for any organization (profit or nonprofit) to experience success in this paradigm shift-filled twenty-first century, it must embrace three key elements:

- excellence (Total Quality Management)

- innovation

- anticipation

Excellence is the price for entry into the marketplace of the next century, and innovation is the key to having a chance to compete successfully in that marketplace, but the real key to success is being able to *anticipate* the right time and place for introducing that innovative product. Barker explains that one must also be able to anticipate paradigm shifts by first being aware of what influences one's own perceptions of the way things are supposed to work (one's own paradigms) and then watching for trends as well as watching for people who are attempting to change the rules. Only by predicting and/or initiating a paradigm shift can one hope to be ready for handling the inevitable change and finding solutions for the new problems that are surely approaching.

The author discusses the appearance and evolution of paradigms based on the three phases of a *paradigm curve*. According to Barker, in phase A, an organization is still learning about the boundaries and rules of the existing paradigm in regard to problem solving; thus, the number of effective solutions is small and slow in coming. However, in the next phase, the organization demonstrates its knowledge of and maneuverability within the new paradigm by the greatly increased number of problems solved. Once it reaches phase C, the organization has saved the more difficult problems for last, and the number of solutions decreases—the time has come for a paradigm shift. Unfortunately, to recognize the need for a paradigm shift at this stage is to have fallen behind, for at this point, it is too late to avoid Barker's *going-back-to-zero rule,* which states that when a paradigm shifts, everyone goes back to zero—except those folks who precipitated the need for change! According to Barker, new paradigms often appear in phase B, but because things are going so well at this stage, new paradigms tend to be rejected, and an organization's success eventually begins to taper off because the organization is secure within and attached to what is known and what has been producing positive results up to now. Thus, it is important to recognize both the potential narrowness of one's own paradigm and the need for change.

Barker further explains that outsiders are typically the ones who come into an organization and initiate paradigm shifts, for they are not a part of the old paradigm—they have no commitment to that set of rules and approach problems from a fresh perspective. Oftentimes, those who are blinded by their own paradigms perceive these change agents to be upsetting the apple cart; fortunately, there often are other individuals, *paradigm shift pioneers,* who also recognize the need for change, have faith in the new set of rules, and courageously follow their intuition to move toward that change despite the comfort of the old way of doing things. The author provides an extensive selection of paradigm shift examples, some of whose predictions were heeded, and some of whose were not.

Barker next explores the significance of the Total Quality movement, predicting it to be the most significant paradigm shift to come out of the twentieth century, based on its offerings of increased innovation, self- management, the return of artistry and craftsmanship, and the return of spirit to the workplace. He also focuses especially on the difference between managing and leading TQ organizations, suggesting that "You manage within a paradigm. You lead between paradigms" (p. 164). The main point of this section is that managers must demonstrate *paradigm pliancy*, facilitate interdepartmental cross talk, and really *listen* to new ideas in order to gain a special leverage in the area of innovation.

The book concludes with an extensive and varied selection of trends and paradigm shifts for the nineties as well as encouragement toward *paradigm pliancy* and a warning against *paradigm paralysis.*

CRITICAL EVALUATION

Barker effectively presents his case for organizations' needing to become aware of, to anticipate, and to prepare for imminent paradigm shifts of the twenty-first century in order to be successful. Not only does he quote such experts in the fields of leadership, TQM, and paradigms as Benning, Deming, Drucker, Juran, and Kuhn, but he also provides very specific, concrete examples from real life as well as from the world of business to demonstrate his ideas. In addition, he offers clear steps for learning to recognize the need for change and for identifying and encouraging those individuals who can help initiate that needed change, thus making the book very practical. Furthermore, Barker's ideas on paradigm shifts and their significance are in keeping with the ideas of Bennis and Nanus (1985) in Leaders: *The Strategies for Taking Charge*, and the ideas of Covey (1990) in *Principle-Centered Leadership*. One assertion of Barker's that does not completely follow the majority of the literature in the area of leadership is the idea that "most leaders are not visionaries" (Barker, p. 169). Interestingly, authors such as Benning and Nanus (1985), Conger (1989), Covey (1990), and a host of others in the field of leadership emphasize the need for leaders not only to be visionaries but also to be clear *communicators* and *leaders* of their vision. Barker, on the other hand, suggests that effective leaders know how to identify those individuals who are visionaries as well as how to tap into others' visionary ideas and select particular visions that they wish to lead. In my estimation, effective leaders must be visionaries; otherwise, such individuals fall more along the lines of Barker's and Benning's category of a manager—someone who knows how to administer rather than how to innovate.

IMPLICATIONS

The implications of Barker's book are significant regarding both the fields of business and leadership and the content of this course. The author has captured the essential components of the paradigm shift phenomenon in such a readable format that not only is the phenomenon easily understood, but the theory can be easily applied. In fact, as I was reading the book, I found myself applying the author's concepts to my own experiences as a member of a local community college, particularly regarding the institution's recent reorganization and move toward TQM, and the reaction of the faculty and staff to this paradigm shift. Furthermore, I anticipate that the different concepts of organizational theory that will be discussed this term—the trends, the movements, the paradigm shifts—will be directly connected to the "rule-changing" discussed in Paradigms: The Business of Discovering the Future.

References

Bennis, W. & Nanus, B. (1985). Leaders: *The strategies for taking charge.* Harper Perennial.

Conger, J. (1989). *The charismatic leader: Behind the mystique of exceptional leadership.* Jossey-Bass.

Covey, S.R. (1990). *Principle-centered leadership.* Simon & Schuster.

Again, note that social science papers that include research require APA-style documentation. Format papers as described in Chapter 8.

Scholarly reviews oftentimes involve pulling together articles on a general topic, summarizing those articles, synthesizing their main ideas, judging how effectively the subject matter in each article is handled, and then drawing conclusions about the findings. Such assignments might be made in a social or behavioral science class.

First, if possible, select a topic of interest to you. Let's say that you have decided to review a series of articles on genetically altered grain research performed within the last year. Your next step is to locate recently published primary research articles, those articles that report firsthand results of scientific studies.

Once you have selected the articles to review, your task is to glean the main points of each of the articles, weighing the credibility of each researcher's findings and drawing your own conclusions based on what you have read. As you analyze each article, ask the following questions:

1. Is this article significant to understanding current genetically altered grains research?

2. Is the article's information accurate?

3. Are the terms used in the article clearly defined?

4. Is the article a primary source or a secondary source?

5. Are there other potentially useful articles listed in the references?

6. What main points does the article present about current thinking on genetically altered grains?

7. Are there any gaps or weaknesses in the information presented?

As in any other type of research, once you have gathered your information and have a sense of the current thinking regarding your topic, organize your information into an outline and develop a thesis statement and essay blueprint. Then, you are ready to write the paper using the appropriate citation format for the discipline in which you are writing. In essence, you are simply writing a mini-research paper.

Writing about Literature

As mentioned in the previous chapter, when you analyze something, you break it down into its parts. By looking at its components, you hope to develop a better understanding of the whole. For example, if you are feeling tired and sluggish, you may go to your family doctor to find out what is wrong. One of the first steps she may take is to order a blood test for you. The lab technician will take a sample of your blood and then analyze its various components that could be impacting your condition. By looking at the lab results, your doctor may have a good idea as to what is causing your tiredness and sluggishness. Thus, by analyzing just a small part of your physical body, the doctor can make some judgment about your overall health.

This same idea holds for writing a literary analysis, except the whole you are looking at is a work of literature, whether a novel, short story, play, or a poem. In a literary analysis, your goal is to help your reader achieve a better understanding of a particular work of literature. To achieve this goal, you break down the literary work into its components. Then by discussing one of these components in depth, you help your reader achieve a greater insight into the work as a whole.

Chapter 12 will guide you in writing a literary analysis by reviewing the elements of literature.

Objectives

- define the components of a short story or novel;

- delineate the parts of a literary analysis essay;

- differentiate among the analyses of fiction, drama, and poetry;

- explain the process of analyzing a short story.

▼ ELEMENTS OF LITERATURE

Before you can analyze a work of literature, you need to know the elements that go into the making of that work. For example, if you are asked to write a literary analysis of a short story or even a novel, you need to be able to identify the basic components of these genres of literature. Below is a description of these various components of a short story or novel and some suggestions as to how you could approach each in writing a literary analysis.

PLOT

The plot is the series of events or incidents that occur in the work of fiction. The plot always has a conflict as its basis. The series of events builds this conflict until the opposing forces meet and a resolution results. The point in the literary work where the two forces collide is called the climax.

Types of Conflict in Works of Fiction	**human vs. human:** one person confronting another person **human vs. society:** one person against a group of individuals or against the mores of society **human vs. self:** one person facing an internal struggle **human vs. nature or environment:** one person confronting some natural element **human vs. animal:** one person in a struggle against an animal **human vs. the supernatural:** one person against fate, a god, or some miraculous power

When you are writing a literary analysis that looks at plot, you are analyzing the conflict. You tell your reader what that conflict is and discuss the major events that illustrate this conflict in the literary work. You point out the climax of the plot and what the resolution of the conflict is. Because your goal is to help your reader understand the whole work, you explain what the conflict and resolution mean for the theme or message of the work.

CHARACTER

When you think of character, you think of the people in the literary work. The main character or the person on whom the plot centers is called the *protagonist*. The literary work may contain one or more major characters and some minor characters.

The important aspects of character in a literary work are personality traits and motivations of the people involved. These traits or motivations cause the conflict that occurs. Is a character naïve, suspicious, or aggressive? Does a character behave out of fear, greed, or ambition? Also, you want to look at the growth of a character in the literary work. Is the character static or dynamic? If the character is static, that character's personality or understanding or level of maturity does not change in any way during the series of events that unfolds. If the character is dynamic, however, that character does experience some type of personal growth. Keep in mind that the growth can be positive or negative. Whatever the case, the character at the end of the story is not the same person he or she was at the beginning.

When you write a literary analysis based on character, you look at the personality traits or motivations of that character. You give illustrations from the literary work that show a particular trait and discuss how this trait impacts the conflict. By looking at the climax of the work, you can draw some conclusion about the growth of the character. Does the character undergo a change, or is the character still the same person? Based on this growth factor, you can draw some conclusion as to the message of the story that the author is trying to convey.

POINT OF VIEW

Closely related to character is point of view. Someone tells the story you are reading. That person is called the narrator. There are four main types of narrators: first-person, third-person limited, third-person objective, and third-person omniscient.

A first-person narrator tells his or her story. The events are either happening to that person or being witnessed by that person. The use of the pronoun "I" is the trademark of a first-person narrator. Once in a while, you may find a first-person plural narrator. In this situation, the story will be told from a "we" point of view. With first-person narration, the narrator can only relate the action that occurs when he or she is present and can only relate his or her own thoughts, and not the thoughts of other characters. The narrator can speculate as to what another person may be thinking but can never know another person's thoughts.

With a third-person narrator, the story is about someone other than the person telling the story. The use of the third-person pronouns "he" or "she" is an indication of a third-person narrator. There are three types of third-person narrators. A third-person limited narrator means the story is being told about someone else but through that person's eyes. It would be like viewing the action while standing behind that person throughout the whole story. Because the narrator is limited, we can know the action only when that character is present, and we can know the thoughts of only that one character.

A third-person objective narrator is as the name indicates: a narrator that does not get involved in any way with the telling of the story. The third-person objective narrator tells the story as it unfolds and does not delve into the thoughts and motivations of the characters. The narrator just stands back and relates what happens.

A third-person omniscient narrator is an all-knowing narrator. Like the other two third-person narrators, this type of narrator is telling a story about someone else, but can relate the action that happens to any of the characters at any place and at any time. In addition, the third-person omniscient narrator can relate the thoughts of any of the characters.

For a literary analysis, you can analyze the narrator. If the narrator is a key participant in the story as you might have with a first-person narrator, you can analyze the narrator as you would any character. If you feel the type of narrator used has an impact on the telling of the story or is vital to the theme of the work, you can discuss this aspect.

Setting

Setting refers to the location and the time period of the series of the events. You may have a story that takes place in one particular location during a relatively short period of time or a story that takes place in multiple locations during an extended period of time. Some stories take place in the past; some, the present; and some, the future. Some stories may shift back and forth between multiple time periods. Shifting to a scene in the past from the present is called a flashback.

Whatever the location or time frame, when you write a literary analysis based on setting, you are discussing how the setting has an impact on the plot or the characters. How does the setting affect the series of events that occurs? How does the setting affect the behavior of the characters?

You can also analyze how the setting reflects the theme of the story. Is the setting reflective of the message of the story? If so, discuss how the locale and atmosphere of the setting reflect the author's views in the story.

Theme

Every literary work will have a theme. The theme is the main point or the central idea or the message of the work that the author is trying to convey to the reader. It is important to remember that the theme does not always have to be a message, such as, "Crime doesn't pay," or, "Honesty is the best policy." The theme may be an illustration of some societal condition, such as "people's inhumanity to others," or "the emptiness of the rich." The theme may present some insight into the human life cycle, such as a boy's transition into manhood or the dissolution of a relationship. The theme may just present a picture of a human characteristic, such as courage or pride.

No matter which elements of a story you decide to analyze, your goal is to help your reader to achieve a better understanding of the theme. You can choose, though, to analyze a story by directly looking at the theme. Let your reader know what the theme of the story is, and then show how that theme is developed in the story. Take excerpts from the story to support your analysis.

Besides these basic components of a short story or novel, you might consider analyzing two other aspects of a work of fiction.

LANGUAGE OR STYLE

Language refers to the words an author uses. Style refers to the way those words are expressed in sentences. Good writers choose their words carefully. The words not only reflect the background and education of the characters and narrator but also convey the appropriate meaning intended. The words may convey their literal meaning, but they may also have an ironical or satirical meaning. The style of the author is also reflective of the characters and narrator and is appropriate for the theme. The author may use short, simple sentences; long, complicated sentences; or even stream of consciousness.

For your literary analysis, you may want to analyze language and/or style. Tell your reader how the author uses words and style to convey or reinforce the theme of the work. Select key passages from the text that show this use.

SYMBOL

A symbol refers to an object or person that represents an idea or concept. For example, a rose is a flower, but it could represent a person's love. A flag is a piece of cloth, but it could represent a country or the concept of patriotism. Many times in a work of literature, the author will use symbols to help convey the theme. If you write a literary analysis based on symbol, select the object or person that you find to be symbolic and tell what that object or person represents. Of course, you will explain to your reader how you arrived at that interpretation. Finally, show how the symbol relates or conveys the theme of the literary work.

▼ LOOKING AT A SHORT STORY

To get a better understanding of these literary elements, let us take a look at the short story "Hills Like White Elephants" by Ernest Hemingway.

Ernest Hemingway (1898-1961)
Hills Like White Elephants

The hills across the valley of the Ebro were long and white. On this side there was no shade and no trees and the station was between two lines of rails in the sun. Close against the side of the station there was the warm shadow of the building and a curtain, made of strings of bamboo beads, hung across the open door into the bar, to keep out flies. The American and the girl with him sat at a table in the shade, outside the building. It was very hot and the express from Barcelona would come in forty minutes. It stopped at this junction for two minutes and went on to Madrid.

"What should we drink?" the girl asked. She had taken off her hat and put it on the table.

"It's pretty hot," the man said.

"Let"s drink beer."

"Dos cervezas," the man said into the curtain.

"Big ones?" a woman asked from the doorway.

"Yes. Two big ones."

The woman brought two glasses of beer and two felt pads. She put the felt pads and the beer glasses on the table and looked at the man and the girl. The girl was looking off at the line of hills. They were white in the sun and the country was brown and dry.

"They look like white elephants," she said.

"I've never seen one," the man drank his beer.

"No, you wouldn't have."

"I might have," the man said. "Just because you say I wouldn't have doesn't prove anything."

The girl looked at the bead curtain. "They've painted something on it," she said. "What does it say?"

"Anis del Toro. It's a drink."

"Could we try it?"

The man called "Listen" through the curtain. The woman came out from the bar.

"Four reales."

"We want two Anis del Toro."

"With water?"

"Do you want it with water?"

"I don't know," the girl said. "Is is good with water?"

"It's all right."

"You want them with water?" asked the woman.

"Yes, with water."

"It tastes like licorice," the girl said and put the glass down.

"That's the way with everything."

"Yes," said the girl. Everything tastes of licorice. Especially all the things you've waited so long for, like absinthe."

"Oh, cut it out."

"You started it," the girl said. "I was being amused. I was having a fine time."

"Well, let's try and have a fine time."

"All right, I was trying. I said the mountains looked like white elephants, Wasn't that bright?"

"That was bright."

"I wanted to try this new drink. That's all we do, isn't it—look at things and try new drinks?"

"I guess so."

The girl looked across at the hills.

"They're lovely hills," she said. "They don't really look like white elephants. I just meant the coloring of their skin through the trees."

"Should we have another drink?"

"All right."

The warm wind blew the bead curtain against the table.

"The beer's nice and cool," the man said.

"It's lovely," the girl said.

"It's really an awfully simple operation, Jig," the man said. "It's not really an operation at all."

The girl looked at the ground the table legs rested on.

"I know you wouldn't mind it, Jig. It's really not anything. It's just to let the air in."

The girl did not say anything.

"I'll go with you and I'll stay with you all the time. They just let the air in and then it's all perfectly natural."

"Then what will we do afterward?"

"We'll be fine afterward. Just like we were before."

"What makes you think so?"

"That's the only thing that bothers us. It's the only thing that's made us unhappy."

The girl looked at the bead curtain, put her hand out and took hold of two of the strings of beads.

"And you think then we'll be all right and be happy."

"I know we will. You don't have to be afraid. I've known lots of people that have done it."

"So have I," said the girl. "And afterward they were all so happy."

"Well," the man said, "if you don't want to you don't have to. I wouldn't have you do it if you didn't want to. But I know it's perfectly simple."

"And you really want to?"

"I think it's the best thing to do. But I don't want you to do it if you don't really want to."

"And if I do it you'll be happy and things will be like they were and you'll love me?"

"I love you now. You know I love you."

"I know. But if I do it, then it will be nice again if I say things are like white elephants, and you'll like it?"

"I'll love it. I love it now but I just can't think about it. You know how I get when I worry."

"If I do it you won't ever worry?"

"I won't worry about that because it's perfectly simple."

"Then I'll do it. Because I don't care about me."

"What do you mean?"

"I don't care about me."

"Well, I care about you."

"Oh, yes. But I don't care about me. And I'll do it and then everything will be fine."

"I don't want you to do it if you feel that way."

The girl stood up and walked to the end of the station. Across, on the other side, were fields of grain and trees along the banks of the Ebro. Far away, beyond the river, were mountains. The shadow of a cloud moved across the field of grain and she saw the river through the trees.

"And we could have all this," she said. "And we could have everything and every day we make it more impossible."

"What did you say?"

"I said we could have everything."

"We can have everything."

"No, we can't."

"We could have the whole world."

"No, we can't."

"We can go everywhere."

"No, we can't. It isn't ours any more."

"It's ours."

"No, it isn't. And once they take it away, you never get it back."

"But they haven't taken it away."

"We'll wait and see."

"Come on back in the shade," he said. "You mustn't feel that way."

"I don't feel any way," the girl said. "I just know things."

"I don't want you to do anything that you don't want to do—"

"Not that isn't good for me," she said. "I know. Could we have another beer?"

"All right. But you've got to realize—"

"I realize," the girl said. "Can we maybe stop talking?"

They sat down at the table and the girl looked across at the hills on the dry side of the valley and the man looked at her and at the table.

"You've got to realize," he said, "that I don't want you to do it if you don't want to, I'm perfectly willing to go through with it if it means anything to you."

"Doesn't it mean anything to you? We could get along."

"Of course it does. But I don't want anybody but you. I don't want any one else. And I know it's perfectly simple."

"Yes, you know it's perfectly simple."

"It's all right for you to say that, but I do know it."

"Would you do something for me now?"

"I'd do anything for you."

"Would you please please please please please please please stop talking?"

He did not say anything but looked at the bags against the wall of the station. There were labels on them from all the hotels where they had spent nights.

"But I don't want you to." he said, "I don't care anything about it."

"I'll scream," the girl said.

The woman came out through the curtains with two glasses of beer and put them down on the damp felt pads. "The train comes in five minutes," she said.

"What did she say?" asked the girl.

"That the train is coming in five minutes."

The girl smiled brightly at the woman, to thank her.

"I'd better take the bags over to the other side of the station," the man said. She smiled at him.

"All right. Then come back and we'll finish the beer."

He picked up the two heavy bags and carried them around the station to the other tracks. He looked up the tracks but could not see the train. Coming back, he walked through the bar-room, where people waiting for the train were drinking. He drank an Anis at the bar and looked at the people. They were all waiting reasonably for the train. He went out through the bead curtain. She was sitting at the table and smiled at him.

"Do you feel better?" he said.

"I feel fine," she said. "There's nothing wrong with me. I feel fine."

WAYS TO ANALYZE "HILLS LIKE WHITE ELEPHANTS"

In the Hemingway short story you just read, the author tells of an American man and a girl waiting on a train in the countryside of Spain. While they are waiting, they begin discussing an unnamed topic, which we come to understand to be abortion.

This story can be analyzed from any of the elements described in the previous section. If you were to look at the story based on plot, you would look at the various developments in the conversation. How do we see the conflict between the two individuals? You would find the climax of the conversation and determine what the resolution will be for the issue at hand. Because the emphasis is always all on the theme or message, you would discuss what Hemingway is trying to say in this short story.

Another way this story can be approached is by analyzing one of the two characters. Based on the conversation, you could describe the personality of either the man or the girl. For example, let's say you wanted to discuss the girl. What are the traits you see exhibited based on her conversation? How do her traits contribute to the conflict in the story? How is the girl's personality different from the man's? Does she change in any way during the story, or does she remain the same? No matter which character you decide to analyze, your goal is to show how the character's personality and inner growth reflect the theme or message of the story.

As mentioned previously, you can also analyze the type of narrator found in the story. For "Hills Like White Elephants," Hemingway uses a third-person objective narrator. If you were to analyze this aspect, you could discuss why Hemingway uses this type of narrator for this story. How is the use of this type reflective of the atmosphere and theme of the story?

A fourth way "Hills Like White Elephants" can be analyzed is by discussing the setting. Hemingway tells us that the day is hot and bright, and the countryside around the two characters is "brown and dry." If you were to analyze the setting, you could discuss how the setting reflects the relationship between the two characters and thus the message of the story.

Of course, you can choose to analyze the theme itself. You can begin your analysis by stating what you feel Hemingway's theme is in the story and then show how you arrived at determining this theme. You can look at the plot, the characters, the dialogue, and/or the setting in supporting your assertion.

As discussed earlier, there are two other elements you could analyze in a short story: language and symbol. Hemingway's simplicity of word and language in this story is deceptive. The words used have underlying meanings for the characters. When the words "fine" and "good" and "simple" are used, what exactly is being said and felt? By analyzing the language, you can help your reader understand the message of the story.

Finally, you can analyze the symbolism in this story. The title itself cues us into the story's symbolism. What does it mean the hills "look like white elephants" as the girl tells us? What do the hills symbolize for the relationship being presented to us by Hemingway? By answering these questions in your analysis, you help your reader to develop an understanding of the story's message.

▼ OTHER GENRES OF LITERATURE

The previous discussion has concentrated on writing an analysis of a short story or novel, but you could also be asked to write a literary analysis of a play or a poem. The elements of these two types of literature are similar to the elements of a short story or novel. A play contains a plot, characters, and setting. If you were to write a literary analysis of a play, you could analyze the play from the vantage point of one of these elements as already explained. As mentioned, a plot is a series of events that culminates in a climax. Generally, the plot in a play centers on the protagonist seeking some goal, whether that be wealth, power, affection, and so on. You can analyze the various events (scenes) that propel the protagonist towards his/her goal and how these events affect him/her and the other characters. The climax or turning point of the play occurs as Aristotle described it, when the action leads to recognition and/or reversal. *Recognition* means the protagonist goes from ignorance to knowledge and *reversal* means that an action results in an opposite result from what was expected, changing the fortune of the protagonist. In a play, the traits and motivations of the characters are revealed in four basic ways: through their appearance, through their words, through their actions, and through the words and reactions of the other characters. You can use their four aspects to analyze characters' wills, desires, and objectives. The other key element to a play is dialogue. Analyzing dialogue is very much like analyzing the language and style in a work fiction. You will want to look at the choice of words that a character uses. How are those words in keeping with the character's personality? Is the character using words satirically or ironically? Do the words hold double meanings? As with any literary analysis, no matter which element you choose to discuss, your goal is help your reader understand the theme or message of the play. And, of course, you could center your analysis on theme and show your reader how you arrived at your interpretation.

When writing about a play, you can handle citations in several ways. Following is an excerpt from a student-written literary analysis of the play *Cat on a Hot Tin Roof* entitled "Mendacity in *Cat on a Hot Tin Roof.*" In this excerpt, the student gives an example of how lies are used to cover unpleasant truths. For the purposes of her essay the student uses page references to indicate citations from the play since a common text was used. However, you should provide as much information as possible from the text to head the reader locate the original passage. Since this prose play is divided only acts, this student's parenthetical citations could have included the act with the page number such as (73; act 1). If a common text were not being used for the play, then the page number would be irrelevant and your citation would look like (*Cat act 1*).

Another example of mendacity being used to cover up distasteful facts is seen in Maggie's efforts to make her indifferent husband appear as if he has thoughtfully remembered his father's birthday by personally buying a fine gift for him. Fully aware that Brick will forget his father's birthday, Maggie buys the present herself, passing it off as Brick's gift. Upon opening

"Brick's" present for Big Daddy, Maggie gasps, "Oh, look, oh look, why, it's a cashmere robe!" (73).

Poetry consists of many forms. If you were analyzing a narrative or epic poem, you could analyze plot as you would for a work of fiction. Characters can also be present in poetry whether the poet is expressing his or her own feelings and reactions in the work or describing someone else's. Who exactly is the speaker in the poem? Again, you can analyze character in a poem as you would analyze character in a short story or novel. Since poetry is a condensed form of literature, when analyzing poetry, you may want to look at rhythm, order, and/or language. When analyzing rhythm, discuss how the poem flows and sounds by describing the devices the poet uses. Also consider the meter of the poem, if appropriate. Does the poet use the devices of alliteration (a series of words beginning with the same sound) or assonance (a series of words containing the same vowel sounds)? When writing your analysis, show how the rhythm reinforces or conveys the poet's message. Depending on the type of poem being written, the poet may have to follow certain conventions relating to arrangement and order of lines. Because of this constraint, an important component of poetry is imagery. Poetry relies heavily on images or word pictures to convey ideas. You can analyze a poem by looking at the imagery found in a poem and how that imagery is achieved. A third element you could analyze in a poem is the language. What is the connotative or symbolic meaning of the words? As discussed in the short story section, how does the use of symbol(s) transcend the literal significance of the poem's words and create new mearning? How does this meaning relate to the theme? Poetic language relies heavily on figures of speech, such as simile, metaphor, and personification. You can explain how such figurative imagery used by the poet creates unexpected comparisons contributing to the message or theme.

Writing citing lines from a poem, provide parenthetical documentation similar to that described for a play, except now you will use stanza and/or verse numbers.

▼ WRITING A LITERARY ANALYSIS PAPER

An important consideration before writing a literary analysis is the use of secondary sources. Generally, a literary analysis is your own interpretation of a literary work. You read the piece of literature carefully; draw your own conclusions as to the author's intent and message in the work; look at the various elements of the work and determine which element would best help clarify that message for your reader; and then locate the references from the work itself that will justify your conclusions. However, your assignment may require you to use secondary sources to support your contentions. In this case, look for critiques of the work you are analyzing and use these secondary authors to confirm your contentions. You may find a secondary source that contradicts your viewpoint. In this case, present this opposite opinion but then show how you disagree with the author's contention based on the evidence you find in the literary work.

Like any essay you write, a literary analysis paper should have an introduction, body, and conclusion. Following are some tips to help you approach each of these sections.

INTRODUCTION

Components of Introduction to Literary Analysis	1. The name of the work you are analyzing and its author.
	
	2. A brief summary or overview of the work being discussed.
	
	3. A thesis statement that fulfills three goals:
	
	    a. Identifies the element of the literary work being analyzed
	
	    b. States the point you are making about that element
	
	    c. Relates your point to the theme or message of the story

BODY

In the body of the literary essay, like with any essay, you are supporting your thesis. In this type of essay, though, the majority of the supporting details, if not all of them, are coming directly from the piece of literature you are analyzing. Your goal is to show through direct references from the work that the assertion you made in your thesis is a correct interpretation.

To provide the best support for your thesis and to make sure your reader understands your interpretation, construct your body paragraphs in the following fashion:

1. First, state your topic sentence, identifying the section or part of the work you are going to discuss because it illustrates the point you have established in your thesis.

2. Second, discuss what you feel this section of the work is showing. What is the point you want your reader to grasp about this section you are highlighting?

3. Third, make a direct reference from the literary work that illustrates your assertion. You may quote directly from the literary work, or you may provide an indirect reference to what is found in the work.

4. Fourth, clarify how your reference from the literary work illustrates your point. This clarification is a key component of your analysis. You want to make sure your reader understands how the excerpt from the work illustrates your point.

5. Fifth, if your assignment is to include critiques from an outside source, you now, through quoting, paraphrasing, or summarizing, take a reference from your outside source to support or reinforce the point you have made. You are using your outside source to provide an authoritative stamp to your assertion.

CONCLUSION

The conclusion of your literary analysis should be brief. Because the purpose of your literary analysis is to help your reader develop a better understanding of the work's message or theme, you want to reinforce in your conclusion what that theme is and how the element you just analyzed in your essay conveys that theme.

Some Points to Remember	• You are writing your literary analysis to an informed reader. You write from the assumption that your reader is familiar with the work being analyzed. Thus, you do not have to provide your reader with extensive summaries of the work. Your goal is to help your reader interpret the work, so any excerpts from the work are to show where your interpretation can be supported from the work itself. • All references to the literary work should be written in the present tense because a literary work exists throughout time. • Because you generally write a literary analysis for a particular course you are studying, the piece of literature you are analyzing will probably be from a common text. Consequently, you do not need to document the source of the work. However, give the page number from the textual source if it is a short story or novel; the act, scene, and line numbers if a play; and the stanza and/or verse numbers if a poem. Include these numerical references as part of your sentence introducing your textual example, or place them in parentheses after the example. If you are not using a common text, then, give the full textual citation for your source on your works cited page. If you are using a secondary source in your paper, however, document this source as you would any source in a research paper, using proper in-text and works cited format as discussed in Chapter 7 of this textbook.

Following are three sample literary analysis essays. The first is an analysis of "Hills Like White Elephants" that includes secondary sources. The second is a student-written comparative analysis of the non-fiction book *Indian Creek Chronicle* and the movie *Into the Wild*. This analysis relies only on primary text. The third example is an excerpt from a literary analysis of the play *Cat on a Hot Tin Roof*.

An Analysis of "Hills Like White Elephants"
by Paul Rankin

Although it would overstate the matter to suggest that a single critical consensus exists regarding the resolution of Ernest Hemingway's "Hills Like White Elephants," a summation of the majority opinion might produce something along these lines: in an impressive feat of dialogue-driven narrative prose, Hemingway's unnamed American male protagonist dominates the meeker, weaker-sexed Jig—the other in terms of her femaleness, her youth (she is the girl as opposed to the woman who tends bar), and her foreignness (because he receives the specific national identification, we may deduce that it's meant to distinguish his from hers)—until, broken, she submits to his will and consents to aborting the child. Frederick Busch phrases it most succinctly when he argues that Jig "buries her way of seeing as she will bury her child" (762). Other critics have suggested that "the male's language [of distance and control] overpowers [Jig]" (O'Brien 22–23) and that "Jig [. . .] knows that she will never bear the child she is carrying" (Abdoo 238). A closer look at what Janet Burroway refers to as the pattern of shifting power, however, reveals a more subversive current in the dialogue—one in which Jig, the xenofeminine, outwits her boorish American inamorato and manipulates both the conversation and the man at each turn to control the shared destiny of her and the unborn child (36). Read according to this pattern of subversion, the story emerges as a series of parries that demonstrate Jig's superiority in terms of her cognitive and conative intelligence, as well as her experience, her scathing wit, and her facility with ironic sarcasm, all of which culminate in the absolute straightforwardness of the last line, a line that incidentally coincides with Jig's own dramatic epiphany: There's nothing wrong with me. I feel fine.

In the economies of such notable theorists as Carl Gustav Jung and Karen Horney, the man's attempt to bully pregnant Jig, although certainly by no means justified, should come as no surprise. We need look no further than Jung's valuation of the mother "for whose sake everything that embraces, protects, nourishes, and helps assumes maternal form" (qtd. in Wilmer 40) to begin to comprehend the nature of the man's feelings of inadequacy and inferiority in the face of Jig's imminent transformation from "the girl" into motherhood. Horney goes Jung one step further, contending that man's fundamental lack of "life-creating power," with which woman is imbued, has motivated the creation of such historically masculine enterprises as "[s]tate, religion, art, and science" in man's attempt to compensate for that insurmountable deficiency (366–67). Unfortunately, however, "even the greatest [. . .] achievements [. . .] cannot fully make up for something for which we are not endowed by nature" (Horney 367). Thus we may expect to encounter, in extreme cases, such attitudes as the man's in "Hills," whose "notion of behaving 'reasonably'" cannot include "birth of any sort" (Busch 761).

As the man persists in opposing the continuance of Jig's maternity, he grossly oversimplifies the issue, even to the point of self-contradiction, calling the abortion first "an awfully simple operation," and then "not really an operation at all" (212). Here and elsewhere, the excessive modifiers like "awfully" and "really" indicate the man's awareness that this will not be an easy sale and belie his understanding, whether he would be willing to acknowledge this or not, of Jig's formidable intelligence and will. We perceive these attributes directly from Jig as well, as she demonstrates an increasing awareness not only of the gravity of the situation, but also of the man's self-centered and insecure motivation for pursuing the abortion. Consider, for example how Jig initiates the story's action by asking what they should drink, and also makes the first significant observation in the story, noting that the hills "look like white elephants" (211). At first glance, these details may appear unimportant in the context of the decision they are at odds over, but in a relationship where "all [they] do [is . . .] look at things and try new drinks," these particular activities carry a substantial amount of weight.

By way of contrast, the man's first three lines are entirely reactionary and essentially passive in nature. To Jig's question about drinks, he replies, "It's pretty hot" (when we have already learned in the opening paragraph that "It was very hot"); to her follow-up suggestion that they drink beer, he calls out, "two beers"; and to the bartender's question "Big ones?" he assents, "Yes. Two big ones" (211). At least initially, the man has nothing to offer, nothing to contribute to the story, just as he has nothing more to contribute to Jig's pregnancy now that he has invested his "minute share in creating new life" (Horney 367).

We encounter further evidence of the man's inferiority complex in his severe response to Jig's playful banter about the similarity between hills and elephants. Having already admitted that he has never seen white elephants, the man angrily berates Jig, saying, "Just because you say I wouldn't have doesn't prove anything" (211). In a story of exchanges, Jig's reaction here speaks volumes—she makes another observation and changes the subject. Jig's ability to take in her surroundings and find ways to diffuse the man's anger demonstrates her resourcefulness at the same time it raises the problematic question that drives the story: Is Jig merely ceding her will to the superior and dominant male's, or is she, rather, manipulating him (and the situation as a whole) to her advantage by giving him the illusion of the upper hand?

To answer this question, we must look backward and forward in the story and put this particular exchange in context. Our backward glance reveals that what set the man off was Jig's access to knowledge and experience that the man cannot have, the first-hand knowledge of what white elephants look like. Recognizing this truth as well as the bamboo curtain, Jig shifts the focus from something she knows that the man does not to something he knows that she does not. Even that ignorance of Anis del Toro, however, appears questionable when we arrive at the manifest sarcasm of her response to his blithe observation that "that's the way with everything," to which she replies, "Especially all the things you've waited so long for, like absinthe." Her awareness of the drink's composition indicates that she knew more than she let on when she inquired about the curtain, and thus we can conclude that something other than curiosity or ignorance motivated her question. Thus, we see Jig powerfully asserting her will, and doing so in such a way that she averts unnecessary confrontation several paragraphs before we encounter the discussion of the "operation."

As we do come to that discussion, as the confrontation becomes entirely necessary, the flurry of verbal punches only serves to intensify Jig's resistance as she grows more explicit in her refusal. "No, we can't," she repeats several times, ironically refuting his assent to her own sarcastic declaration that "we could have everything." Demonstrating his now-characteristic inability to understand her point of view, the man assumes that she is still referring to "the whole world" when she says, "It isn't ours any more." Still subversive, still subtle even as the exchange heats up, Jig corrects him once and for all, saying, "No it isn't. And once they take it away, you never get it back." When the man acknowledges that "they haven't taken it away" yet, perhaps without even realizing it, perhaps still imagining she means the world (and all it has come to signify in terms of their unfettered experience and his selfish desire to hang on to that), he proves Jig's point and effectively closes off any further negotiation (213).

What remains is primarily denouement, where the man and Jig return to their drinks and wait for the train. As he attempts to broach the subject, the girl shuts him down completely, and even though the point of view follows him as he passes through the bar, drinks more Anis, and returns, ultimately, Jig gets the last word: "There's nothing wrong with me" (214). The man has heretofore treated Jig's pregnancy like a burden or an illness, whereas Jig, in the cross- talk that emerges from the "no-we-can't" volley, equates the pregnancy, and by implication the child, with "the whole world."

In the final analysis, contenders on either side of the debate must acknowledge that, much like Frank Stockton's "The Lady or the Tiger," this story leaves us at the brink of enlightenment. Unlike Stockton's resolution, which hinges solely on the whims of chance, Hemingway has endowed us with sufficient elements of characterization—Jig's wit, resourcefulness, and strong will as opposed to the man's quick temper, self-centeredness, and irresponsibility—to make an educated guess as to the direction of their immediate future. In a story built on irony and sarcasm, it is almost paradoxical how sincere Jig's final declaration reads: "There's nothing wrong with me," she says, and we understand finally that the white elephant was never the abortion or even the unborn child itself—it was always the man.

Works Cited

Abdoo, Sherlyn. "Hemingway's Hills Like White Elephants." Explicator 49.4 (1991): 238–40. Print.

Burroway, Janet. *Writing Fiction: A Guide to Narrative Craft.* 6th ed. New York: Longman, 2003. Print.

Busch, Frederick. "On Hills Like White Elephants." *Norton Anthology of Short Fiction.* Ed. R. V. Cassill and Richard Bausch. 6th ed. New York: Norton, 2000. 761–62. Print.

Hemingway, Ernest. "Hills Like White Elephants." *The Complete Short Stories of Ernest Hemingway.* New York: Collier, 1987. 211–14. Print.

Horney, Karen. "The Distrust Between the Sexes." *A World of Ideas.* Ed. Lee A. Jacobus. 6th ed. Boston: Bedford/St. Martin's, 2002. 357–71. Print.

O'Brien, Timothy D. "Allusion, World-Play, and the Central Conflict in Hemingway's 'Hills Like White Elephants.'" *Hemingway Review* 12.1 (1992): 19–26. Print.

Stockton, Frank. "The Lady or the Tiger." 1882. *East of the Web.* Hyperfiction, 2003. Web. 3 August 2005. <http://www.eastoftheweb.com/shortstories/UBooks/>.

The Lady or the Tiger and Other Stories. New York: Garrett Press, 1969. Print.

Wilmer, Harry A. *Practical Jung: Nuts and Bolts of Jungian Psychotherapy.* Wilmette, IL: Chiron, 1987. Print.

William Herndon

Professor Dominique Dieffenbach

ENC 1102

16 July 2014

Romantic Notions and Suicide by Hubris

The struggle to find one's identity is common to many young adults, but few are willing to go the extremes that Chris McCandless, played by Emile Hirsch, and Pete Fromm choose to pursue. Sean Penn and Jon Krakauer collaborate in telling Chris' tale in the movie *Into the Wild*, which is based on Krakauer's book of the same name and his prior article, "Death of an Innocent." Author Pete Fromm describes his experiences and self-revelations while guarding salmon eggs through seven months of an Idaho winter in his book, *Indian Creek Chronicles.* Chris and Pete are two very different individuals who choose to follow similar paths of discovery. Their personalities, motivations and even their choices in preparing for this adventure are very different, but there are some similarities in the lessons derived from their life-changing experiences.

The personalities and motivations of Chris and Pete play an enormous role in each of their stories of isolation in the wilderness. Chris is an intense young man trying to learn all he can about life by immersing himself fully in the experience of an aesthetic existence. The friends he makes along the way and his journals make it clear that he is intelligent, charismatic, and even extroverted. However, Chris also displays an arrogance and foolishness that prevent him from listening when a number of friends try to reason with him. Some of this stubbornness is natural to him, but his toxic relationship with his parents seems to have magnified and turned it bitter. The discovery of his father's infidelity and his own status as a "bastard" child only heightens his need for this exploration. Despite his faults and difficulties, Chris is universally described as a good and moral person who is easy to like and hard to forget.

Pete is also a smart, likeable young man searching for himself and his role in the world. His romantic notions about the mountain man stories that he enjoys reading, and his desire to have stories of his own, lead him into the Idaho backwoods. Before his adventure even begins, he realizes that he is in over his head and wishes he could find a way to back out without appearing foolish. Pete Fromm writes, "If the wardens had called saying the project was off and I wouldn't be able to go in after all, I would have danced a naked jig down Main Street" (15). Pete is embarrassed by any greenhorn mistakes that he makes and hopes no one sees them, but he does recognize and learn from them. While these two young men share similarities such as likeability and intelligence, there are some very marked difference in their personalities and motivations. Chris seems to be fleeing from his family and the corrupting influences of civilization while Pete hopes to bring something of the wilderness back to share with his family and friends.

Chris is very self-assured and confident in his ability to survive any situation that could arise. He wants to get lost in the wild and discover things for himself. Because of this, Chris decides not to take any reasonable amount of equipment or even sufficient supplies for the amount of time that he has planned to stay. As Krakauer reports in "Death of an Innocent,"

Chris "admitted [to Jim Gallien who had picked him up hitching] that the only food in his pack was a 10 lb bag of rice. He had no compass; the only navigational aid in his possession was a tattered road map he had scrounged at a petrol station, and when they arrived where Alex asked to be dropped off, he left the map in Gallien's truck, along with his watch, his comb, and all his money, which amounted to 85 cents." The little bit of survival training he engages in involves conversations with a hunter who does not seem to have much of a clue himself. He decides not to learn about the area he plans to live in or even take a good map of the area. The most sensible choices Chris makes are to take a .22-caliber rifle, and an extensive manual on the local flora and fauna. While Jim Gallien, playing himself in the movie *Into the Wild,* is dropping Chris off at the trailhead in Alaska, he convinces Chris to take his rubber boots because Chris' supplies are so insufficient. Chris compounds these mistakes by failing to explore the area once he sets up camp in the bus. Many of these mistakes are conscious decisions made out of ignorance and an overabundance of self-confidence.

Pete also has a habit of making rash decisions without really thinking through them very well. However, he is self-conscious enough to question his decisions and ask for help. Once committed to the job, Pete and Rader begin serious preparation for a winter of rough seclusion. They gather a pile of supplies that include more food than Pete could eat, wilderness survival manuals, two rifles, tools, and game traps. He also takes some needed company with him in the form of Boone, a puppy that Rader and Lorrie chose for him (Fromm 12–16). After a visit from Rader and Sponz goes bust, playing with Boone saves him from loneliness: "Soon we were in the meadow, where the rain had turned back into snow, and we scurried after each other in the darkness, me shouting and Boone barking, the heavy, sodden trees soaking up all traces of our voices" (Fromm 130). Pete's camp site is chosen for him by park rangers, and they help set up the tent and show him how to gather firewood. Once he is alone, Pete cuts more wood than he could possibly need for a single winter in an effort to just to avoid the loneliness (Fromm 35–36). A description by Fromm of his attempts at baking eloquently expresses the fact that loneliness seems to be his worst enemy:

> Small failures like that could set off some desperate swings-to loneliness so powerful it could make me fight for breath. Then tiny victories, like pulling my first golden loaf of bread from the wood stove, would send me into idiotic charges through my meadow, laughing and carrying on as if I'd just won the lottery.
>
> Each one of those victories, as minor as they were, cut a piece out of the loneliness that always skulked nearby, in the dark patches of trees, in the black water trying not to freeze over, even in the way the river talked at night, taking on voices it never had in the day. (39)

Keeping that desperation at bay is important to keeping one's sanity intact, and activities such as hiking, cooking, trapping and hunting provide very necessary distractions for Pete. Preparation is a key factor in wilderness survival. Chris disregards common sense in his attempt to live off the land and intentionally leaves important tools and supplies behind. Pete, on the other hand, seeks guidance from his friend, Rader, and then overprepares to such an extent that he has more food than he can eat and tools he doesn't even know how to use when he arrives. The obvious difference in their preparations condemns Chris to ultimate disaster and saves Pete from a similar fate.

It would be impossible to remain unaffected by the ordeals these two men go through. Through the adversity and loneliness of their experiences they learn important lessons about themselves and come to appreciate their environments. Prior to his time in the "magic bus," Chris is pushing people away and cutting all ties. Even the people he seems to care about are hurt and cut off in his attempt to separate himself from the world. He seems incapable of accepting responsibility for his mistakes, even going so far as blaming the animals for not being there to be killed when he is hungry. After he wastes the moose kill, he falls into a short-lived despair from which he begins to accept his mistakes and learn from them. Before he dies of starvation, Chris comes to the realization that "happiness is only real when shared" (*Into the Wild*). Unfortunately, Chris' revelation comes too late because he is trapped by a river swollen by a thaw he fails to anticipate and his own lack of preparation. His death is a great loss for his family and friends and a world that will never know what he could have become.

His time in the Idaho backwoods changes Pete in ways that are more visible to his friends than to him. While in isolation, Pete learns many of the skills necessary for survival, but those skills are not the most important lessons. He gains independence, self-confidence, and seriousness that he was lacking before his adventures began. His journey teaches him to value his own skills and knowledge and to realize that everyone has his or her own strengths and weaknesses. Pete comes to appreciate the valley where he lives in a way that cannot be understood by an outsider who doesn't live there. He begins to value the stories he has more than can be equated to money. Rather than sell the bobcat skin, he concludes, "There was no point in selling it. Anyone who saw it afterwards would only see pretty fur. I didn't need the money so badly it was worth killing the cat's story" (163). Pete begins his quest to be a mountain man as a self-conscious youth, and he matures into a confident, conscientious man. This experience plays a pivotal role in the development of Pete Fromm into the author and man that he is today.

These two narratives depict similar journeys into frozen frontiers and each player's struggle to survive on such a stage. Chris and Pete display the foolishness of young men in their metaphorical attempts to grow up, and both learn much about themselves in the process. While there is no real need for either of them to embark on the journeys they choose, neither will develop into the men that they become without their sojourns into the wild. They are both intelligent young men with great potential, but with very different personalities. Ultimately, it is Chris' overconfident disregard for his own safety that leads to his death, not any lack of ability. Even in the end there is no detectable remorse in him for how his disappearance and death will affect those he is leaving behind. In contrast, the uncertainty Pete feels going into his venture ensures that he will seek advice and prepare as best as he is able for his endeavor. Unlike Chris, Pete often thinks of his family and relishes their correspondence. Despite the fact that he comes to love his valley and its isolation, he looks forward to the company of his friends and family. Ironically, when he does return to civilization with his stories, he is no longer sure how he should tell them or if anyone would even be able to understand. These two young men trek into wilderness adventures for different reasons and learn many life lessons, each leaving a different legacy.

Works Cited

Fromm, Pete. *Indian Creek Chronicles.* New York: Picador, 1993. Print

Into the Wild. Dir. Sean Penn. Perf. Emile Hirsch, William Hurt, Marcia Gay Harden, Hal Holbrook, Vince Vaughn, Jena Malone. Warner, 2007. DVD.

Krakauer, Jon. "Death of an Innocent." *Outside Magazine* 11 Apr. 1993: N. pag. *The Independent.* Web. 21 Nov. 2013.

Chapter 13

Writing for Business

Writing for the workplace is similar to the academic writing you have been studying. You must pay attention to your grammar and sentence structure, and you must give as much attention to detail and accuracy as required for your argumentation and essay writing. Also, the need to take personal responsibility for what you write is a major requirement for business writing; remember, if the reader does not understand what you write, it is *your* fault, and your business may suffer for the lack of understanding. But, there are a few differences between essay writing and business writing that will affect the way you present your material. First, most business writing is personal in tone. When you write a memo, letter, or report, you are generally addressing that document to a specific person or group. Essay writing usually has a more general audience and has a less personal tone.

Second, business writing is usually more content-specific; that is, the document you are writing usually has a single purpose: to order some material, to report the progress of a project, or to convey a specific bit of information. Consequently, a business document is generally much shorter than an essay.

Finally, business writing is heavily formatted. Depending on the type of document being generated, you will need to adhere to specific guidelines for writing and formatting its content. While the format may vary depending on the document and the organization for which you are working, most business formats are standardized and follow certain guidelines. Chapter 13 will guide you in writing and formatting documents for the workplace.

Objectives

♦   provide an overview of the process for writing for the workplace;

♦   differentiate among the formats for correspondence writing such as the memo and the letter;

♦   explain the elements of the technical report;

♦   discuss the format of the letter of application and the resume.

▼ PLANNING

Before you actually write your document, you must first make several key decisions about its style and tone. The first decision, of course, is *who* will read it. Knowing your audience is critical to constructing the appropriate document. How many people will read your letter or report? What is your relationship to your audience? Remember that the more *power* you have over your audience, the more formal you must be. A memo to a peer who has the same authority you have may be informal and on a first-name basis, but a memo to someone distant from you in the organization or community will probably not allow such informal liberties.

Another question you must ask is what the purpose of the document is. Most technical writing is done to *persuade, to inform,* or to *instruct.* If you are submitting a recommendation report to your supervisor, urging him or her to purchase a new scanner/copier for the office computer, present the factual data that supports your recommendation and provide enough information to allow an appropriate decision. Emphasize how your reader will benefit from the new technology, and address your supervisor's obvious questions: How much will it cost? Will the scanner/copier increase or enhance production? Is it compatible with existing equipment?

If your intention is not to persuade your supervisor, but simply to inform him or her about the status of office equipment, then an informational memo may be the appropriate choice. Decide what information your reader needs, and anticipate potential questions that might arise. Document your sources of information, and offer alternatives if necessary.

Additionally, if a scanner/copier is purchased, you may have to construct a document educating the office staff on how to use and maintain the new equipment. What does your audience need to know? What are the dangers of operating the equipment, and how should you convey these dangers so that all your readers will be aware of them?

Finally, before you begin the writing process, you must determine the *tone* your document will convey. Tone is usually dictated by your purpose and by the audience who will read your document. If your intention is to offer your employees a raise, your tone may be less formal than if you were telling your employees there will be no raises this year. Also, the make-up of your audience will have a lot to do with the tone you use. You already know from your essay writing that you write differently for a younger audience than for an older one, or for a professional audience than for a group of novices. Always consider your audience before you decide what tone to take with your document.

▼ DRAFTING YOUR DOCUMENT

Once you have identified your purpose, audience, and the tone you want to convey, you are ready to write a draft of your technical document. Technical writing is direct and simple. Your audience needs to know what you know, and it's your responsibility to convey that information. Don't make your document any longer or any more complicated than is required to accomplish your goal. Use a standard subject-verb-object sentence pattern, and choose words that will be readily understood by your reader. Once again, remember that if your audience doesn't understand your document, *it is your fault*. Most importantly, choose an appropriate format and follow the guidelines of that format. Most of your technical documents will take the form of a *memo, letter,* or *report.*

THE MEMO

Most memos you will write will be pre-formatted. Many companies and organizations have standard memo formats for you to use for correspondence with your co-workers, staff, or other members within the organization. Though memos are usually brief and often informal in tone, the need for accuracy and clear expression is essential. The main elements of the memo are the heading, the body, and the signature.

Heading

The memo requires you to identify the reader, the writer, the date, and the subject in the heading. Look at the following memorandum:

FLORIDA STATE COLLEGE AT JACKSONVILLE
4501 Capper Road
Jacksonville, FL 32221

MEMORANDUM

TO: BJ Hausman, Dean of Student Success
FROM: Luther T. Buie, Campus Achievement Leader
DATE: March 18, 2013
SUBJECT: <u>Tuition Reimbursement Request</u>

I am sending this memo requesting tuition reimbursement for a Technical Writing course I am completing at Florida State College at Jacksonville.

As the Campus Achievement Leader, I am responsible for designing office publications, developing marketing plans for student success and retention initiatives, and receiving and responding to student concerns. This course is preparing me to respond to student and college correspondence utilizing an array of writing forms.

Through this course, I am acquiring additional knowledge of researching a topic, making oral presentations, working effectively and efficiently in teams, and addressing ethical issues. These skills will make me a stronger technical writer, a better student retention specialist, and overall a better Florida State College at Jacksonville employee.

Thank you for your time and consideration. I look forward to the opportunity to share my newly acquired skills.

cc: Barbara Darby, North Campus President

Notice the heading aligns the names, date, and subject. Also, information in the subject line should be emphasized in some way—underlining, boldfacing, or using all uppercase. Titles of individuals are best placed on the same line as the name.

The Body

The body of the memo resembles that of a letter. You may start with a purpose statement or provide some brief background information necessary to understand the message. The next section provides the gist of the document and should contain whatever essential information or data the reader needs. Finally, the conclusion of the memo should be a brief statement of thanks, or a reminder of what is to happen next. Notice that a memo does not have to be centered on the page. The body begins two or three lines below the heading and may leave considerable white space if the memo is short.

The Signature

There are several ways to sign a memorandum. Many companies prefer that the writer simply write his or her initials next to the name in the heading. Others prefer a full signature next to the name. If there is no preference, you might consider the formality of the memo; if it is simply an informational memo, or if you know there are no other employees in the company with your initials, using your initials will be appropriate. If your memo may have legal implications or others may have the same initials you have, then a signature may be required.

The memo is designed to provide brief communication within an organization. It is an efficient way to transfer information, but the writer is no less obligated to insure the accuracy of the information conveyed.

THE LETTER

The letter is generally used to convey information more formally. It is a preferred format to communicate outside the organization. While there are several letter formats that businesses may use (block, modified block, simplified), they all generally have the same basic elements. The following example is written in block format.

FLORIDA STATE COLLEGE AT JACKSONVILLE
11901 Beach Boulevard
Jacksonville, FL 32246

May 15, 2014

Ms. Judy Bradshaw
Learn to Read Jacksonville
Downtown Main Library
P.O. Box 2178, Jacksonville, FL 32203

Dear Ms. Bradshaw:

Thank you for submitting your grant proposal for Learn to Read for the 2014–2015 fiscal year. The college has received your request for $38,000, and we are working quickly to review all applications for the 2014–2015 Adult Literacy Grant.

Our grants selection committee will begin the screening of all community agency proposals no later than June 5, and a Learn to Read representative will be invited to attend that public meeting once the date and time are set. The committee's goal is to allocate 2014–2015 grant dollars to all of our community partners no later than Monday, June 16. Your agency should expect to receive any allocated dollars no later than mid-July.

Enclosed, you will find the templates for monthly tracking, mid-year reporting, and end-of-year reporting. Please send us a copy of your finalized tutor training schedule and your classroom instruction schedule by June 30.

We look forward to working with your adult learning program again in the coming year. We are very excited about the changes in adult education that are happening at the college, and our partnership with Learn to Read is an important component to meeting the adult literacy needs of our community.

Sincerely,

Margo Martin, Ed.D.
Dean of Arts and Sciences

Enclosures (3)

MM/mwk

The Heading

The business letter requires your address or that of the company and the date. All elements of the address should be spelled out with the exception of the state postal abbreviation if you use it.

The Inside Address

The inside address provides the name and address of the person or organization receiving the letter. If known, include the title and position of the person. As with the heading, avoid abbreviations except with the most common titles (Mr., Ms., Dr.). If you do not know the name of the person, you may address the letter to the company or organization. When possible, include the specific agency or department within the company to insure your letter gets delivered.

The Salutation

The salutation is common in most business letters. Use "Dear" followed by the person's title and name and a colon.

Dear Ms. Bradshaw:

If you don't know the name of the person, you may address your letter to the department or position.

Dear Adult Literacy Program:

or

Dear Director of Learn to Read Jacksonville:

Avoid using the old *"Dear Sir:"* salutation since it makes an assumption about the sex of the recipient.

The Subject Line

Often, you will find it helpful to use a subject line in order to route your letter or more clearly define its intent. The subject line begins with the word *Subject* or *Re* followed by a colon. You may also choose to place emphasis on your subject line by boldfacing, underlining, or capitalizing major words.

Subject: Confirmation of 2014–2015 Adult Literacy Grant Proposal

The Body

The body of your letter is single-spaced with double spacing between paragraphs. The opening paragraph usually introduces the subject of your letter, the middle paragraphs provide the substance, and the closing paragraph usually expresses a social message. Keep your letter personal and to the point; remember your reader is a person who responds to a natural voice. Don't lose your human tone in contrived professional language. Look at this paragraph written with the intention to impress someone:

> In reference to the aforementioned request for grant funding, I am of the opinion your organization was substandard in performance in that my reception of the report templates followed the previously agreed mailing date by several weeks. Consequently, my nonprofit organization experienced grievous curtailment of our client services due to budget deficit.

Does anyone really talk this way? Couldn't this paragraph have been better written in another way?

> The grant report templates that I requested from your organization did not arrive until two weeks after the agreed-upon mailing date; therefore, we were late in submitting our final report and have not received our fourth-quarter funding. As a result, we have been unable to provide adequate services to our clients.

It is important that the message you convey in your letter be readily understood by the reader. Use your natural voice and avoid jargon.

The Complimentary Close

Most professional letters end with the standard *"Sincerely"* followed by a comma and your signature. If you are familiar with the person you are addressing, you may use a more personal close such as *"With best regards"* or *"Yours truly."*

The Signature

Your handwritten signature appears directly above your word-processed signature. When you sign your name, make it legible. Nothing is gained by giving your reader a signature he or she cannot read; if anything, it suggests you are a disorganized individual. Place your title underneath your printed name if you are representing your organization.

> Sincerely,
>
> Margo Martin, Ed.D.
> Dean of Arts and Sciences

Additional Notations

If you enclose additional documents in your letter, you should note that in your letter after the signature. If there is only one additional item, simply use the word *"Enclosure."* If there are multiple enclosures, you may indicate the number in parentheses. You may also identify the enclosure by name:

Enclosures (3)
Enclosure: Report Template

If you did not type your letter, you should identify the typist. Your initials will appear first in uppercase by followed by a slash or colon and the typist's initials in lowercase:

MM/mwk

Another notation is required if you send copies of your letter to a secondary reader or readers. You should list them in alphabetical order. Such acknowledgement is important in legal documents since the reader has the right to know who else may have received a letter. Use a lowercase **cc** followed by a colon and the name of the person. It may also be important to list the person's title in important correspondence.

cc: C. Martin
     M. Smith

Final Notes

Your letter should be centered on the page as much as possible, with 1-to 1-1/2-inch margins at the top and 1-inch margins on the sides. If your letter is more than one page, do not use letterhead stationery for subsequent pages. Place the addressee's name at the upper left margin, the page number in the center, and the date in the right hand corner:

Judy Bradshaw 2 May 15, 2014

THE FORMAL TECHNICAL REPORT

In your profession, you may be asked to do an extended report for your employer. Reports take many forms and may be *informal* or *formal,* depending on the purpose of the assigned task. Informal reports may take the form of an incident report, an inspection analysis, a laboratory report, or a progress report. Formal reports require more careful preparation and detail, and generally follow a standard format, regardless of the purpose of the report. This format consists of seven parts arranged in a standard order: the *title page, table of contents, summary, introduction, body, conclusions,* and *recommendations*. The formal report may also have an *appendix* and *reference page* if supplementary documents are included or research is required. If the document is formally transmitted to a particular person or department, *a letter* or *memo of transmittal* may be necessary, serving as a "receipt" of contract completion. This letter will identify the purpose of the report, the content, the conclusions and recommendations, and a statement of project completion, and will accompany the report to its delivery point.

The Title Page

The title page conveys four main points of information: the *title of the report, the author of the report* (either an individual or a department or company), the *recipient's name,* and the *date the report was completed.* The placement of these items varies, though the title should be given dominant position on the page. If a visual is included on the title page, it should not detract from required elements. Note: remember, white space *is* a visual design element and should determine how your elements are presented. The title page should be clean and visually balanced, not cluttered.

REPORT FOR
BICYCLE SAFETY WORKSHOP:

FLORIDA STATE COLLEGE OF JACKSONVILLE
KENT CAMPUS

Prepared for:
Professor Stephanie Powers
Technical Report Writing Instructor
Florida State College at Jacksonville
Jacksonville, Florida

Prepared by:
Stephanie Hughes
ENC 2210 Student

February 25, 2013

The Table of Contents

The table of contents lists the contents and initial page numbers of the report, beginning with the *Summary* or, if there is no summary, the *Introduction.* Like the title page, the table of contents page should be well balanced with all elements aligned. Often, depending on the number of visual elements in your document, you can also include the *list of illustrations* on the same page as the table of contents. If you have a large number of illustrations, however, list them on a separate page.

Table of Contents

The Summary

The summary, sometimes referred to as the executive summary or abstract, is often the first element of a formal report and allows the recipient to briefly review the report's purpose, findings, conclusions, and recommendations. The summary should contain all the essential information without the visuals or lengthy discussion of the complete report. Generally, it should be no more than one page with an introductory paragraph explaining the purpose and scope of the report. A second paragraph should list the major findings, and a final paragraph should present the conclusions and recommendations.

SUMMARY

Safety among students that attend FSCJ, Kent Campus is important. Having a Bicycling Safety Workshop at Florida State College at Jacksonville (FSCJ) Kent Campus would benefit many students that attend school at this location.

The main purposes of the Bicycling Safety Workshop at FSCJ Kent Campus is to go over safety when riding a bike and to help the students to physically map out the safest possible routes to get to Kent Campus. Going over basic bicycle safety will be beneficial to students whether they are riding to school or anywhere around town.

Through the Bicycle Safety Workshop, students will meet local community bicycling advocates who will be facilitating the workshop and will find a connection with the local bicycle community. They will also gain an increased knowledge of safety measures to be taken while riding bicycles. They will be made aware of the laws governing bicycles through discussing the Florida State Bicycle Laws. This workshop will help students to physically map out safe bike routes to and from school. The students will also be given an information packet that contains many websites with helpful information as well as some important resources on bicycling in Jacksonville. There are many statistics that show how Jacksonville is a dangerous place to be a cyclist. A survey administered to Kent Campus students revealed that students are interested in participating in a Bicycle Safety Workshop and that there is a concern among students about the safety of riding bicycles in Jacksonville.

This workshop will be free, facilitated by local bicycle community leaders who have committed to donating their time to teach the workshop. If a room is unavailable for the workshop to take place, then it shall be held in the Kent Campus courtyard. This arrangement will ensure that the cost of the workshop is absolutely free to students and the Kent Campus.

The Introduction

The introduction section may include a number of elements, including a *background* or *history* section, a *scope* section, and a *procedure* statement.

The background or history statement presents the origins of the problem being studied, pointing out important elements leading up to the current study. The background statement can be helpful in understanding the parameters of the problem and the significance of the study and recommendations.

A scope statement defines the limits of the study. In a particularly complex problem, the report may deal with only one aspect, leaving other areas for future studies and recommendations. In a business setting, the scope statement may clearly delineate the contractual agreement, insuring there is no misunderstanding about what the report's recommendations cover.

The Discussion

The discussion is the body of the report and is usually divided into *criterion* sections. These criteria are usually defined in the table of contents and serve as headings for each of the sections in the discussion. Since the discussion is the content of the report and is the major part of the report's preparation, it is often done first, with the other report elements (the *summary, introduction,* and *table of contents*) done afterwards. Note, too, that most of your visuals are placed within the discussion.

In your discussion, remember that all visuals must be cited *before* they appear in your document. The citation should include an introductory remark and a brief explanation of what the reader will see in the visual. Refer to all visuals as either a *Figure* or a *Table*. Tables are textual explanations laid out in a logical and accessible format. Figures are photographs, diagrams, charts, or graphs that depict the textual information symbolically. There are a number of ways to introduce your visual. For example, you might begin with a tag line such as the following:

> "As you can see in Appendix A, the *National Alliance for Biking and Walking 2012 Benchmark Report*, there are still many cyclist injuries that happen around the city. Here are a few statistics for Florida and Jacksonville ..."
>
> or
>
> Appendix A, the *National Alliance for Biking and Walking 2012 Benchmark Report*, shares statistics for Florida and Jacksonville, demonstrating that there are still many cyclist injuries that happen around the city.

Whatever pattern you use, be sure to cite the table, figure number or appendix number and tell the reader what is significant. Most importantly, after you cite your visual in the text, place the visual immediately afterwards. Readers don't enjoy having a visual cited on page 4 appearing four or five pages later in the discussion.

Another important thing to remember in your discussion is to cite all your sources of information, just as you would in a formal research paper. Citing your references may require you to add a *references* page at the end of your report, an element that would also be listed in your table of contents.

The Conclusions

Following your discussion, most reports require you to draw some conclusions based on the data. These conclusions appear on a separate page immediately after the discussion section, and the conclusions should address each of the criteria you discussed. For example, if your discussion sections consist of three topics: the *Bicycling Statistics, Student Survey,* and *The Workshop,* you should draw conclusions for each of these four sections. The conclusions can be written in bullet format or as paragraphs, but there should be at least one conclusion for each of the areas discussed.

The Recommendations

The final required element of your formal report is usually a recommendation page, which presents the report's findings on a course of action. If the purpose of your report is to decide which sites should be developed under the existing evacuation plan and which sites might be developed with a modified plan, your recommendations should address those decisions, based on the study of the two plans and the costs involved in both (assuming the company asked you to do a cost analysis). A recommendation might be positive or negative; many reports recommend a project not go forward based on the report's findings (too speculative, too costly, politically unfeasible). Formal technical reports provide businesses and agencies with the information and recommendations on which to base their final actions; consequently, the reliability and integrity of the report are critical. Technical reports should be as honest and as factual as possible.

Following is a sample technical report using the format presented in this discussion. While the formal report is only one model of the many kinds of technical reports you may be asked to write, it is a standard format common to many. A number of excellent technical writing books are available today, and the Internet offers a wide variety of models and resources for you to explore. Check with your librarian or instructor if you have particular questions or if you need help finding a technical writing reference document to assist you in your business writing.

Report for
Bicycle Safety Workshop:
Florida State College of Jacksonville
Kent Campus

for
Professor Stephanie Powers
Technical Report Writing Instructor
Florida State College at Jacksonville
Jacksonville, Florida

by
Stephanie Hughes
ENC 2210 Student

February 25, 2013

Table of Contents

Abstract

Safety among students that attend Florida State College at Jacksonville (FSCJ), Kent Campus is important. Having a Bicycling Safety Workshop at FSCJ, Kent Campus would benefit many students that attend school at this location.

The main purposes of the Bicycling Safety Workshop at FSCJ Kent Campus are to review safety procedures when riding a bike and to help students map out physically the safest possible routes to get to Kent Campus. Going over basic bicycle safety will be beneficial to students whether they are riding to school or anywhere around town.

Through the Bicycle Safety Workshop, students will meet local community bicycling advocates who will be facilitating the workshop and will find a connection with the local bicycle community. They will also gain an increased knowledge of safety measures to be taken while riding bicycles. They will be made aware of the laws governing bicycles through discussing the Florida State Bicycle Laws. This workshop will help students to physically map out safe bike routes to and from school. The students will also be given an information packet that contains many Web sites with helpful information as well as some important resources on bicycling in Jacksonville. There are many statistics that show how Jacksonville is a dangerous place for a cyclist. A survey administered to Kent Campus students revealed that students are interested in participating in a Bicycle Safety Workshop and that there is a concern among students about the safety of riding bicycles in Jacksonville.

This workshop will be free, facilitated by local bicycle community leaders who have committed to donating their time to teach the workshop. If a room is unavailable for the workshop to take place, then it shall be held in the Kent Campus courtyard. This arrangement will ensure that the cost of the workshop is absolutely free to students and the Kent Campus.

Introduction

Jacksonville, Florida, is the largest city by area in Florida and the contiguous United States; it is also the largest city in Florida by population. As population grows, along with public awareness of the importance of living more sustainably, many people are seeking out alternative means of transportation rather than driving personal vehicles. Many people do walk to where they need to go, but because Jacksonville is spread out, a large number of people choose to ride a bicycle.

Many students ride a bicycle to FSCJ's Kent Campus. Riding a bike has many health benefits as well as financial pluses. For some students though, finding the safest route to school can be quite a challenge. Many students choose to take their vehicles to school instead of their bicycles because of the risks involved in bicycling. Many students have never been told about what safety measures they should take when riding a bicycle.

Steven Tocknell, chairman of Jacksonville's Bicycle and Pedestrian Advisory Committee under the city's planning department, has stated that a significant part of the problem [cyclists' safety] is the lack of bike lanes. If the city did increase the amount of bike lanes, that would help to improve the quality of bicycling in Jacksonville; however, students should be prepared on how to properly use those lanes.

What would the workshop entail?

- Meet local bicycle community advocates who will be facilitating the workshop
- Make connections to the local bicycle community
- Learn safety procedures while riding a bicycle
- Learn Florida State Bicycling Laws
- Gain assistance from local bicycle community leaders in mapping out the safest routes to school from students' homes
- Get an information packet containing important bicycle information and resources

These key points will increase bicycling safety for students at Kent Campus through this free workshop. The workshop will be led by experienced community leaders, and they give students some helpful knowledge that will increase their safety while riding a bicycle.

Data Collection

Bicycling Statistics

There are many efforts to increase safety and awareness for cyclists in Jacksonville; most are facilitated by community-based groups that advocate bicycling. Despite their gracious and heroic efforts to make Jacksonville more "bike-friendly," there are still many cyclist injuries that happen around the city. Statistics for Florida in general and Jacksonville in particular can be found in Appendix A, the *National Alliance for Biking and Walking 2012 Benchmark Report*:

- Between 2006 and 2010, 534 bicyclists died in traffic crashes on Florida roads and highways, and 3,744 were seriously injured (Florida Department of Transportation).

- Some people will not ride bicycles on busier roadways, even where lane-sharing with motor vehicles is not necessary, and strongly prefer to ride on sidewalks or paths. Where sidewalk riding is allowed, it is not necessarily safe or convenient (Florida Department of Transportation, 2012).

- "In 2008, in Jacksonville, Florida alone, there were 566 pedestrians and bicyclists who were hit by vehicles in 2008. Of this number, 20 died from the accident-related personal injuries. In 2009, these figures rose to 604 pedestrians and bicyclists who were hit by a vehicle with 29 dying from accident-related injuries. The Jacksonville Sheriff's Office also maintains statistics as to injuries and fatalities. According to JSO, there have been 124 bicycle riders and pedestrians who have been killed in Duval County since 2006" (Larry Hannan, *Florida Times-Union*, 2010).

- Jacksonville ranked as the third-worst large city for safest places for biking (National Alliance for Biking and Walking Benchmark Report, 2012, p. 52).

- Jacksonville is considered one of the least-safe major cities for bicycling with 14.2 bicyclists killed per 10,000 daily bicyclists, respectively (*National Alliance for Biking and Walking Benchmark Report*, 2012, p. 53).

These statistics prove a clear point, that Jacksonville is a dangerous place to ride bicycles. With the workshop, students will learn about ways to prevent accidents and to ensure their safety. This knowledge will benefit not only the individual student, but also the city of Jacksonville as well since it will help students to be safe cyclists.

(See Appendix A for full *National Alliance for Biking and Walking 2012 Benchmark Report*.)

5

Student Survey

During my research, I created a survey to administer at Kent Campus to assess the feasibility of student participation in the Bicycle Workshop. After conducting the survey, I analyzed the results. To ensure a broad range of participants, the students were chosen at random on four different days of the week, at different times of the day, and in different locations around Kent Campus. Following are the survey questions and the analyzed results.

All questions were answered in Yes/No/NA (not applicable) format:

1. Do you currently own a bicycle?
2. Do you ride a bicycle to FSCJ Kent Campus on regular basis (two or more times a week)?
3. Are you familiar with bicycle safety procedures?
4. If you do ride a bicycle to school, do you feel the route you currently take is safe?
5. If there were a free Bicycle Workshop available at FSCJ Kent Campus that went over bicycle safety procedures and that helped you map out the safest route for you to take to school, would you be interested in attending?
6. If you own a bicycle, would you be more inclined to ride a bicycle to school after attending the workshop?
7. Do you feel like Jacksonville is a "bike-friendly" city?

Survey Results:
Total number of students that filled out survey: 50

Question No.	No. of Students That Answered Yes	No. of Students That Answered No	No. of Students That Answered N/A
1	34	16	0
2	23	11	16
3	8	41	1
4	2	21	17
5	39	7	4
6	33	1	16
7	4	45	1

6

Summary of Survey Results:

- Of the students surveyed, 68% own a bicycle.
- Out of the students who <u>do</u> own bikes, 67.6% of them ride them to FSCJ Kent Campus two or more times a week.
- Of <u>all</u> the students surveyed, 82% were not familiar with bicycle safety procedures.
- Of <u>all</u> the students surveyed, 78% said they would be interested in attending the Bicycle Safety Workshop, including the 16 students who do not even own a bike.
- Out of the students that <u>do</u> own a bicycle, 97% said they would be more inclined to ride a bicycle to school after attending the workshop.
- Only 8% of <u>all</u> the students surveyed answered "Yes" they felt like Jacksonville is a "bike-friendly" city.

From the data collected through surveying students at Kent Campus, there is evidence that many students (even those without bicycles) are interested in attending a Bicycle Safety Workshop. Since such a low number of students are aware of bicycle safety procedures, this class will be very beneficial to students who have no prior knowledge of what bicycle safety procedures are. Also, since such a high number (97%) of students who own bicycles said that they would be more inclined to ride a bicycle to school after attending the workshop, this result shows that a Bicycle Safety Workshop would greatly benefit those students who own bikes.

Many students (16 out of 50) do not currently own bicycles. Since there will be interactions and communication with local bike community leaders through the Bicycle Safety Workshop, there is a possibility that the students without bikes could get some assistance with obtaining one. Helping to find students a bicycle is great possibility that will be beneficial to students who do not currently own one, or students who have bicycles that are not in serviceable condition. The facilitators of the workshop have access to many resources that participate in community events, where many bicycles and bicycle parts are donated.

The Bicycle Safety Workshop

The workshop will cover five main topics: Connecting with the Local Bicycle Community, Practicing Safety Measures for Riding Bicycles, Understanding Florida State Bicycle Laws, Finding Safe Bike Routes for Students, and other Learning about Helpful Information and Important Resources.

Connecting with the Local Bicycling Community
Facilitators of the Bicycle Safety Workshop:

- Harley Henry, Cofounder of The Jacksonville Bicycle Coalition, Local Bicycle Community Event Advisor, Bicycle Advocate
- Troy Sharpe, Founder of The Skids Bicycle Association, Creator of the 24-Hour help line for bicyclists—(904)-458-SKID, Local Bicycle Community Event Coordinator, Bike Advocate
- Stephanie Hughes, Community Organizer for Local Bicycling Events, Author of this Formal Report for a Bicycle Safety Workshop for FSCJ-Kent Campus

Local Bicycling Community Connections
Mr. Henry, Mr. Troy, and I are very involved with the bicycling community in Jacksonville. We all currently reside in Riverside and attend Kent Campus. When presented with the idea of a workshop to educate students on bicycling safety at Kent Campus, these community leaders agreed to donate their time and to help facilitate the workshop.

Although we have never done a workshop like this at Kent Campus, after interviewing both Mr. Henry and Mr. Sharpe, we are all confident that the workshop will be a successful event. Past community bicycling events that we have collaborated on include Weekly Organized bike rides through Downtown, Riverside, and Murray Hill neighborhoods; the Annual Duval Bike Olympics; Jacksonville Bike Polo Tournaments, and many more. All of these events were fun and educational for the community and local cyclists.

Through this workshop, students will be given a list of this year's local community bicycling events. There are weekly, monthly, and yearly events that the students will be made aware of and invited to. All of these opportunities will connect the students with fellow cyclists and give them a chance to get involved with the local bicycling community. The workshop will be connecting students to the bicycling community around the Jacksonville area, and through those connections they can make friends, meet other bicyclists, and plan future events.

8

Safety Measures for Riding Bicycles

Key safety measures for riding in or around traffic that will be covered in detail during the workshop include (but not limited to) the following strategies:

- Cyclists should always wear helmets.
- Cyclists on the road should act and be treated as if they were driving a vehicle. This strategy is important because it will increase the cyclist's visibility to motorists.
- A cyclist is safer when riding with the flow of traffic rather than facing into traffic.
- Cyclists who ride their bicycles facing into oncoming traffic increase their risk of getting hit by a vehicle by two to four times.
- Cyclists should stay alert and be aware of the traffic and obstacles around them.
- Cyclists should wear clothes that make them more visible (light colors). Avoid wearing very loose clothing, as it can get caught in the bicycle's moving parts.
- Cyclists should always have reflectors and bicycle lights on the rear and front of the bike.
- Cyclists should follow rules for riding in groups and understand how group riding differs from riding alone.
- Cyclists should protect their bikes from theft by locking bikes and should learn and practice preventative measures that reduce the likelihood of theft.
- A cyclist should ensure that the bike is adjusted to fit him or her. Feet should rest on the ground while in the seated position. Brakes should be working correctly. Handlebars should be firmly set in place. Wheels should be full of air with no bubbles in tire tubing; wheels should also be straight and secure in place.
- A cyclist should always use hand signals when slowing down, stopping, or making left/right turns.

All of these rules and tips will be shown visually to the students. Through demonstration of all of these key safety measures and explanations as to why they are important to bicycling safety, the students will have a thorough understanding of bicycling safety procedures. These safety guidelines have been adapted from the Florida Bicycling Association's user's manual, *"Bicycling Street Smarts: Riding Confidently, Legally, and safely"* (see Appendix B).

9

Florida State Laws for Bicycling

During the Bicycle Safety Workshop, the facilitators will cover some of the important laws that the State of Florida has put in place regarding cyclists.

Bicycle Drivers and the Florida Uniform Traffic Control Law as set forth in Chapter 316 of the Florida Statues will be discussed. These are the important points that are governed by this code (see Appendix B for full Bicycle Drivers and the Florida Uniform Traffic Control Law):

- Bicycle is classified as a vehicle
- Lighting equipment
- Brakes
- Wearing of headsets
- Carrying a passenger
- Use of helmet
- Driving on right side of roadway and roadway position
- Yielding and other Traffic Laws for all drivers
- Not driving under the influence
- Riding two abreast
- Signaling a turn or stop
- Riding on a sidewalk or crosswalk

The *Florida Bicycle Law Enforcement Guide,* 12th edition, from the Florida Bicycle Association (cited from the 2012 Florida Statues) will also be discussed during the Bicycle Safety Workshop. This resource will show students what laws will be enforced and what is considered a violation (see Appendix C for full copy of the Florida Bicycle Law Enforcement Guide).

- Challenge of bicycle traffic enforcement
- Legal status of cyclist
- Equipment and Passengers
- Laws for all drivers (motorists and cyclists)
- Laws for bicycle drivers
- Laws for sidewalk riders: operating as a pedestrian
- Bicycle crash investigation
- When is a lane shareable

This workshop will give a full scope on what the law expects from cyclists. It will benefit the students' safety by making them aware of current laws that are in place to protect and ensure the safety of cyclists.

Finding Safe Bike Routes for Students

An important aspect of the Bicycle Safety Workshop for students at Kent Campus is for the participants to receive assistance from the workshop facilitators to find safe bike routes to Kent Campus. In the survey, 39 out of 50 participants answered "Yes," that they were interested in attending a free Bicycle Workshop at Kent Campus that explained bicycle safety procedures and that helped to map out the safest route to take to school (see Student Survey page 4).

It is important to know safety procedures and the laws that the State of Florida has in place for bicycles, but it is just as important to know the safest bicycle routes between the school and the students' homes.

How will it work?

The students who attend the Bicycle Safety Workshop will have a form to complete, requesting the facilitators to help them to find a safe route(s) to and from Kent Campus. The facilitators will use maps, GPS, and personal knowledge as experienced riders of the neighborhoods around Kent Campus and Jacksonville to figure out the safest route(s) for the student to travel. This task may take up to a week or longer to identify the safest possible route(s) to and from school for the students; therefore, the form will have a place for the students to give the facilitators their contact information. After the facilitators have mapped out the students' individual route(s), they will contact the students with that information.

The students do not need to give their actual home address. Any landmark close to their home will suffice. This process will ensure the students' privacy. Also, the facilitators will ride the routes to ensure that they are the safest possible ways for students to travel.

Helpful Information and Important Resources

A copy of the essay titled *"The Path Less Paved"* will be submitted to the school's newspaper, *The Campus Voice,* to be published along with the date and time of the workshop, pending approval of the workshop (see Appendix D). The purpose of the essay is to get students interested in riding bicycles to school and attending the free Bicycle Safety Workshop.

Additionally, there are many Web sites that have reliable and helpful information for cyclists. At the end of the workshop, the students will be given an information packet with a list of Web sites and other helpful information and important resources that students can use.

11

Websites

- www.floridabicyle.org
  The Florida Bicycle Association—Advocating a bicycle-friendly Florida. We envision a state where people of all ages see bicycling as an enjoyable, practical, and safe activity and transportation option, and where all who lawfully use the roadways, motorists, and bicyclists alike, respect and appreciate each other's use.

- www.pedbikesrc.ce.ufl.edu
  Florida's Pedestrian and Bicycling Safety Resource Center—Promotes safe pedestrian and bicycling activities for citizens and visitors, young, and old, by providing educational materials and information to advocate groups in the state.

- www.bikejax.org
  Bike Jax—Our mission is to establish Jacksonville as a city that is increasingly safe, accessible, and friendly to bicycle transportation.

- www.nfbc.us
  North Florida Bicycle Club—Our mission as the North Florida Bicycle Club is to encourage all people to participate in bicycling—a fun activity that can be recreation, transportation, fitness, and competition. We serve the North Florida community in promoting safer conditions for cyclists and other road/trail users. We are committed to support bicycling through social activities, education, and leadership by example and civic involvement.

- www.jaxbikecoalition.org
  The Jacksonville Bicycle Coalition—Fighting for Our Right-of-Way: A Duval-based order advocating for the rights of cyclists.

- www.bikesbelong.org
  Bikes Belong—From helping create safe places to ride to promoting bicycling, we carefully select projects and partnerships that have the capacity to make a difference.

12

Contacts

- Florida Department of Transportation—Safe Routes To School
  Tony Nosse, P.E.
  Safety Engineer
  anthony.nosse@dot.state.fl.us
  (386)-943-5334

- Joan Carter
  Pedestrian/Bicycle Coordinator
  joan.carter@dot.state.fl.us
  (386)-943-5335

- 24-Hr Bicycle Helpline
  The Skids Bicycle Association
  (904) 458-SKID

- Jacksonville Fire and Rescue Department
  For non-emergency
  (904) 630-0434

- Jacksonville Sheriff's Office
  (904) 630-0500

- For Emergency Assistance
  Dial 911

- Florida Bicycle Association
  PO Box 916715
  Longwood, FL 32791-6715
  Phone: (850)-238-5328

- Safety Office
  Florida Department of Transportation
  Tallahassee, FL 32399-0450
  (850)-245-1500
  (800)-828-7655

- Florida's Pedestrian & Bicycling
  Safety Resource Center
  2114 NE Waldo Rd, Gainesville, FL 32609
  352-273-1680

13

Conclusion

Summary of Findings

Jacksonville is a dangerous place for bicyclists. There are, however, many preventative measures people can take to try to ensure their safety while riding a bicycle. Many students feel that Jacksonville is not a "bike-friendly" city and are interested in finding out how to ensure their safety when riding their bicycles to school.

Interpretation of Findings

Based on all the information documented in this Formal Report, there is a clear need for action to be taken to protect students who bicycle to FSCJ's Kent Campus. It is not only beneficial to the city's status as the third-worst large city for bicyclists, but also to the overall health and safety of students who use a bicycle to commute to school.

Recommendations

By having a free Bicycle Safety Workshop at Kent Campus, students will be exposed to useful safety procedures for bicycle riding. The students will also benefit from an awareness of the laws that are designed to protect cyclists in the State of Florida. They will also receive aid in finding safe bike routes between school and home. Students will additionally meet with local bicycle advocates and leaders of the Jacksonville bicycling community. Students will receive free informational packets that include helpful cycling resources.

Having a free Bicycle Safety Workshop for students who attend Kent Campus will be the most cost-effective and practical way to educate the students on bicycling safety.

Appendix "A"
Reports Available
National Alliance for Biking and Walking 2012 Benchmark Report

15

Appendix "B"
User's Manual
Florida Bicycling Street Smarts Riding Confidently, Legally, and Safely

16

Appendix "C"
Report Available
Florida Bicycle Law Enforcement Guide

17

Appendix "D"
Path Less Paved
By Stephanie Hughes

Have you ever been late for work or school because of a traffic jam or because your car broke down? Have you ever seen grey smoke billowing from the car in front of you or wished you didn't have to smell those nauseating fumes while filling your gas tank? How often do you notice yourself turning up the radio to drown out the honking and beeping of the cars around you? Many people begin their day with the frustrations of rush hour traffic. Imagine starting the day with the sight of blooming flowers, the scent of fresh cut grass, and the sounds of chirping birds on the journey to your destination. Riding a bike rather than taking a vehicle is not only more peaceful and aesthetically pleasing, it is better for your wallet, health, and the environment.

Using a bicycle for transportation can be beneficial to your bank account. The expenses associated with owning a bike are low in comparison to the insurance, oil changes, new tires, and car payments that accompany the ownership of a car or truck. With a bike you only need to fill up on water, unlike a car with gas and oil. If you consider the recent prices of gas, that alone can save a tremendous amount of money. Also, there are no payments associated with purchasing a bicycle; they are usually bought all at once and are drastically cheaper than purchasing a car. A set of bike tires can last years, and there is no need to rotate them, unlike a car. The overall maintenance of a bike is considerably less than a vehicle. You can save a truck load of money by not driving a truck!

Many people in today's fast-paced world have hardly any time to exercise. By simply biking to work or school you can kill two birds with one stone. Bicycling is considered to be a low-impact exercise that people of all ages can enjoy. On an average, people burn more than 30 calories riding a bike just one mile, which are more calories than walking out the front door to the car. There is also the concept that adding one healthy activity to your life will lead to other healthy lifestyle choices. When riding a bike people are less likely to get food from a drive-thru, and more likely to drink water; which is really healthy for you and can definitely benefit the waistline. It is easy to get stuck in a rut, so if you can take the "Where are my keys?" out of the morning routine and replace it with "Where is my bike lock?", then you are well on your way to living a healthier lifestyle.

Riding a bicycle is a fun alternative to driving that is good for our bodies and our planet. Vehicles are a major source of air and noise pollution that can be reduced with your help! Every car that is taken off the road, even for just a few hours or days a week, helps to reduce the growing amount of automobile pollution.

The environment is struggling to keep up with the amount of carbon emissions coming from the tailpipes of cars and trucks. The burning of fossil fuel is increasing the temperature of the atmosphere and will continue to do so. We only have one precious Earth, so we need to take good care of it.

There are many reasons why the health benefits and aesthetic value of using a bicycle for transportation outweigh the expenses and environmental degradation of driving a personal vehicle. The amount of money to be saved by is probably the biggest reason for most people to give up their car keys; but for me the health benefits and reducing pollution keep me pedaling instead of pumping gas. The memorable sights and sounds of my trips to school make every bike ride more enjoyable than the last one. Everyone should try the "bike" path less traveled; it will make all the difference.

References

Allen, John S. (2001). *Bicycling Street Smarts: Riding Confidently, Legally, and Safely.* Retrieved from http://www.floridabicycle.org/resources/pdfs/StreetSmartsintro_2012.pdf

Florida Department of Transportation. (2012, August). *Florida Bicycle Law Enforcement Guide.* Retrieved from http://www.floridabicycle.org/resources/pdfs/PEGLEG_2012.pdf

Hannan, Larry (2010, April 6). *Drivers an increasing danger for bicyclists and pedestrians in Jacksonville.* Retrieved from http://mayportmirror.jacksonville.com/news/metro/2010-04-05/story/jacksonville-pedestrians-and-cyclists-struggle-avoid-getting-hitch

National Alliance for Biking and Walking. (2012). *National Alliance for Biking and Walking 2012 Benchmark Report.* Retrieved from http://www.bikewalkalliance.org/resources/benchmarking

▼ WRITING THE RESUME

Most of you are currently in school seeking a degree that will ultimately lead you to a profession of your choice. Whether you are planning to be an educator, a lawyer, an engineer, or a scientist, to get the job of your choice you are more than likely going to go through a hiring process. Getting hired entails gathering your credentials, submitting applications, and being interviewed, and you may have to experience this process a number of times before you are successfully employed. Many job seekers dread the experience, but if you are prepared, persistent, and patient (the three *Ps* of job hunting!), the process can be a positive one for you.

One of your first tasks is to prepare your application materials, which usually include a *letter of application* and/or a *resume.* Remember, the purpose of both these written documents is not to get you immediately employed, but instead to get you to an interview. Most potential employers use the letter of application or the resume to make the first critical cut of applicants, so it is imperative that these documents truly represent you in the best way.

THE LETTER OF APPLICATION

Before starting the letter of application, examine the advertisement for the job in which you are interested. The advertisement will state what skills and abilities the employer is seeking. For example, the employer may require a bachelor's degree and three years of supervisory training, as well as knowledge of numerous software applications. Your success in getting the position will depend on your ability to match *your* skills with the employer's needs. Use the terms in the advertisement to construct your letter of application.

Like the business letter, the letter of application has an *introduction,* a *body,* and a *closing.* The introduction paragraph should be a brief statement informing the employer what position you are seeking, how you became aware of the position, and a brief summary of your basic qualifications.

> I am seeking the position of General Manager at the Inn and Club at Ponte Vedra that was recently advertised on the jobs.jacksonville.com website last week. I am confident my educational background, my past supervisory experience as a hotel catering manager, and my proven communication skills make me an excellent candidate for the job.

The second section, the body, may be several paragraphs long and should match your skills and abilities with the stated needs of the employer. Provide the necessary details that will convince the employer that you are, indeed, not only qualified for the position, but that you are the preferred candidate. If the advertisement says the position requires a bachelor's degree, spend a paragraph detailing what degree you have, where your degree was obtained, and what courses and experiences you had in acquiring that degree that directly relate to the job requirements.

> I received my bachelor of business administration degree in Hospitality Management from the Florida Atlantic University in December 2010 and took extensive coursework in personnel management, hotels and resort management, and meetings and events management. Additionally, I did my field experience in hospitality management at the Boca Raton Resort & Club, a Waldorf Astoria property, working as a supervisor-trainee in their personnel department.

If the job requires at least three years of supervisory training, your letter should outline your job experience, with emphasis on the supervisory responsibilities inherent in each position.

> In the summer of 2011, I was employed full-time by Marriott Hotels as Manager of Catering Services at the Marriott at Sawgrass, supervising a staff of 45 employees. In the spring of 2013, I was promoted to the position of Senior Manager of Catering Services at the hotel, and have remained in that position to date, with responsibility for supervising a staff of more than 100 employees.

Finally, if the position calls for specific computer or other technical skills, list the skills that directly relate to the position.

> My current job requires me to be proficient and current in all the latest computer and telecommunication software related to hotel management. I recently attended a week-long training session in the new XXX personnel records system and will be implementing the program at the Marriott at Sawgrass in the next few weeks. The new system is expected to reduce the processing time for new employees by over 30%, saving the company considerable expense.

Your conclusion should be brief, requesting an interview and stating ways you can be reached.

> I would like to have the opportunity to meet with you to discuss my qualifications for the position of General Manager. You can reach me during the day at (904) 666-5897, Ext. 445, or on my mobile phone at (904) 653-8854. I believe I can contribute a great deal to the resort management needs at the Inn and Club at Ponte Vedra, and I look forward to meeting with you soon.

THE RESUME

Recent advances in workplace technology and practice have changed the way most employers go about the business of screening and hiring personnel. One very visible change has been in the way resumes are formatted. While the information in the resume has remained basically the same, the new technologies available to the applicant allow him or her to adjust the content of the resume to meet the requirements of each job for which he or she is applying. As a result, the applicant can basically construct a different resume for each job application, emphasizing personal qualities and achievements specific to the job requirements.

RESUME CONTENT

There are two basic types of resumes, the *traditional* and the *functional*. A traditional resume is preferred if you are a recent graduate of high school or college and are seeking a job in a profession for which you were trained. A functional resume is more effective for an individual who has a wide range of job experiences or who has had little or no college training. Both types of resumes, though, have some basic elements in common.

CONTACT INFORMATION

Your name and address are critical elements and should be placed at the top of the page. Use boldface and a larger font than in the text to increase visibility. Be sure the address and phone number are current so that a potential employer will have no problem reaching you.

Career Objective

A career objective statement is no longer required in a resume, but it can be effective if it addresses precisely your career goal. Avoid making meaningless statements about seeking opportunities for personal growth or professional challenges; if you want to be a veterinary assistant, state that as your career goal.

Employment History

You need to include your work history, listing your jobs in reverse chronological order. Be sure you identify the specific job title you held, the name and location of the employer or company, the dates of your employment, and the job duties. Do *not* leave any major gaps in your work history. Be honest in your explanation of those gaps; if you were out of work a year for severe depression, state that temporary medical problems kept you from working. You need not go into detail; you can always address the issue more thoroughly if it comes up in an interview.

Education

If you have attended college, you need to list your educational experience. Do not list your high school graduation date unless you have no college experience. Be sure to include the degree you are seeking or have received, the name of the school and its location, and the years attended. You may also include your grade point average if it is notable, any academic honors or special recognitions, and any coursework that might be relevant to the job you are seeking. As with your work experience, explain any breaks in your education chronology. If you took a year off to work so that you could pay for your tuition, state that.

Personal Information

You may decide not to include this section, though it may be useful to include if you have some unique qualities that might prove helpful. For example, you might be fluent in a foreign language, know American Sign Language, or have some unique hobbies or recreational skills such as being an accomplished pianist or holding a black belt in martial arts. Don't include this section in your resume unless the personal data truly sets you apart and is relevant to the job you are seeking. Note: do not include your sex, religion, birthdate, marital status, or a picture of yourself. Employees cannot use these pieces of information in considering your qualifications.

References

You need to maintain a list of references, but need not include these in your resume. Many contemporary resume writers leave this section out altogether, opting to have a separate list available "upon request" or covering the information in the reference section of most job application forms. Remember that your references should not be relatives and should be included only if they can give you a positive evaluation. If you had a bad experience with a previous employer, he or she will probably not provide a good reference for you.

RESUME STYLE

Generally, resumes are written in "bullet" format, using lists and phrases instead of complete sentences. When you cite your work experience or accomplishments, use active verbs to begin your statement, as follows:

- Directed three major research projects in a two-year period

- Managed several departments and four separate task forces

- Supervised 58 full-time employees

- Operated eight-wheeled transportation vehicles

- Completed advanced CPR training

- Implemented a successful employee orientation program

- Initiated contacts with major corporate partners

- Organized a 3-day departmental leadership retreat for 60 staff members

- Trained all incoming computer assistants for the corporate headquarters

Whenever possible, quantify the activity. Providing specific information allows the potential employer to understand more clearly the requirements of the task and to relate your accomplishments specifically to the requirements of the job for which you are applying.

Another important element of your resume is the effective use of "white space." Remember, your reader needs to be able to look at your document quickly and easily. You don't want to pack it with long sentences or give too much detail so that the reader has difficulty finding the specific information he or she needs to determine your qualifications. Often, the resume is screened strictly for educational qualifications, or the reader only needs to know that you have supervisory experience. A clearly formatted resume, grouped in the major sections mentioned earlier and separated by white space, will allow the employer to find the information he or she needs quickly and effectively.

THE FUNCTIONAL RESUME

If you have no traditional educational training, but have work skills that are necessary for the job you are seeking, use the functional resume format. Start with listing your *Professional Skills* instead of your education or work history. These professional skills might include key skills you can perform, special training you've received on the job, leadership and management skills you've demonstrated, manuals or techniques you've developed on the job, and any special recognition or awards you've been given for your services. Include any professional affiliations such as professional or service clubs, unions or business associations. If you have military service experience, you may want to list a separate *Military Service* section. The branch of service, the dates you served, your record of promotions, and any special training or responsibilities you acquired would be components for this section.

Look at the following examples of effective traditional (reverse chronology) and functional resumes:

Traditional (Reverse Chronology) Resume

ROMANA LOPES
12209 Rocky Ridge Road
Jacksonville, FL 32217
(904)555-5359
RomanaLopes@hotmail.com

OBJECTIVE
To provide support in an executive-level office setting in higher education.

EDUCATION	**August/2012**

B.S. Degree, Social Science
B.S. Degree, Sociology
Florida State University

WORK EXPERIENCE

Pathways Academy, Jacksonville, FL	**July 2012–Present**

- Oversee and maintain the financial budget utilizing Orion software.
- Purchase equipment and supplies for the Academy.
- Train and support clerical administrators.
- Utilize proprietary software to verify student information; inform and assist parents and students through the application process while specifying specific requirements needed for acceptance into the Pathways program.

Florida State College Jacksonville, FL	**July 2008 to July 2012**

- Assisted the Dean of Liberal Arts in managing various disciplines within the department.
- Performed all clerical responsibilities with the utmost discretion concerning personnel and student issues.
- Compiled, collected, and presented data; maintained and balanced numerous budgets.
- Acted as a liaison between faculty, adjuncts, and students.

Florida Community College, Jacksonville, FL	**March 2006 to June 2008**

- Assisted the Associate Dean of Communication in managing the department.
- Performed clerical responsibilities which included creating reports, maintaining records, and encoding classes.
- Prepared for and helped facilitate meetings.

Florida Times Union Newspaper, Jacksonville, FL   **May 2003 to March 2006**
- Contacted customers concerning delinquent status of classified accounts and assisted in resolving problems or discrepancies utilizing PBS invoicing software.
- Responded to customer correspondences.
- Communicated with advertising agents and supervisors on customer-related matters.

Georgia Pacific Corp, Jacksonville, FL   **September 2000 to March 2003**
- Reconciled customer accounts utilizing Infinium accounting software and researched discrepancies.
- Electronically pulled wire transmissions from various banks.
- Trained employees and facilitated meetings.

Old Dominion University, Norfolk, VA   **October 1994 to May 1998**
- Scheduled production jobs via Control-M software.
- Created reports and troubleshot errors utilizing JCL.
- Verified schedule's accuracy.
- Managed year-end processing.
- Served as relief computer operator and helpdesk.

ACTIVITIES AND RECOGNITIONS
- Volunteer, Women Build, Beaches Habitat for Humanity 2011–2012.
- Volunteer, Learn To Read 2009–2011.
- Volunteer, Second Harvest Food Bank 2009.
- Employee of the Month Award, FSCJ South Campus October 2009.

REFERENCES
Available upon request

Functional Resume

REBEKAH TROTTER
1907 Elm Street
Jacksonville, FL 32202
(904) 555-1704
Btrotter1999@gmail.com

OBJECTIVE
To secure a position as an executive assistant in a high-tech company in Northeast Florida.

PROFESSIONAL SKILLS
- Analyze, review, compute, record, and proofread data and other information, such as records or reports.
- Prepare memos, letters, invoices, reports, financial statements, expense reports, and other documents, using word processing, spreadsheet, database, or presentation software.
- Manage and maintain multiple executives' schedules, and coordinate events for committee, board, and other meetings.
- Operate office equipment and troubleshoot problems such as computer hardware, software, copiers, printers, scanners, fax machines, and phone systems.
- Perform at a highly organized and detail-oriented level, self-directed with strong administrative and PC skills.
- Demonstrate excellent customer service and written and verbal communication skills.
- Work independently with minimal supervision, multitask, and interact with all levels of management with strict confidentiality.
- Use an array of software with high proficiency: Microsoft Office (Windows 7, 2010, Vista, XP): Word, Excel, Outlook, PowerPoint, Publisher, Access, Visio, Lotus Notes, OnTime Bug Tracking, Ilient Helpdesk, Adobe Acrobat and Reader, and AS400.

WORK EXPERIENCE

Student Assistant	FSCJ, South Campus	2013-Present
Temporary Administrative Assistant	Snelling Staffing	2006–2013
Temporary Sr. Staff Assistant	FSCJ, South Campus	2012
Transportation Clerk	Harte Hanks, Inc.	2007–2008
Administrative Assistant—Loss Prevention	The Pantry, Inc.	2007
Temporary Executive Secretary—Legal	Westaff	2007
Administrative Assistant—IT	Logix3	2005–2006
Executive Assistant	TEKsystems, Inc.	2005
Temporary Administrative Assistant	On Call Staffing	2003–2005
Staff Assistant—Engineering	JTA	2001–2003
Executive Assistant	HomeSide Lending, Inc.	2000–2001

EDUCATION
- Florida State College at Jacksonville
- Bachelor of Applied Science, Computer Systems Networking and Telecommunications, anticipated graduation May 2015
- Associate of Arts, May 2013, graduated with honors, Dean's and President's Lists
- Lansdale School of Business
- Associate in Science, Secretarial Science, May 1989

REFERENCES
Available upon request

Writing an In-Class Essay

As a college student, you will frequently find yourself having to demonstrate your knowledge and understanding of new information through timed in-class writing. In some cases, you may be required to complete short-answer types of questions, which involve writing a few sentences to a few paragraphs. In other testing situations, your instructor may expect you to write one or more complete essays during class time. Whatever your writing task may be, it is important that you are adequately prepared *before* the testing period, and that you have a plan for completing the writing assignment successfully *during* the testing period. Chapter 14 will guide you in preparing to write more confidently in a timed, in-class setting.

Objectives

- discuss strategies for preparing to write in class;

- provide steps for planning the in-class essay;

- establish a plan for writing the essay;

- recommend proofreading and editing techniques.

▼ Preparing to Write in Class

No amount of writing skill can take the place of adequate preparation for in-class writing assignments. Regular class attendance, good note-taking skills, careful reading, and participation in a study group are all factors that, if you make them a part of your learning regimen, will help you to succeed in comprehending, retaining, and applying new information. Once you've learned new information, though, your instructor will want you to show that you can do something with it. One means for demonstrating your level of understanding is through timed writing.

The point of in-class writing is not simply to dazzle your instructor with what you know. Rather, the goal is for you to make connections, show relationships, develop themes, synthesize information, and draw conclusions based on your new knowledge and current understanding. While your instructor may provide you with your in-class writing topics in advance so that you might prepare your responses more thoroughly, in most instances, an in-class writing assignment requires you to develop your responses quickly, with little indication of the specific topic given ahead of time. However, you do not have to approach an in-class writing task as though you are leaping into the great unknown.

Reviewing Your Text and Lecture Notes

The best clues for determining potential in-class writing topics can be found in your assigned reading and your lecture notes. The likelihood of your being asked questions that are not discussed in the assigned reading or that are not mentioned during class is highly unlikely. Therefore, begin your preparation by carefully reviewing the information that you have read and that your instructor has presented in class.

As you have probably already noticed, textbook chapters are usually organized into major and minor sections, which are indicated by boldfaced headings and subheadings. Take a closer look at the chapter you are now reading. Note that it is divided into four major sections: preparing to write in class, planning the essay, writing the essay, and proofreading and editing. These four sections highlight the areas of in-class writing that we authors consider to be important. As you review any chapter in a textbook, note the concepts that the author of that text presents as major ideas, and consider these concepts as potential test topics.

Now compare the main ideas from the text with the main ideas presented in class. Unfortunately, not all instructors lecture in an organized, outlined fashion such as the way information is presented in most textbooks. As a result, you may have to work a little harder to organize your class notes. Clues to look for in your notes include ideas that the instructor stated more than once during class or highlighted in out-of-class materials as well as concepts that you also encountered in the assigned reading.

As you review your text, your lecture notes, and additional materials provided by the instructor, develop a list of key concepts that might be included on the exam. Consider how these concepts might be converted into short-answer or essay questions.

CREATING POSSIBLE ESSAY QUESTIONS OR TOPIC PROMPTS

In most instances, you will not know exactly what questions your instructor will ask. Even so, don't panic. If you have participated in class and completed all assignments, you already have the tools necessary to predict the general areas that will be covered on the test and to develop practice questions that will be similar to those that your instructor might ask.

For example, let's say that you are studying the Civil Rights Movement in your history class. As you prepare for your exam, which will cover several chapters, you remember that the instructor spent an entire class period discussing the Civil Rights Movement in the U.S., and you find that this topic spans several pages in your textbook. You would be wise to expect a short-answer question such as this one to be on the test:

> What were three major events in the Civil Rights Movement, who were the key players in these events, and what were the significant outcomes of each event?

Note that instead of a question, your instructor may ask you to respond to a complete or partial statement, also known as a *prompt*. For example, a topic prompt on the Civil Rights Movement might look like one of the following:

> Describe three of the key turning points in the Civil Rights Movement and explain their significance in moving the country toward equal rights for all citizens.
>
> or
>
> Discuss the influence and impact of Presidents Eisenhower, Kennedy and Johnson on the Civil Rights Movement.

Whether your instructor gives you a question or a prompt, your task is the same: respond adequately yet concisely. Try writing a solid response or at least developing an outline for all of your practice questions and prompts. Be sure to think of a few specific examples to support your general ideas.

While there is no way to predict exactly what your instructor might ask in a timed writing session, you can certainly prepare yourself generally to write an essay response to any question related to the material your instructor has covered. Even if your practice questions and prompts do not match the test questions exactly, you will have increased your level of confidence by thoroughly familiarizing yourself with the material and drafting possible responses.

PLANNING THE ESSAY

In-class writing may involve several minutes or several hours, depending upon the context of the writing situation. For now, let's assume that you are in a testing situation in which you have been given sixty minutes to complete one essay. Therefore, budgeting your time is imperative. Rather than diving headlong into the topic, consider devoting the first ten minutes of the testing period to establishing a plan or blueprint for your essay.

ANALYZING THE QUESTION OR TOPIC PROMPT

To begin, read the question or the topic prompt at least twice. What exactly are you being asked to do? Break the question or prompt into its parts. Specifically, look at the verb or verbs in the question. Typical essay questions or prompts often include one or more of the following verbs: *identify, list, illustrate, define, analyze, discuss, explain, trace, compare, contrast,* and *evaluate*. Does the question ask you to give an answer in two or more parts? Perhaps the prompt indicates that you are to limit your response to only one reason or effect. Whatever task is expected of you, your first step is to make an effort to understand exactly what you are being asked to do.

Let's imagine that your 60-minute topic prompt is the following:

> In a well-developed essay, identify and describe the necessary and sufficient causes for a significant event in your life.

What ideas come to mind? Perhaps you can think of several events, such as completing basic military training, winning first place in a major marathon competition, or having your first child. At this point, many students might say to themselves, "Ah, I'll write one paragraph about each of these three events, which will result in a five-paragraph essay." Look again at the topic prompt: it asks you to write about the causes that led to *one* major event, not several. So now you must focus on one event—let's choose your big marathon win.

Next, notice the verbs in the prompt: *identify* and *describe*. Not only must you list the causes that resulted in your finishing the marathon in first place, but you must also describe each cause in detail, using specific examples to support your response.

Students often make the mistake of writing more than what is asked of them or writing completely off topic. The key to staying on target in a timed writing situation is to familiarize yourself with the types of essay questions and topic prompts that are frequently encountered in a testing situation and to have a strategy for handling each one.

TYPES OF ESSAY QUESTIONS AND PROMPTS

Following are some of the most common types of essay questions and topic prompts that you might encounter in an in-class writing situation.

Definition

Definition questions require you to provide meaning for a concept or idea. That does not simply mean that you can give a basic definition and move on to the next question. Oftentimes, you are expected to provide an explanation that includes examples that illustrate your points. Verbs often associated with definition questions are *define, explain, illustrate, clarify, state, identify, discuss,* and *describe*. Consider the following prompt from a psychology test:

> Identify and define the four lobes of the cerebral cortex, and describe the sensory and motor functions of the cortex, using examples that are not in your textbook.

This prompt has two parts: first to identify and define, and then to describe by using examples. Initially, you could list each of the four components, providing a definition for each one. In a separate paragraph, you could then develop an extended example of the cortex's four lobes. This prompt lends itself well to a four-paragraph essay response if you include an introduction and a conclusion.

Division and Classification

Division and *classification* questions involve breaking an idea into two or more parts or creating categories to describe a concept. Verbs often associated with dividing and classifying are *categorize, analyze, identify,* and *list*. Look at the following combination of a prompt and a question on a political science exam:

> In the area of health care, identify three goals that should be pursued by federal leaders. Which institutions of government must work to achieve those goals?

This question requires two things to occur: to identify three goals and to identify an unspecified number of governmental institutions connected with each goal. First, divide the issue of health care into three specific goals, devoting a paragraph to each goal. Next, develop each goal paragraph by including at least one government agency. Don't forget to use specific examples!

Comparison and Contrast

Comparison and *contrast* questions call for the student to discuss similarities and differences, respectively. Verbs often used in this kind of question are *compare, contrast, distinguish*, and *differentiate*. Try this question from a test on child development:

> Four-year-old Megan and seven-year-old LuAnn come to the college's Early Learning Laboratory for assessment. In what ways will their cognitive abilities be different?

This question requires you to complete one task: to show the differences between the cognitive abilities of two children. One way to approach this question might be to spend one paragraph discussing Megan's cognitive abilities and to devote another paragraph to LuAnn's cognitive abilities. While the question does not ask for a definition, it might be helpful to define cognitive development in the introductory paragraph. Be sure to draw your conclusions regarding the specific differences between the two two girls' cognitive abilities in a final paragraph.

Argumentation and Evaluation

Argumentation and *evaluation* questions involve making a case **for** or **against** an idea. Verbs frequently used in this kind of question are *agree, disagree, defend, argue, criticize, prove, justify,* and *evaluate*. Consider this statement and the following question taken from a philosophy exam:

> Many American believe that the war on terror has contributed to the growing abuse of human rights. Do you agree or disagree with this statement? Explain your answer.

In this instance, you are expected to think critically, taking a stand on the specific issue of the war on terror and the general notion of "sacrificing some freedoms for the good of the majority." The temptation you may face with this kind of question is to give a simple "I agree" or "I disagree" answer with a sketchy example or two. Try to come up with two or three solid reasons that either support or refute the statement, and then write a well-developed paragraph for each of your points, including concrete examples to support each of your reasons.

Cause and Effect

Answering a *cause* question involves identifying and explaining why a particular event happened. On the other hand, answering an *effect* question entails identifying and relating the end result or results of an event that has occurred. Some essay questions require you to explore both causes and effects in your response. These types of questions are readily identified by words such as *cause, effect, result, outcome,* and *reason.* Consider the following history exam question as an example:

What were the main effects, both immediate and long-term, of the removal of American Indian tribes from lands east of the Mississippi River? Support your argument with reference to specific events and ideas.

What is your task? First, you must identify effects, and then you must include related events and ideas. One way to handle this question might be to write one body paragraph for each effect. If you regard the possible effects as social, political, and economic, you will end up with a five-paragraph essay.

Process Analysis

Process analysis questions require you to explain how something occurs or how something has already occurred. This kind of question often can be recognized by the verbs *trace, explain,* and *explore* as well as by the adverb *how.* For example, consider the following topic prompt from a humanities final exam:

Trace the fortunes and political power of the noble classes in Russia, Austria, and Prussia from about 1300 to the mid-1700s.

Remember, process analysis depends greatly on chronological order, so one way to respond to this question might be to discuss the Russians, Austrians, and Prussians in separate body paragraphs. That way, you can clearly relate the development of wealth and power for each set of nobility by following time order. This organizational plan will result in a five-paragraph essay.

GENERATING IDEAS

Once you have read the question or topic prompt carefully and understand what you are expected to write, you need to do a little brainstorming. Rather than relying on your memory, jot down your ideas as they pop into your head so that you can see them in front of you. Consider the 60-minute topic prompt again:

In a well-developed essay, identify and describe the necessary and sufficient causes for a significant event in your life.

You know that you will focus on one event—your first-place win at a state-level marathon competition. What causes led to your success in this running event? Make a list:

- winning local and regional races

- having an uncle who won many running competitions

- participating in school-sponsored track and field events since middle school

- running regularly since you were nine years old

- having sports-oriented parents

- having a good coach

- running against competitive opponents

Now consider how you might organize the ideas on your list. Rather than writing seven body paragraphs, one for each idea, how might you group certain ideas? One way might be to discuss the people who influenced you in one paragraph, your practice regimen in another paragraph, and your competitive running experiences in a third body paragraph. Also consider the order in which you will address each group of ideas. Is there a logical order that needs to be followed? Perhaps you should write in chronological order or maybe even in order of importance. Whatever topic you choose to write about first and last, be sure the order makes sense. A rough outline for your marathon topic might look like this one:

1. Influential people
    Coach Alison Smith
    Uncle Frank
    Dad and Mom
2. Practice routine
    Running for fun
    After-school practice in middle school and high school
3. Race competition
    Competitive opponents
    Track meets
    Race wins

Hashing out a rough, informal outline before you begin to write will provide you with a plan or blueprint to follow as you develop each paragraph during your timed writing. You should not feel restricted by this outline, however. In fact, as you begin to write, you may very well think of other good examples to include in your paragraphs. If they do not stray from the topic, include them! The advantage of starting with an outline is that the chances of your getting off topic, forgetting an important point, or developing writer's block during a testing period are greatly reduced if you have an outline from which to work.

WRITING A THESIS STATEMENT AND ESSAY BLUEPRINT

One effective way to ensure that your essay will focus on the essay question or topic prompt at hand is to use the important elements of the prompt as the foundation for your thesis statement. For example, let's refer once again to our topic prompt:

In a well-developed essay, identify and describe the necessary and sufficient causes for a significant event in your life.

Minimally, your thesis statement needs to include the term *causes* and to state the major life event that you plan to discuss. Try this possibility:

Several necessary and sufficient causes led to my winning first marathon in the Southernmost Marathon competition hosted by the city of Key West, Florida..

By making the significant elements of the topic prompt part of your thesis statement, both you and the person who scores your paper will be clear that you are sticking to the topic. Now you need to include an essay blueprint sentence, which will establish the essay's organizational plan topically. Try this one:

Several necessary and sufficient causes led to my winning first place in the Southernmost Marathon. *The influential people in my life, my rigorous practice routine, and intense competition all contributed to my achieving my personal best in a sport that I truly love.*

Now you have established a blueprint to follow as you flesh out the body of the essay, and you can be certain that your response will be in keeping with the assigned topic prompt.

▼ WRITING THE ESSAY

While this text has emphasized the importance of writing multiple drafts to refine a paper's quality, it is important that you regard the first draft of in-class timed writing as the *only* draft. In-class writing, while it must be legible, is generally not scored on its appearance; rather, it is scored on its depth, accuracy, and clarity in answering the exam question or developing the topic prompt.

As mentioned earlier in Chapter 1, an essay must contain three main parts: an introduction, a body, and a conclusion. If you refer once again to the sample marathon essay topic, note that you already have a portion of the introductory paragraph written: the thesis statement and the essay blueprint, which may appear at the beginning or the end of the introductory paragraph. Including a few sentences in the introduction to gain the reader's interest is, of course, a good idea, but if you get stuck here, do not allow your brain to become paralyzed. Instead, move on to the body paragraphs. You can always come back later and add more ideas to the introduction.

DEVELOP YOUR MAIN POINTS

Your rough outline and your essay blueprint should clearly indicate to you how the body paragraphs of the essay should unfold. Each body paragraph needs a topic sentence, supporting details, and specific examples. Look again at the outline for your marathon topic:

1. Influential people
      Coach Alison Smith
      Uncle Frank
      Dad and Mom
2. Practice routine
      Running for fun
      After-school practice in middle school and high school
3. Race competition
      Competitive opponents
      Track meets
      Race wins

The first body paragraph should be about the people who influenced your development as a long-distance runner. Your topic sentence should include the three people mentioned in the outline: your folks, your coach, and your uncle. The supporting details of the paragraph should explore not only who these people are in relation to you, but also how their influence caused you to excel in the sport of running. Remember that you must continuously connect your response to the topic prompt that you have been given. Stick to the topic prompt!

The second and third body paragraphs should unfold in a similar manner, once again following the order established in your rough outline and essay blueprint. Don't forget to include transitions within as well as between paragraphs. They will help to keep both you and the person scoring your work on track.

PACE YOURSELF

Consider the number of questions that must be answered or the number of paragraphs you will need to write to complete your timed-writing assignment, and make a conscious effort to balance the remaining time accordingly. For example, if you have been allotted sixty minutes to write a five-paragraph essay such as our sample marathon essay, and you have already spent ten minutes planning the essay, you should spend approximately seven minutes on each paragraph, which will leave you fifteen minutes to look over your final product.

LEAVE ROOM FOR REVISING

One way to make your quickly written paper neater and easier to edit, read, and score is to double space as you write. By leaving a clean line between each line of writing, you will give yourself enough space to make any changes as you proofread the paper. Also, your instructor will have plenty of room to write glowing comments about your work!

▼ PROOFREADING AND EDITING THE ESSAY

Students are often tempted to recopy their drafts in the remaining minutes of an in-class writing session, thinking that neatness will improve their scores. Unfortunately, what frequently happens is that students end up creating more careless errors such as missing words and phrases rather than polishing their work. Instead of spending the last few minutes of the testing period attempting to recopy your essay response, use this precious time to look over your paper carefully to identify and correct any careless mistakes you may have made.

CREATING A PERSONAL ERROR CHECKLIST

Very few people can write error-free on a timed in-class essay assignment, and error-free writing is not what your instructor will expect from you. Even so, you will want to do your best to eliminate careless errors from your written responses. A few errors that often find their way into students' in-class writing assignments include mistakes in grammar, punctuation, spelling, and content.

If you are aware of one or more errors that consistently turn up in your own writing, consider developing a mental checklist of your own personal errors so that you can be certain to check specifically for those mistakes when you are proofreading your work.

READING FOR CARELESS ERRORS

During a short in-class writing session, students generally do not have a lot of time to get away from their writing so that they might see their essays with fresh eyes. When every moment counts, you cannot afford to turn your paper over, twirl your pen, and think about something else for awhile, especially at the end of the testing session. One way to break away briefly from the content of your paper and to focus more clearly on the mechanics of what you have written is to read your paper backward. Really!

Start with the very last sentence of the paper—not the last word, but the entire sentence. Read that last sentence to yourself. Check for misspellings, fragments and run-ons, missing words, awkward phrasing, and so forth. No problems there? Good! Then, trace your finger up to the beginning of the second-to-last sentence. Read this sentence to yourself, checking for errors. You may want to consider your own personal error checklist at this point. Continue editing your paper this way, sentence by sentence, until you reach the beginning of the essay.

Reading your paper backward *first* will help you to isolate spelling, grammar, punctuation, and sentence structure errors. It will also help you to distance yourself somewhat from the subject matter of your writing so that you can now read for errors in content and unity.

READING FOR CLARITY AND COHERENCE

After you've read your paper backward, your brain should be better equipped to identify content and unity mistakes. As you read your paper a second time, this time from beginning to end, check for missing examples as well as any information that is unrelated to the assigned topic. Also check to see that you have included transitions to link ideas within and between paragraphs. If you discover a point or an example that you need to add, then do so—that's why you've double spaced! If you spot a sentence or two that ramble away from the assigned topic, then neatly mark out the ideas that do not belong in this particular essay.

MAKING CHANGES

One final point: should you discover an error, do not attempt to obliterate it. Remember, you want to keep this single draft as clean and as legible as possible. Instead, draw one neat line through the error and write the correction on the blank line above it. If you add or change the location of information, don't hesitate to insert carets, to draw arrows, or to use numbers to help your reader to follow your revisions. Remember, the key is to respond to the essay question or topic prompt as clearly and as succinctly as possible, not to win an award for penmanship.

INDEX